GW00373939

INSIGHT GU

SRI Lanka

APA PUBLICATIONS
Part of the Langenscheidt Publishing Group

ABOUT THIS BOOK

Editorial

Project Editor
Edmund Bealby-Wright
Editorial Director
Brian Bell

Distribution

UK & Ireland
GeoCenter International Ltd
The Viables Centre
Harrow Way
Basingstoke
Hants RG22 4BJ
Fax: (44) 1256-817988

United States
Langenscheidt Publishers, Inc.
46–35 54th Road
Maspeth, NY 11378
Fax: (718) 784-0640

Worldwide
APA Publications GmbH & Co.
Verlag KG (Singapore branch)
38 Joo Koon Road
Singapore 628990
Tel: (65) 865-1600
Fax: (65) 861-6438

Printing

Insight Print Services (Pte) Ltd
38 Joo Koon Road
Singapore 628990
Tel: (65) 865-1600
Fax: (65) 861-6438

© 1999 APA Publications GmbH & Co.
Verlag KG (Singapore branch)
All Rights Reserved
First Edition 1992
Fourth Edition 1999

CONTACTING THE EDITORS
Although every effort is made to
provide accurate information in
this publication, we live in a
fast-changing world and would
appreciate it if readers would
call our attention to any errors or
outdated information that may
occur by writing to us at:
**Insight Guides, P.O. Box 7910,
London SE1 8ZB, England.
Fax: (44 171) 620-1074.
e-mail:
insight@apaguide.demon.co.uk**

Paradise was the word visitors once used to describe Sri Lanka – a lush, tropical island surrounded by glorious beaches and crystal-clean blue waters. Now, paradise is torn by inter-mittent ethnic conflict. And yet, as the authors of this book have found, visitors are not put off travelling to Sri Lanka, such is the richness of its culture and natural beauty. It is an island particularly well suited to Insight Guides' in-depth approach.

How to use this book

Insight Guides have a proven for-mula of informative and well-written text paired with a fresh photojournalistic treatment. The books are structured both to convey a better understanding of a destination and its culture and to guide readers through it:

◆ The first section, with a yellow colour bar, covers the region's rich **history** and lively modern **culture** in authoritative **features** written by experts.

◆ The **Places** section, with a blue bar, gives a run-down of all the places worth seeing. Places of particular interest are cross-referenced to specially commis-sioned full-colour maps.

◆ The **Travel Tips** section at the back of the book offers recom-mendations on everything from travel to hotels and restaurants. Information may be located quickly by using the index printed on the back cover flap, which can also serve as a con-venient bookmark.

◆ **Photographs** are chosen not only to illustrate the geography of Sri Lanka and the beauty of its towns and villages, but also to convey directly to the reader the island's unique atmosphere.

The contributors

Tania Brassey, part-Sinhalese, part-Irish, led from the front. Having left Sri Lanka at the age of 13 – to avoid an arranged marriage – she has been back often, and recently completed a novel set in Sri Lanka in the 1950s. Whilst writing *Festivals*, *Food and Drink*, *Gems*, *Veddhas*, *Colombo*, *Up Country* and *East Coast* chapters herself, she also sought out the very best writers to take care of the rest.

Jeanne Thwaites, who comes from one of Sri Lanka's oldest Burgher families, contributed the Tamils and *Snapshots of Sri Lanka* essays, while **Feizel Mansoor**, himself of Muslim descent, wrote *Muslims*. **Dr H. Tamitegama** indulged his penchant for Sinhala history and indigenous medicine in the sections on *The Sinhalese*, *Tea*, *Ayurveda* and *Kandy*. Leading biologist and conservationist **Dr Ranil Senanyake** contributed the *Sanctuary* essay. **Ralph Fouldes**, environmental scientist, wrote *Exploring the Outdoors*.

The sections on *Polonnaruwa* and *Anuradhapura* were written by **Samantha Elepatha** (of German and Sinhala extraction), while Tania's daughter, **Pikka Brassey**, had the chance to visit old haunts while penning the *Crafts*, the *South* and *West Coast* chapters. **Dr Vessantha Abeysekera** wrote *Sigiriya*. **Kochika Sangrasagra** had the task of compiling *Travel Tips*.

The romp through Sri Lanka's complex history was provided by **Rowlinson Carter**, who also contributed the features on boy monks, pearl diving, and many other issues.

Insight Guide Sri Lanka was creatively edited by **Edmund Bealby-Wright**, who has visited the island many times since he met his Sinhalese wife.

Photographer **Dominic Sansoni** has left his mark firmly on this guide, as he did also on the *Pocket Guide to Sri Lanka*. **Lesley Player** also toured the island on Insight's behalf.

Eric and **Katerina Roberts**, familiar themselves with Sri Lanka, proofread the book, and **Salima Hirani** edited Travel Tips.

Map Legend

▬ ▪▪	International Boundary
▬▬	Province Boundary
─ ─ ─	District Boundary
─•─	National Park/Reserve
─ ─ ─	Ferry Route
✈ ✈	Airport: International/Regional
🚌	Bus Station
P	Parking
❶	Tourist Information
✉	Post Office
✝ ✝ ✝	Church/Ruins
✝	Monastery
☾	Mosque
✡	Synagogue
🏰	Castle/Ruins
∴	Archaeological Site
∩	Cave
🗿	Statue/Monument
★	Place of Interest

The main places of interest in the Places section are coordinated by number with a full-colour map (e.g. ❶), and a symbol at the top of every right-hand page tells you where to find the map.

CONTENTS

Detail of a
Hindu
doorway in
Sri Lanka's
Hill Country

Travel Tips

Places

REMEMBER MY NAME

Sri Lanka's many changes of name over the centuries
are a reflection of its fascinating history

The island currently going by the name of Sri Lanka has had a string of other identities and has been known under a range of nicknames and pseudonyms. To Prince Vijaya and the founding fathers it was, in their Sanskritic language, *Tambapanni*, after the copper-coloured beach on which they landed, either at Mannar or Puttalam but in any case on the west coast. In the reign of the Roman Emperor Claudius, a sea captain working for Annius Plocamus, a tax collector in the Red Sea, suffered the misfortune of catching a monsoon that swept his boat off course and dumped him on the island 15 days later. For him, and other Roman and Greek callers, *Tambapanni* was too much of a mouthful and became *Taprobane*. The geographer Ptolemy rang a slight change by showing it as *Taprobanam* on his famous 2nd-century AD map.

Arab traders could have told Annius Plocamus's captain that if he waited a while a different monsoon would blow him back to Arabia or, if he liked, East Africa. They relied on these winds to go back and forth, knew the island well and called it *Serendib*. This name is a corruption of the Sanskrit *Sinhaladvipa*. Cosmas Indicopleustes, the Byzantine author of *Christian Topography*, twisted the Arabic into *Sielediba*, but the 18th-century English novelist Horace Walpole stuck to the original for his fairy tale, *The Three Princes of Serendib*, and used it to coin "serendipity," meaning discovery by happy accident. Another variant, *Sirinduil*, as yet awaits a neologist to give us a definition of "sirinuility."

Edward Barbosa, a Portuguese captain who visited in 1515, tried to persuade his countrymen to adopt Tennaserim, which in some ancient Indian language meant "Land of Delights," but they had already settled on Celao, which had started as the Chinese *Si-lan* and, thanks to medieval Europeans like Marco Polo, become *Seylan*. The Dutch worked out their own derivation to produce *Zeilan*; the English compromise was Ceylon.

Through all of this, the Sinhalese had long ago decided it was *Lanka*, and it officially changed to Sri Lanka in 1972 (the prefix means beautiful). The words *Prajathanthrika Samajavadi Janarajayi* (Democratic Socialist Republic) were tacked on in 1978. The trick with these tongue twisters is to work your way along the word pronouncing everything, as in Italian. Of course this tactic won't help you guess which syllable to emphasise, but any mispronunciations will be forgiven. After all, the Sri Lankans have got used to people getting their name wrong. ❑

PRECEDING PAGES: father and son fishermen netting their catch on the South Coast; Tamil pluckers pursue the perfect cup of tea – two leaves and a bud; Kandyan dancers, dripping with silver and oozing charm, stop the traffic; playful dwarves, no two alike, line the walls of Kelaniya Temple outside Colombo.
LEFT: one of the Buddha images that make up the Gal Vihara at Polonnaruwa, where solid rock becomes transcendental.

THE LAY OF THE LAND

A fertile island warmed by the tropical sun and watered by monsoon rains,
Sri Lanka has been moulded by its position and shape

The shape of Sri Lanka has evoked visions of a teardrop on India's cheek, a pear, a mango, a pearl and, in Dutch eyes somewhat insensitive to the misgivings of Muslims and vegetarian Buddhists who live on it, a Westphalian ham. Even more politically incorrect, the Portuguese poet, Camoens, vividly described how:

Ceylon lifts her spicy breast,
And waves her woods above the
watery waste

A contour map will show just how accurate his image is, and the evidence of geology shows that Sri Lanka was indeed once under the sea, before it thrust itself skywards. The fossilised remains of prehistoric creatures formed the limestone rock that rose out of the watery waste. Its woods waving in the monsoon-bearing tradewinds are far less abundant than they once were, but otherwise the poet has summed up the island well; mountains, forests and sea.

Mountains and monsoons

The highest pinnacle is Pidurutalagala, at a very pert 2,524 metres (8,200 ft), which, as Herman Hesse commented, sounds very lofty in English feet, but climbing it is "a walk." More people choose to climb Adam's Peak, which is not a walk but a pilgrimage. Until properly surveyed, this mountain was thought to be the tallest on the island. It managed to fool everyone by standing against a low backdrop.

Apart from providing gentle exercise for German novelists, the mountainous region affects the climate of Sri Lanka as the dumping ground for monsoon rains. The island greedily sucks up not one but two monsoons, coming from different directions at differrent times of the year. Colombo and the South West get a drenching from April to October, and in peaceful days the

---

LEFT: cloudy hills, once covered with dense jungle, were cleared to be planted with coffee, then tea. A few trees were left for shade.
RIGHT: wild birds in Bundala Park.

more fortunate would avoid it by taking a holiday on the East coast, which receives its payload of water from November to January.

Equatorial variations

The monsoons give Sri Lanka its only seasons, because being situated so close to the equator,

the temperatures are high throughout the year, staying close to the average of 27°C (80°F) in Colombo, although when humidity increases it feels a lot hotter. The island's equatorial position is an asset for astronomers, who are able to observe the Southern Cross, the stars depicted on the Australian flag, as well as the Great Bear.

Even those for whom the setting sun provokes nothing more than a Pavlovian response to reach for the drinks cabinet will find themselves pondering why they are plunged into total blackout before the second pink gin. Twilight hardly exists at this latitude, the sunsets are magnificent, but there are no curtain calls.

A choice of perpetual seasons

There are wide variations in climate, but they are not seasonal. Like the rains, they are provided by the mountains. The higher you go, the cooler it gets, so you can pick your climate with your altitude. At Nuwara Eliya on the higher levels you have a permanent warm springtime, averaging 16°C (61°F), with bright sunny days ending in chilly evenings when the unprepared tourist will yearn for a cardigan. They even suffer the occasional light frost, which is dreaded for the damage it does to the tea plants.

A little lower down, at Kandy, a Mediterranean summer reigns all year round, not the least attraction of this extraordinarily beguiling city. At the coast the altitude cannot help cool you down, but the sea breeze will take over.

The impact of humans

The first inhabitants of Sri Lanka, huntsmen who arrived in the Stone Age, had a wondrously small impact on the environment. Later settlers from India who glimpsed these naked men disappearing into the jungle without a sound reckoned them to be ghosts or spirits. These newcomers cultivated rice, and they began to make a major impact on the island with increasingly ambitious irrigation projects.

Like the ancient Egyptians and Mesopotamians, irrigation was a spur to civilisation. Vast reservoirs were constructed to collect the monsoon rains which enabled the people to have a year-round growing season. The countryside that once concealed nothing but a few hundred thousand hunter gatherers now sustained a population of around 10 million and still had surplus rice to export.

The colonial masters who subsequently exploited the island's riches had no interest in irrigation and so the tanks gradually fell into disrepair, turning much of the countryside into malarial swampland. By 1900 the population was just 3½ million.

The importance of forests

The Sinhalese owe the preservation of their culture to the thick forests which protected the Kandyan kingdom from European armies. Once the hilltops were in the possession of the British, planters cleared the waving woods described by Camoens, burning innumerable priceless trees to plant coffee, and later tea.

Despite the felling, there are still tracts of scrub jungle, rainforests and high-altitude cloud forests in Sri Lanka, some areas of which have

NEXT STOP ANTARCTICA

If you set a southerly course from Dondra Head, the southernmost tip of the island, expect to run into penguins, since your next landfall will be Antarctica.

the island a most picturesque appearance." Not surprisingly, these beaches are now lined with hotels. The low coastline encircles the mountain zone, the most prominent member of which is Adam's Peak, towering "like a mountain monarch amidst an assemblage of picturesque hills."

Sailing around the southern tip of the island ships met precipitous rocks, and only the largest of them could approach the shore. Coming to Trincomalee mariners found a magnificent basin, "perhaps unsurpassed in extent,

continued to provide concealment, this time for Tamil Tiger guerrillas.

Circumnavigating the island

Until recently all travellers to the "utmost Indian Isle" came by sea, their first vision of the island was described as "truly beautiful." The west and south coasts are uniformly low, and fringed with coconut trees "which grow to the water's edge in great luxuriance, and give

LEFT: the Parakrama Samudra, one of the huge reservoirs that were built to retain the monsoon rains.
ABOVE: the exception that proves the rule, the Manalkadu Desert near the island's northernmost point.

security and beauty by any haven in the world."

Rounding the north of the island was made difficult by "numberless sandbanks, rocks and shoals" which almost join it to India. A passage was deepened to allow large vessels through, avoiding the rocks of Adam's Bridge. The island's northern tip includes a miniature Sahara of shifting dunes called Manalkadu Desert. Further on, the sight of the copper coloured sands that gave the island one of its names, *Taprobane*, told the mariners that they had completed the circumnavigation. Of course, today's traveller has only to shuffle through the arrivals lounge of Colombo Airport. That's progress. ❏

Decisive Dates

PREHISTORY

Circa **10,000 BC** The first Stone Age culture emerges in Sri Lanka, and is related to early settlers in Australia, the Nicobar Islands and Malaysia, etc. Stone Age factory in Bandarawela uses fire to shatter quartz to make tools (microliths).

Circa **500 BC** So-called Balangoda culture in Ratnapura district. Appearance of simple pottery.

Circa **300 BC** Pomparippu Cemetery, simply decorated pots and large urns buried in the ground, containing bones.

EARLY HISTORICAL PERIOD

543 BC Year 1 of the Buddhist era in Lanka. The first entries in the *Mahavamsa* or "Great History" date from now. Arrival of Sinhalese led by Prince Vijaya.

300 BC The Greek historian Megasthenes describes the pearls of Ceylon.

273–236 BC In India, the reign of Asoka, the "Constantine of Buddhism," sends missions to all parts including Lanka. Inscriptions in Brahmi characters on cave shelters show first Buddhist communities.

EARLY ANURADHAPURA PERIOD

Circa **250–210 BC** Reign of Devanampiya Tissa; introduction of Buddhism; Mahinda comes to Mihintale; arrival of the slip of the Bo tree under which the Buddha found enlightenment. Foundation of the Mahavihara and Thuparama monuments.

Circa **204–161 BC** Reign of Tamil general Elara.

199 BC Death of Mahinda.

161–137 BC Reign of Dutugemunu; defeat of Elara, unification of Sri Lanka under a single monarch for the first time. Religious foundations at Mihintale and Anuradhapura.

103–102 BC First reign of Vathagamani; interrupted by Tamil attacks.

89–77 BC Restoration of Vathagamani; first dissensions in the Buddhist community.

35–32 BC Pali scriptures committed to writing.

AD 45 Four Lankan envoys visit Rome; Pliny mentions Sri Lanka in his histories.

214–136 Reign of Voharika Tissa; progress of Mahayana Buddhism.

276–303 Reign of Mahasena; and the foundation of the Jetavanarama, the largest *dagoba* or stupa in the world.

303–331 Reign of Sirimeghavana; arrival of the Tooth relic; apogee of first Anuradhapura period.

412–413 The Chinese scholar Fa-hsien visits Anuradhapura.

428 Embassy to China; nuns sent to Nanking.

432–459 Tamil invasion and domination; end of first Anuradhapura period.

LATE ANURADHAPURA PERIOD

459–477 Reign of Dhatusena; end of Tamil domination. Dhatusena murdered by his son, Kasyapa.

477–495 Reign of Kasyapa; construction of Sigiriya. Kasyapa is killed in battle while facing the army led by his brother, Mogallan, who had determined to avenge their father's death.

495–512 Reign of Mogallan I; capital returned to Anuradhapura; arrival of the Hair relic.

575–608 Reign of Aggabodhi I. Irrigation works.

608–618 Reign of Aggabodhi II. Rebuilding of the Thuparama.

618–684 Internecine struggles; Tamil interventions; finally Pallava domination.

684–718 Reign of Manavamma; alliance with the Pallavas.

772–777 Reign of Aggabodhi VII, which brought temporary abandonment of Anuradhapura in favour of Polonnaruwa.

835–853 Reign of Sena I. Pandyan conquest.

840 Anuradhapura plundered.

853–887 Reign of Sena II; alliance with Pallavas against Pandyas.

Circa **925** Pandyan king asks for aid against the Cholas and takes refuge in Sri Lanka.

Circa **947** Chola expedition; Anuradhapura is plundered, the king flees to Rohana.

956–972 Reign of Mahinda IV. Rebuilding takes place at Anuradhapura.

993 Capture and sack of Anuradhapura. Mahinda V takes refuge in Rohana.

Circa **1000** Rajarata annexed to Chola empire.

1017 Mahinda V captured by Cholas; Chola viceroy at Polonnaruwa. Collapse of irrigation system and destruction of many religious foundations.

POLONNARUWA PERIOD 1073–1215

1055–1110 Reign of Vijayabahu; kingdom liberated from Cholas.

1070 Vijayabahu crowned at Anuradhapura.

1073 Capital transferred to Polonnaruwa. Religious foundations and irrigation works.

After 1110 Three rival princedoms compete; all have separate capitals.

1153–86 Reign of Parakrama I (The Great). Polonnaruwa becomes the undisputed capital, beginning a period of political, religious and material reconstruction. First Gal Vihara sculptures carried out.

1187–96 Reign of Nissanka Malla; further grandiose buildings erected.

PERIOD OF EPHEMERAL CAPITALS 1214–1597

1214 Kalingan Invasion.

1215–36 Tyranny of Magha, leader of the "Giants of Kerala." Destruction of Polonnaruwa.

1236–70 Reign of Parakramabahu II.

1270–1508 A succession of kings, up to Parakramabahu VIII.

1254–1324 Marco Polo visits Seilan (Ceylon).

1505 Portuguese arrive; they soon occupy the island's coastal areas.

1550–97 Dom Jão Dharmapala set up as puppet king by the Portuguese.

1554–93 Rajasinha I rules most of the island. The Jaffna kingdom also holds out against the Portuguese.

KANDYAN PERIOD 1597–1815

1597 Capital moved to Kandy.

1629–87 Reign of Rajasinha II.

1656 Dutch arrive and oust Portuguese after both land and sea battles.

PRECEDING PAGES: an Esala Perahara procession celebrates the arrival of Buddha's Tooth relic. **LEFT:** praying before the Bo tree at Anuradhapura, the oldest recorded tree in the world. **RIGHT:** Dudley Senanayake and Indira Ghandi, prime ministers of Sri Lanka and India, in the late 1960s.

Circa **1660–80** Robert Knox, an English sailor, is captured by the king of Kandy.

1796 Dutch surrender to the British, who have become interested in Trincomalee's fine harbour.

1798–1815 Reign of Sri Wickrama Rajasinha.

BRITISH COLONIAL PERIOD 1802–1948

1802 Ceylon becomes a Crown Colony.

1815 Last Kandyan king deposed and exiled in Madras.

1826 Ola parchments found at Mulgirigala that led to understanding classical Pali scripts, and the translation of the *Mahavamsa*.

1870 Coffee plantations blighted.

1886 Ruins of Polonnaruwa rediscovered.

1931 Universal franchise granted.

INDEPENDENCE 1948–PRESENT

1948 Independence declared.

1959 S.W.R.D. Bandaranaike assassinated.

1960 Mrs Bandaranaike becomes world's first woman prime minister.

1972 Ceylon becomes Republic of Sri Lanka.

1978 New constitution introduced.

1987 Indian peacekeeping troops, rioting JVP.

1989 Ranasinghe Premadasa becomes president.

1993 Premadasa assassinated.

1994 Chandrika Bandaranaike becomes president.

1998 50th anniversary of Independence.

ANCIENT CIVILISATION

Sri Lanka's ancient chronicles stretch back into a far distant past

where history melts entertainingly into myth

Sri Lanka has inspired more legends than it can comfortably accommodate, with the result that some legends have to bunk up together. The worst example of mythical over-crowding is found at the top of a mountain called Sri Pada, or Adam's Peak, at the summit of which is a sort of fossilised footprint. According to preference, the footprint was left by the Hindu god Shiva performing the dance of creation, or by Adam serving a thousand-year sentence on one leg for misconduct in Paradise, or by Buddha on an early evangelical mission to the island, or by the doubting Christian apostle St Thomas before his martyrdom in Madras. Consequently, it rewards in equal measure the panting piety of Buddhist, Hindu, Muslim and Christian pilgrims alike.

With the four main religions of the world, you get a free bonus theory that the footprint was left by a eunuch attached to the Queen of Sheba, named Candace, but so far he hasn't inspired many pilgrims. Whoever it was had big feet; the print is about 1 metre (3 ft) long.

An abode of demons

Sri Lanka appears in Hindu legend with a status comparable with that of the city of Troy in Homer's *Iliad.* In the Hindu epic *Ramayana* the siege of Lanka is described at great length with grotesque humour, as Prince Rama sets out to avenge the abduction of his wife Sita who had been whisked away by the 10-headed, 20-armed demon king of Lanka. Rama is aided by an army of monkeys led by Hanuman, who is still revered by Hindus as the apotheosis of loyalty and unselfish energy. They have to get past the guardian devils, *rakshasas,* and then overcome their king, Ravana.

This is a story full of beings who can change their shape or fly like Superman, but it is also

---

LEFT: the Summit of Adam's Peak draws pilgrims of all religions.
RIGHT: guardstones depicting mythical Naga kings, such as this one in Polonnaruwa, are still doing sentry duty at the foot of temple steps.

remarkable because Ravana flies around in the oldest flying machine in world literature; a peacock-powered sky chariot, the *dandumonara.* You may see one at Colombo Airport, because the flying machines operated by Air Lanka, the national airline, have a stylised *dandumonara* on the tail-fin.

Chronicles of kings

In the 5th century AD, Buddhist monks began writing the *Mahavamsa* ("Great History") on palm-leaf tablets. Like the Old Testament, it is a chronicle of ancient kings interwoven with the theme of a Chosen People guided by the True Faith. In this case the heroes were the Sinhalese, who today make up about 70 percent of the population, and this national story was (and still is) a way of asserting their claim to the island. It was written at a time when the Sinhalese capital, Anuradhapura, was beset by armies from Southern India who threatened to imitate the Visigoths and Vandals that had (half a world away) recently sacked Rome.

The lion tribe

The Sinhalese royal family traced their lineage to the union between a lion (*sinha*, hence *Sinhalese*) and a princess. While some commentators propose, with a polite cough, that the lion was merely symbolic, the chronicle makes no bones about it. "Very fair was she and very amorous," it says of the princess, who was travelling in a caravan that was attacked by the lion in question. The others ran away, but she went up to it and "without fear she caressed him, stroking his limbs." She gave

STONE AGE FINDS

Evidence of neolithic cultures have been found, with quartz tools manufactured in Bandarawela and simple pottery found at Balangoda.

in the guise of a raven-haired temptress called Kuveni. She was sitting by a pond, innocently spinning. The first of the renegades sidled up to her suggestively and for his pains was pitched into the pond. The rest tried the same line, and all with the same result. However, Vijaya was protected by a magic thread and, grabbing Kuveni by the hair, threatened to cut off her head. Kuveni had a better idea. She agreed to release the men and, making herself younger (the chronicle says her age dropped to 16) and even more beautiful, nod-

birth to twins, a boy and girl who later married and produced "16 twin sons."

The eldest son was Vijaya, the chronicle's somewhat tarnished hero, who was guilty of such misconduct at home that there were calls for him and his cronies to be put to death. Instead, the king had their heads shaved on one side and packed all 700 into a boat, telling them to push off.

The half-shorn Sinhalese no sooner landed on the island when a mythical being or *yaksa* appeared to them in the form of a bitch. Deducing that where there were dogs there must be people, especially females, they chased after it. Waiting for them was another *yaksa*, this one

ded in the direction of "a splendid bed, well-covered around with a tent and adorned with a canopy."

Although "looking forward to the time to come," Vijaya insisted on certain pre-nuptial conditions: Kuveni had to give him a kingdom even if that meant betraying her people. They married and had two children but were not really compatible. Vijaya's marching orders to her were businesslike: "Go thou now, dear one." No amount of gold would make him change his mind, so back to the jungle she went, only to be stoned to death by her unforgiving people. The children escaped to live as man and wife, and it was their progeny who became the Veddhas.

The shortage of women emphasised by these stories was relieved by importing brides from south India, the beginning of a tradition in which loyalty to a particular caste seemed to transcend religious differences. As Vijaya's subsequent marriages failed to produce an heir, the establishment of a Sinhalese royal dynasty depended on inviting a relative over from the north. The choice fell upon a nephew from a branch of the family who lived in Bengal, and when he landed at Trincomalee it was with 32 of his own followers. Linguistic and other evidence tends to support the view that Aryan immigration occurred in two waves.

At first the Sinhalese were confined to "low country" river valleys, the only areas suitable for the cultivation of their staple, rice. In the interior large tracts of the island were impenetrable jungle and, except for the Veddhas, uninhabitable. A great plain in the north and a smaller one in the southeast were inviting but impractical. Whilst it received regular monsoon rainfall, the earth baked hard in the dry season. The solution was to store the rainwater in large reservoirs, so that the paddy fields could be irrigated all year round. Such ambitious projects demanded a high degree of centralised authority, which in turn was rewarded with taxable agricultural surpluses. Sri Lanka was booming; it was a source of precious stones, first-class elephants and spices, and local cinnamon was much superior to the mainland variety.

The arrival of Buddhism

The *Mahavamsa* chronicle indulges in a spot of wishful thinking when it recounts Buddha's three visits to the island when the only inhabitants were *yaksas* and *nagas* (by implication the ancestors of the surviving Veddha population) who flitted through the jungle so elusively that they could have been spirits and demons. Although Buddha's appearance struck fear into their hearts, they were not suitable disciples.

The chronicle also asserts that just as Prince Vijaya and his followers reached Sri Lanka, Buddha, in a remote part of Tibet, lay down between two *sala* trees and attained *nirvana*. His parting words, according to the *Mahavamsa*, were to pronounce a blessing on their enterprise.

LEFT: a 19th-century photograph of Veddhas records a way of life that was unchanged for millennia.
RIGHT: elephants, the bulldozers of ancient Lanka.

Prosaic history records that in 543 BC, the traditional date of Prince Vijaya's landing, Buddha would have been about 16. He died around 60 years later, after eating some off-colour pork prepared by a disciple named Chunda.

For two centuries after Buddha's death, his "Middle Way" between hedonism ("low and ignoble") and extreme asceticism ("sad, unworthy and useless") met with only moderate success. The turning point was its appeal to the emperor Asoka the Great. With the characteristic zeal of a new convert, he dispatched missionaries in all directions, including Egypt, Syria and Greece. Lanka, however, was a spe-

IRRIGATION

The brilliant solution to the problem of conserving rainwater was invented in the 3rd century BC. Working like a modern sluice-gate, the *bisokotuwa* or valve-pit meant much larger reservoirs, known in Sinhalese as *wewa* and to the British as "tanks," the largest covering many square kilometres. A network of canals fed the surrounding area. The ancient engineers demonstrated their prodigious skill maintaining a steady gradient of less than 20 cm per kilometre (1ft per mile) over distances that eventually stretched to 80 km (50 miles). Thousands of these man-made lakes dot the lowlands, with 11,200 in the Northern Province alone.

cial case, and its conversion was entrusted to his own son Mahinda. Asoka directed his son to King Tissa of Anuradhapura, who was pre-eminent among a number of kings.

The mango tree test

King Tissa was hunting deer on a mountainside at Mihintale, not far from his palace, when he was confronted by Mahinda. The missionary prince tested the king with searching questions about mango trees, an interrogation which survives verbatim but is more or less unintelligible to anyone not steeped in Buddhist theology. The king's replies were totally satisfactory and,

texts that Mahinda brought over with him were translated into Pali, the language of Sinhalese scripture, and Anuradhapura blossomed with grand buildings in honour of the new religion. Lanka was on the verge of a civilisation that would last 1,000 years and be ranked among the wonders of the ancient world.

Tamil threat

Although a few Tamils settled in the north of the island and perhaps in the east in the 3rd century BC, the main migrations did not occur until the 10th century AD. Today they represent about 19 percent of the population. The Sin-

in turn, he was left in no doubt about the validity of Buddha's beliefs. His conversion was sealed by the new title Devanampiya ("dear to the gods") and the arrival of Mahinda's sister, a nun, with a collection of holy relics: Buddha's begging bowl, his collar bone, and a branch of the sacred Bo tree beneath which Buddha had seen the light. The cutting was planted next to the royal palace and orders were given for the building of a temple to house the begging bowl and collar-bone.

Some 23 centuries later, the tree still stands in the garden – albeit propped up on crutches – as the oldest documented tree on earth and certainly, for Buddhists, the most sacred. The

halese descendants of Prince Vijaya appealed to their south Indian neighbours to form their armies, in order to appease their Buddhist abhorrence of killing anything, even cockroaches, which left them vulnerable. If their Tamil mercenaries mutinied, the Sinhalese could do nothing about it.

In 237 BC, only a few years after Devanampiya Tissa's death, two Tamil captains in the Anuradhapura army staged a coup d'état and ruled Anuradhapura for 22 years before they were murdered. The Tamil general Elara was quick to step into their shoes and his rule lasted 44 years. Some chroniclers accused Elara of turning Anuradhapura into a sepulchre of corruption, blasphemy and filth. To others, he dispensed justice with perfect impartiality to friend and foe alike.

A national hero

Getting about through the jungle was slow and difficult, so Elara had no reason to depart from a Tamil liking for de-centralised government, carving the land into manageable chunks under quasi-feudal barons who called themselves kings. The perfect impartiality referred to by chroniclers suggests that some of these kings, perhaps the majority, were actually Sinhalese.

This was certainly the case in southeastern Ruhuna, the maverick annexe of the Dry Zone, where the king was so satisfied with existing arrangements that at table one day he asked his 12-year-old son and heir-presumptive to swear faithfully that he would never lift a finger against Elara. The prince flung his rice bowl from the table, said he would rather starve to death than make such a pledge, and soon after the meal sent his father some female baubles to show what he thought of his obsequiousness. For his part, the prince took to sleeping in the foetal position: he could not stretch out, he explained to his mother, between a Tamil tyrant and the sea. When the prince had a relic of Buddha set into the shaft of his spear, there could be no doubt that he, Dutugemunu, was the right man to lead the island to independence.

The preliminaries took 11 years and were a matter of picking off the feudal dependencies and their collaborator kings one by one, Dutugemunu sharing the battle honours with his enormous elephant Kandula. On one occasion, when they stormed the gates of a fortress and were showered with rocks and molten lead, the elephant had to dive into a nearby tank to cool off. Then, under a protective shield of buffalo skins, they re-entered the fray and demolished the gates like matchsticks.

All of this was leading up to a dramatic finale with Dutugemunu and Elara in single combat on elephants. Dutugemunu won, but he was magnanimous in victory, giving the fallen general an honourable tomb and decreeing that anyone passing it, even royalty, would dis-

mount out of respect. It is said that as recently as 1817 – that's 2,000 years after the event – a Kandyan noble on the run from the British climbed out of his litter on tottering legs to comply, although these days, curiously, no one seems sure where the Tamil general was buried.

Anuradhapura

Dutugemunu's triumph was celebrated with a dazzling display of new parks, temples and palaces in the capital, the greatest being his copper-roofed Brazen Palace near the sacred Bo tree, not for himself (the chronicles take care to mention) but for monks. It is said that

LEFT: an archaeological puzzle, the small *dagobas* at Kantharodai may have been votive shrines.
RIGHT: an 1864 view of the Thuparama *dagoba* at Anuradhapura, after its first modern restoration.

GUILT CURRY

Dutugemunu stands next to the three Buddhas facing the Ruwaneliseya. He is unique in Sinhalese history in being presented as a tragic hero, one who was haunted not only by the human cost of the war against Elara – the chronicle says 1 million casualties – but also for once absent-mindedly eating a bowl of chillis without offering any to the monks. The issue was not that they were chillis, or the improbability of anyone swallowing a bowl of chillis without thinking, but that the deprived party were holy monks.

It was perhaps the chronicle's *piquant* way of sending a warning to unborn kings and politicians.

Dutugemunu, freed from the foetal position, stretched out along a stone bench to watch his most ambitious project, the Ruwanweliseya, or Great Stupa, slowly rise, the domed shape inspired by the bubble when a stone drops into water. He did not live to see it finished.

However hard-earned, Dutugemunu's unification fell apart in the absence of defined rules of succession. Of Anuradhapura's early kings only 15 ruled for less than a year, 22 were murdered by their successors, six were murdered by other people, four committed suicide, 13 were killed in battle, and 11 were dethroned never to be heard of again. If any of the perpe-

trators had Buddhist inhibitions about using cold steel, more than 50 deadly poisons grew wild on the island. A Queen Anula first poisoned her husband to gain the throne and then reached for the bottle as soon as she got bored with a succession of five lovers, including "a gigantic Malabar named Wattuka." Unable to find any more volunteers to share either the throne or, even fleetingly, her bed, she reigned alone for four months before being murdered by her stepson. The chroniclers could take this sort of thing in their stride; it awaited a Victorian historian to pronounce her "a woman whose wickedness cannot perhaps be paralleled in the history of the universe." On the other

hand, there was a twinge of sympathy for a playful king, Subha, whose party trick was to change places with a servant who was his spitting image. He played the trick once too often and, howling protestations notwithstanding, never got the crown back.

Sigiriya

Murderous royal ambitions could have unexpected results and one example resulted in the creation of the eighth wonder of the world. In 478, King Dhatusena had just completed Anuradhapura's biggest reservoir yet – a 5-km (3-mile) wall of granite – when he was murdered by his son Kasyapa. As was common practice in such circumstances, a second son, Mogallan, ran off to the mainland to see if he could raise an army and take the throne for himself. His negotiations took 18 years, and in the meantime Kasyapa built an impregnable fortress on a 200-metre (650-ft) rock that towered over the forest at a place called Sigiriya. While there was still no sign of Mogallan, he added creature comforts. A water garden, for example, and a gallery of 500 topless beauties so beguiling that generations of graffiti artists poured out their hearts in verse. When Mogallan materialised, Kasyapa went by elephant to meet his Nemesis on the plain below.

The chronicles have little to say about Kasyapa apart from grudging admiration for the way he died. It seems he was leading a charge on the Chola force that Mogallan had at last managed to raise when his elephant sensed they were heading for a hidden swamp and veered away. The troops behind misread this sudden evasion as a signal to retreat and broke up in confusion. Left to face the enemy alone, Kasyapa raised his dagger high, drove it down his throat, re-sheathed the blade, toppled off his elephant and died. Mogallan dispatched 1,000 of his brother's courtiers and returned the capital to Anuradhapura.

Chola invasion

Mogallan's victory betrayed the dangerous reality that the Tamil kingdoms of the Pandyas, Panavas and the Cholas on the mainland were Anuradhapura's king-makers. Interference, however, worked both ways, and Sinhalese kings ran the risk of taking sides in disputes on the mainland. Their worst mistake was to back the Pandyans against the Cholas led by

Rajaraja, a formidable king whose empire eventually stretched to Malaysia and Indonesia, Rajaraja ordering a revenge attack in 993.

The Sinhalese were powerless against overwhelming force. Mahinda V, then king of Anuradhapura, was bundled off to exile in India, the capital was sacked, and Rajaraja annexed the whole island as part of his empire. It seemed that 1,500 years of history had come to nothing.

Although this calamitous state of affairs lasted only 75 years, it did bring the curtain

RELOCATION GAINS

Polonnaruwa had one big advantage over Anuradhapura as a capital: it had fewer mosquitoes.

Polonnaruwa, the medieval city

Anuradhapura was replaced by Polonnaruwa, an ancient military stronghold at the one point where armies could ford the Mahaweli river, the best place to keep an eye on infiltration from the south.

For all Rajaraja's might, the politics of south India were notoriously fluid. Within 50 or 60 years of the invasion, the Cholas were troubled both at home and by a nagging guerrilla campaign lead by Vijayabahu, a young relative of the exiled king, which made them cut their losses and leave in 1070. For the

down on Anuradhapura. A city that once measured 25 km (16 miles) across was in ruins and, when people could no longer read the Pali script, all but forgotten. Some seven centuries later, the Englishman Robert Knox walked by the scene of the Chola's revenge on the city and wrote: "Here and there, by the side of the river, is a world of hewn stone pillars, and other heaps of hewn stones which, I suppose, formerly were buildings..."

LEFT: one of the Sigiriya maidens in an unrestored state, but is she goddess or courtesan?
RIGHT: the ruined temples at Polonnaruwa retain their religious power, though roofless and weather-beaten.

sake of tradition, Vijayabahu had himself crowned in the rubble of Anuradhapura but, like the departed Cholas, elected to rule from Polonnaruwa. Described by the chronicles as "a brave man and distinguished by his good conduct," Vijayabahu kept the peace for over 40 years, being "extraordinarily skilled in the use of the many expedients such as kindness."

Parakrama the Great

The chronicle saved its unbridled adulation instead for Parakrama I, who more than made amends for Vijayabahu's coolness towards the Buddhist clergy. Thus, a tremendous thunderstorm had no effect on a royal procession, when

Parakrama rode with his queen in a tower erected across the backs of two elephants. Not a drop of water touched them, "a striking instance," the chronicle noted, "of the power of Buddha."

But it was another drop which made Parakrama famous and is still very much quoted. When announcing plans for more ambitious irrigation schemes than had ever been attempted in Anuradhapura, he declared that "not one drop of water must flow into the ocean without serving the purposes of man." His showpiece made a mockery of the later British term "tank." At 2,100 hectares (5,600 acres),

deserved her. His successor lasted five days. The rot stopped with the coronation of Parakrama's Indian brother-in-law, Nissanka Malla. The boastful Nissanka Malla ordered teams of elephants to drag a 25-ton rock across 100 km (60 miles) so that scribes could engrave an indelible record of his works.

He oversaw a baroque flourishing of art, with sinuous lotus-stem pillars and elaborately entwined carvings. He also taxed later scholars by adding inscriptions to existing buildings so that other kings' work appeared as his own, but most agree that he commissioned one of the greatest works of sculpture in any age; the

the Parakrama Samudra was more like an inland sea.

Parakrama's huge vision extended to foreign policy, too. He may not have been the first Sinhalese king to send troops to India, but none had contemplated a naval force – commanded by a Malabar general, Adikaram – to invade Burma and, as things turned out, kill its king.

Baroque monarchy

Tangles at court after Parakrama's death had a familiar ring. His nephew Vijayabahu II murdered a shepherd who hesitated to hand over his beautiful daughter and was at once murdered himself by another who thought he better

imposing Gal Vihara, three giant Buddhas carved in different poses out of a single wall of granite.

Kalingan Invasion

If Parakrama's prodigality had stretched the treasury, Nissanka Malla's vanity finished it off. His death without leaving a designated heir triggered the usual chaos and once again there was an opportunist on the mainland ready to step in.

The chroniclers were inconsolable: "This Magha, who was like unto a fierce drought, commanded his army of strong men to ransack the kingdom of Lanka, even as a wild fire doth a forest. Thereupon, these wicked disturbers of the peace stalked about the land hither and thither crying out boastfully, 'Lo! we are the giants of Kerala'." His atrocities are catalogued: the amputation of limbs; rich men tortured until they surrendered their valuables; believers beaten up at their prayers; children flogged wholesale; temples and libraries destroyed; slave labour and so on. "Alas! Alas! Even so did those Tamil giants, like the giants of Mara, destroy the kingdom and the religion of the land... and robbed all the treasures that were therein with all the pearls and precious stones."

When Magha died in 1255 there were no members of the ruling class still around to make a bid for the throne. With the city and its irrigation system left unattended, the jungle closed in. Although the Polonnaruwa era had lasted less than two centuries, compared with Anuradhapura's eight, it was a match in magnificence. Like Anuradhapura, its memory faded until 1886 when S.M. Burrows, a British colonial officer, came across the remains of the Thuparama, the city's best-preserved monument. "The entrance to and interior of this curious building was almost entirely blocked up with fallen masonry and other debris," he wrote. "This has been removed at a considerable cost of labour, for most of the fallen blocks of masonry were so large that they had to be broken up with the pickaxe before removal was possible. But the labour was well expended..."

Ephemeral capitals

Dispersed among the forests, the Sinhalese moved their capital around, the most notable locations being the rock of Yapahuva and Gampola. Udarata, the future Kandyan kingdom, stretched from Batticaloa on the east coast to Kotte near the port of Colombo in the west. The Tamils, whose numbers had grown significantly, looked after themselves in an independent kingdom centred on Jaffna. Thus fragmented from the 13th to 15th centuries, the island was prey to invaders from unexpected quarters. Cheng Ho, a Chinese admiral, carried off one of the Sinhalese kings and his prime minister to China. A Malayan king invaded for reasons

LEFT: the grandeur of Polonnaruwa is reduced to a picturesque ruin in a 19th-century postcard view.
RIGHT: a new threat on the horizon in the shape of Portuguese war-ships.

which remain a mystery, and there is similar uncertainty about incursions by the king of Pegu in Burma or even a sultan of Egypt.

The first Europeans arrive.

The odd European arrived in Greek and Roman times, but the rush began when Marco Polo declared Lanka "better than any other island in the world." He was on a mission for Kublai Khan, to offer the king any city he liked in the Khan's empire in exchange for "the grandest ruby that was ever seen." The king would not let the ruby go but was ready to hand over strands of Buddha's hair, his begging bowl, and

a pair of teeth belonging to Adam, buried on the mountain that bore his name.

The islanders, Marco Polo reported, worshipped idols and went around "nearly in a state of nudity, only wrapping a cloth round the middle parts of their bodies." To supplement their diet of rice and meat they drank a wine bled from trees. They were not keen warriors; they preferred to use foreign mercenaries.

At the beginning of the 16th century a fleet of storm-battered ships appeared off the west coast. The occupants wore armour, carried firearms, and appeared to eat stones and drink blood. It was the island's first sight of the Portuguese, and the chroniclers drew a deep breath. ❏

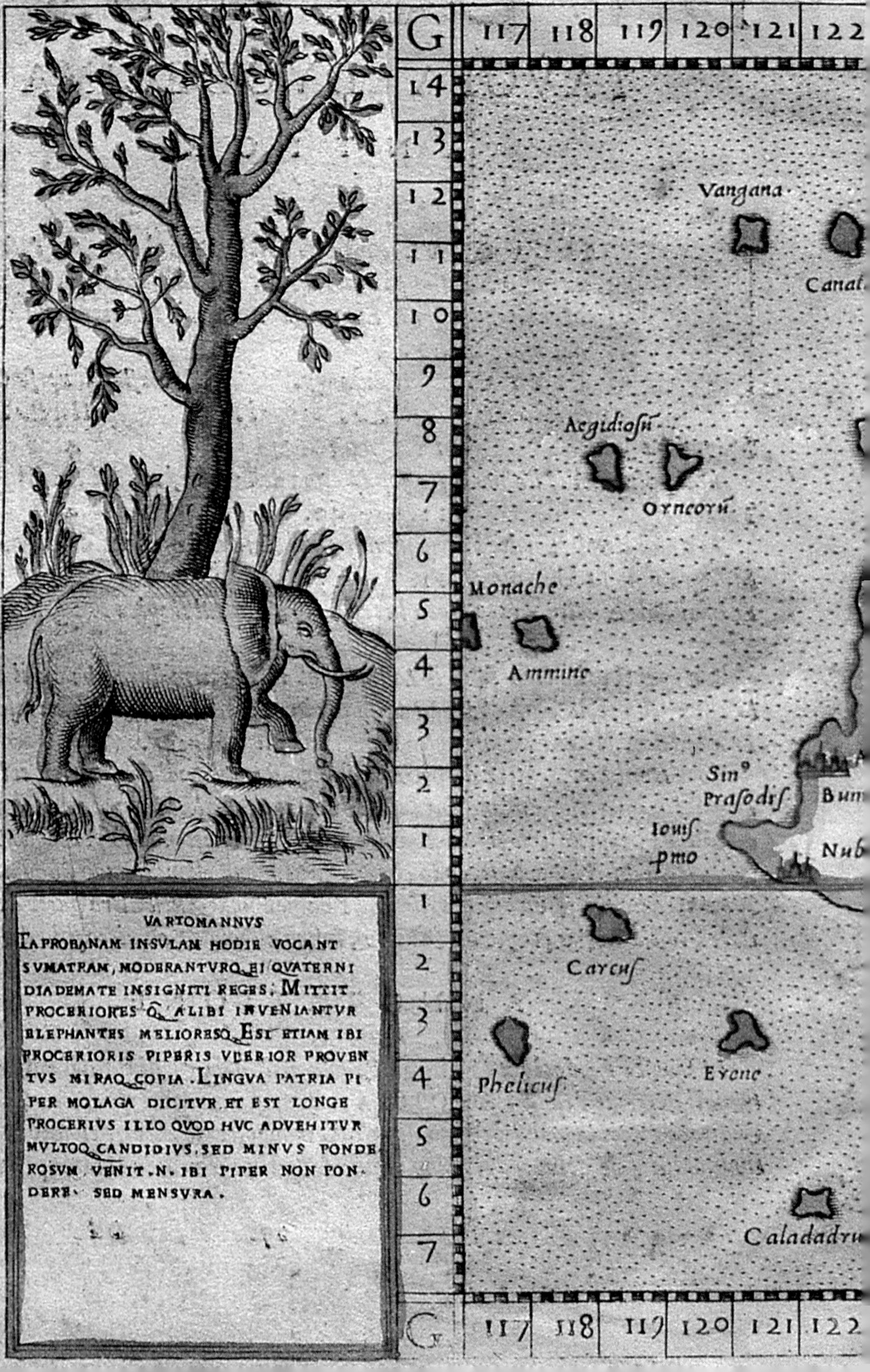

G	117	118	119	120	121	122

14
13
12
11
10
9
8
7
6
5
4
3
2
1

Vangana·

Canal·

Aegidiosu

Oyncoru

Monache

Ammine

Sin°
Prasodis

Iouis
pmo

Bun

Nub

1
2
3
4
5
6
7

Carchus

Phelicus

Efone

Caladadru

| 124 | 125 | 126 | 127 | 128 | 129 | 130 | 131 | 132 | 133 | 134 | 135 | | G |

INDIAE PARS

14

Borcum pmo

13

Susuara

12

11

Talacori Galidi

Modutti

10

MARE INDICVM

Margana Iogana

Anubingara

9

Anurogrammum regia

Nagadiba Maagram mum

Nagadiba

8

Oxia pmo. Procuri

7

Soani Galibi montes Gangesfl:

TAPROBANA

Semm

Adisamu

6

que ante se

solis por

5

Poduce Habet insulas 1578

zibala

4

Abaratha Tarachi

Malea mons.

3

Bocani Bayacus fl.

Bocana

2

Pascua

Elephantum

1

Æquinoctialis

Vlispada Rhogadani

Nacaduna

Nanigiri Bachi oppidum

zaba

1

odoca

Anium prom

Dagana

Corcobara

Gumara

2

3

Arana

4

Alaba

5

Bassa

Balaca

6

7

THE PORTUGUESE MEN O' WAR

The first Europeans to take an interest in Sri Lanka came for spice
but found themselves swept up in political intrigue

In 1497, the Portuguese navigator Vasco da Gama proved that sailing round Africa was a better route to the East than Columbus's course which ran into the unexpected continent that stood in his way. Eight years later, Dom Lourenco de Almeida, a Portuguese naval commander, was hunting for Moorish spice vessels off the Indian coast when bad weather forced his fleet of nine ships to anchor in the very river mouth where the spice-traders collected one of their most valuable commodities: cinnamon.

Their arrival did not go unnoticed. "There are now in our harbour of Colombo," a scout reported to the king of Kotte, "a race of men, exceeding white and beautiful. They wear boots and hats of iron, and they are always in motion. They eat white stones and they drink blood. They have guns which make a noise like thunder, and a ball shot from one of them, after flying some leagues, will break a castle of granite, or even of iron." The mistaken diet of white bread and red wine apart, the newcomers lived up to these terrifying first impressions.

The way to Kotte

The king of Kotte saw the Portuguese as an answer to belligerent Tamil states. He wished to meet de Almeida. To this day, "taking the Portuguese to Kotte" is a wry joke recalling the merry path they were led to disguise the fact that Kotte was just 13 km (8 miles) away and the kingdom quite small. The slog through the jungle took at least three days, some storytellers say weeks. Portuguese annals remember the occasion differently. As the ships fired a cannon on the hour and the roar was always audible, the weary envoys knew what was going on. A Portuguese soldier remarked in his journal that in his opinion every single person born on the island was treacherous.

The king offered 110,000 kg (250,000 lb) of cinnamon a year, an astonishing sum, for Portuguese protection. The Portuguese were slow to realise just how good a bargain they were being offered. The island was strategically placed to defend their trade routes, which

stretched from Brazil to Macao. By the time they re-opened negotiations in 1521, however, local politics had taken a characteristic turn.

Wars of succession

King Vijaya VI and his elder brother were both married to the same queen, so there were

doubts about the paternity of her three sons. The king was more confident about being the father of a fourth boy by a second queen and designated him as heir. That amounted to a double death warrant: for the boy and for the king himself.

The dubious triumvirate carved up the kingdom among themselves, and in 1540 the eldest, who took over Kotte, asked Portugal to guarantee the succession of his favourite grandson. Duly the boy was groomed for the throne with a Christian education and baptised as Dom Jão Dharmapala, whilst his effigy was shipped off to Lisbon and there crowned with great ceremony. The Portuguese even found a way of speeding the boy's accession: his grandfather was taking the air at an open window of the royal pavilion when a shot rang out and hit him square on the head. A Portuguese soldier said he was aiming at a pigeon.

Dom Jão Dharmapala's reign was immediately challenged by his cousin-once-removed Rajasinha who captured Kotte. Portuguese troops were despatched to ensure that this bellicose cousin was indeed once removed, but when the booty in the palace proved less than expected, they resorted to "robbing houses and violating women with great insolence and highhandedness." Under local rules, a Portuguese historian noted, soldiers smashed up property and killed one another but left women alone. "A great disgrace to Christians that Pagans should be more moderate in this."

Realising that they could not hold Kotte indefinitely, the Portuguese installed Dom Jão Dharmapala in Colombo. He was a sitting target, and in due course an uncle managed to get at him with some poison. The dose wasn't fatal, but the hapless Dom Jão lost all his teeth and was a physical wreck for the rest of his long and unhappy life.

A cunning Queen

As Rajasinha campaigned through the jungle, scooping up petty principalities until he had the great prize of Kandy, he left in his wake a flotsam of royal refugees, among them a couple of young princes who washed up on Portugal's doorstep. Unfortunately, there was only one prospective bride, Dõna Caterina, another refugee who had a claim to the Kandy crown which Portugal intended to enforce. This was another death warrant; with polyandrous arrangements now out of the question, one young prince was soon clutching his stomach.

And so the wrangles went on. After the wretched Dom Jão Dharmapala ceded his throne to Portugal, a baptised Christian named Konappu Bandara was engaged to lead the army into Kandy against Rajasinha. The idea was that Bandara would install the son of the king whom Rajasinha had overthrown. Instead, he celebrated the army's victory by seizing the throne for himself as King Vimala Dharma Suriya I. The retreating Rajasinha stood on a bamboo splinter and contracted fatal blood poisoning. The Buddhist chroniclers shed no tears: "Verily this sinner did rule with a strong arm."

Clearly a hard man was needed to sort things out, and none came harder than General Conquistador Pedro Lopez de Souza. It was agreed that he should make a start by getting young Dõna Caterina on the Kandyan throne come what may. In the event, Kandy was taken with hardly any opposition – Vimala Dharma Suriya I was lying in wait for De Souza on his way back to Colombo. The General Conquistador was in for a multiple humiliation: a military trouncing, the capture of Dõna Caterina, and the fact that she then married Vimala Dharma Suriya I, a change of sides that shows she was a consummate political survivor.

A TALE OF CRUELTY

Sinhalese chroniclers reserved the blackest pages in their history of the Portuguese era for Don Jeronimo de Azavedo, a captain-general who was said to throw victims so regularly into a pool of crocodiles that the beasts knew when to drift to the surface with their mouths open. It amused him to pick up children on the end of a spear and hear them, as he put it, crow like cocks.

PREVIOUS PAGES: a reproduction of the Greek geographer Ptolemy's 2nd-century AD map of "Taprobane."
LEFT: Catholic statue from the Portuguese period.
ABOVE: Dom Jão Dharmapala, the puppet king.

Battling for control

Meanwhile Jaffna remained a base for pirates who preyed on Portuguese shipping. In 1560, the viceroy accompanied 1,200 troops from Goa to subdue the north. "The viceroy, whose charger had been shot under him, fought his way to the vanguard on foot amid a cloud of arrows and bullets." The Tamil prince was eventually driven out of the city and the Portuguese went in for the spoils. Among the prisoners was the prince's wife, who afterwards became a Christian. The prince had slipped out of the fortress at night, leaving behind the heads of 12 chiefs who had suggested he might like to make peace with

the Portuguese. He was later reinstated, but proved to be an inveterate plotter. His last successor was sent to Goa to be beheaded. After almost a century, Portugal controlled the whole island apart from Kandy.

Nevertheless, Portugal had lost control of the seas. In 1612, two English ships beat off four Portuguese galleons and 26 frigates, and the Dutch had been investigating the island for a decade. Admiral Joris van Spilbergen had met Vimala Dharma Suriya I in Kandy and offered help against the Portuguese.

His compatriate Sebald de Weert arrived a few months later with a small fleet and went with some of his officers to see the king, inviting him to come back and inspect his ships. The king seemed reluctant to do so, saying that he should not leave his queen alone. The admiral, who had been drinking, unwisely quipped that from what he had heard, it was most unlikely that the queen, Dōna Caterina, would be alone for long. To be fair, the king's precise instructions to his men were *"bandapan me balla"* ("bind this dog"), but one of them took this to mean he should grab the admiral by the hair and split his head open with a sword. On reflection, the king decided this was no bad thing and ordered the other officers to be given the same treatment. The king sent a note, in Portuguese, to the captain of the ships, drawing his attention to the danger of drink.

Vimala Dharma Suriya died of fever in 1604. He was, the chroniclers concluded, "a bold and experienced warrior... tall, of a black complexion with a beautiful symmetry of body and a deep commanding voice..." His favourable obituary ended with a unique concession from the Buddhist monks: "He ridiculed the idea of all religious tenets, permitting everyone free religious exercise according to their own will and pleasure. In fact, he was in every sense of the word, a finished courtier."

The king's half-brother Senerat was a leading contender for the throne, and Dōna Caterina married him, elevating him to the throne with instructions to open negotiations with the Dutch with a view to getting rid of her former guardians, the Portuguese.

Losing control

The campaign to unseat the Portuguese extended to seeking an alliance with, of all people, the Danes. An eager expedition took two years to make the voyage from Denmark only to find that it had been overtaken by fast-moving local events and that their assistance was no longer required.

Faced with the long voyage home, the dejected crew stopped off on the Indian Coromandel coast for supplies, found they liked the place, and decided they might as well start a Danish colony there.

They were not needed on the island because by 1630 the Dutch had the sea-power necessary to blockade Goa, preventing Portuguese

> ### HORRORS OF WAR
>
> As Rajasinha II continued his successful campaign, a chronicler recorded with satisfaction that it was possible to make a pyramid with Portuguese heads.

The bloody finale

Twenty grim years later the Dutch provided the troops and heavy weapons for the climactic siege in Colombo. A Portuguese survivor described the end: "At three o'clock on the afternoon of the 12th May, 1656, we came out of the city, 73 very emaciated soldiers, all that remained there, including some with broken arms and minus a leg, and all looking like dead people... We then entered the house where we met the Dutch general and major, who received us very warmly

reinforcements from reaching the island while Rajasinha II, who had succeeded Senarat, fought his own battles. His forces inflicted a major defeat on the Portuguese commander Constantine de Sa.

But the Sinhalese king was not inclined to gloat when presented with de Sa's head, despite the victory: "How often did I ask thee not to make war on men, nor destroy my lands, but to let me live in peace, the Portuguese remaining absolute lords of the best part of Ceylon."

LEFT: a Portuguese church in Negombo.
ABOVE: a Dutch engraving showing their emphatic victory over the Portuguese.

and gave us a toast..." The Dutch officers said they looked forward to meeting the rest of the brave defenders. They were told there were no more surviving. "At this they changed colour, a great sadness following the cheerfulness with which they had received us."

The Portuguese garrison in Jaffna managed to hold on until 1658, but this was simply a sideshow to Rajasinha's arrival to claim Colombo under his agreement with the Dutch. He found the gates shut against him. In fury, Rajasinha torched everything around the city before withdrawing to Kandy. According to the Sinhalese proverb, "we gave pepper and got ginger." ❏

KANDY – THE HIDDEN KINGDOM

This secret place has the poetic resonance of Samarkand or Mandalay.
Its magic is vividly captured in the diary of a 17th-century sailor

It was as a haven for Sinhalese refugees from the appalling Magha, the tyrant who wrecked Polonnaruwa, that Kandy began to acquire its reputation as a remote and secretive kingdom, a jungle Shangri-la. Here, shunning the trading colonies on the coast and the Tamils to the north and relying on the jungle to preserve

their privacy, were the Sinhalese Kandyans, who saw themselves as the untainted descendants of Prince Vijaya and his 700 followers.

A captive audience

It was in the reign of Rajasinha II that life in Kandy came under an extraordinary microscope. In 1660, a 19-year-old Londoner named Robert Knox was among a party of English sailors who went ashore near the mouth of the Mahaweli river and were taken prisoner by the king's men. Knox kept an account of his "19 years six months and odd days" in captivity. He was allowed enough freedom to move around and talk to people – even to start a busi-

ness and buy a house – and his *Historical Relation of Ceylon* is a priceless document. Unlike the Buddhist chronicles, it is concerned with the lives of ordinary people, not just kings, and it inspired parts of Daniel Defoe's *Robinson Crusoe*.

The first surprise, on Knox's arrival in Kandy, was that he and his ship-mates were not the only European "guests." Rajasinha kept a menagerie of Europeans for his amusement: prisoners of war, shipwrecked sailors, insolent diplomats and so on. The most bad-tempered prisoner, at least to begin with, was Louis XIV of France's personal envoy, M. de la Narolle, who refused to go along with the etiquette expected at court. He was dragged out and kept in chains until he calmed down. Then, like all the European prisoners, he was free to make friends. The many little de la Narolles soon running around Kandy were the progenitors of all the "De Lanarolles" who survive to this day.

The Kandyan way of love

Knox chose not to marry because he wanted to avoid ties that might dissuade him from escaping when the opportunity arose. There was no question of simply bolting. The jungle was dense, the paths through it were carefully watched and no one was allowed to use them without a kind of passport. Nevertheless, Knox liked women, and Kandyan women, it seems, loved men. Even married women, he noted, had affairs with anyone they liked, if necessary leaving their husbands at home to look after the children. Problems only arose "should they lay with a man of inferior quality to themselves." When important visitors called, husbands "commonly will send their wives or daughters to bear them company in their chamber… And for the matter of being with child, which many of them do not desire, they very exquisitely can prevent the same." The treatment, it seems, was a concoction of the plumbago plant.

Men could take women of a lower caste to bed but not sit or eat with them. To marry them was to be automatically demoted to their level. "Both women and men do commonly wed four or five times before they can settle themselves." If a woman deserted her husband, no one would marry her until her husband had remarried. Polyandry, in which two or more brothers shared a wife or one man married a number of sisters, was acceptable but fairly unusual.

A strait-laced Portuguese Jesuit who wrote about Kandy strongly disapproved of polyandry but observed that the institution of marriage under local rules was "the greatest felicity in the world."

Kandy was not a great city of monuments; civil war and foreign invasion led to a style of wooden architecture that could be easily rebuilt. People lived in small clay daubed thatched cottages with a couple of stools as the only furniture. Their diet was rice flavoured with herbs, spices or fruit juices. If they appeared lazy, it was because the moment they acquired anything above the bare necessities of life, it was snatched away by hordes of assessment officers, customs officials, rent collectors and tax gatherers.

Death by elephant

Justice was dispensed by a court of local chiefs and officials, although Knox expressed doubts about an appeal system that worked on the principle that "whoso gives the greatest bribe, he shall overcome." Appeals to the king were risky: he might decide that the petitioners were wasting his time, in which case they could expect a trial by ordeal, which meant plunging their hands into boiling oil. Only the king could order corporal punishment – although never for women – and capital punishment by elephant seemed an effective deterrent because Knox knew of only a few examples.

In the case of execution by elephant, "they will run their Teeth through the body, and then tear it in pieces and throw it limb from limb.

PRECEDING PAGES: Kandyan chiefs padded out with hundreds of yards of fine cloth wound round them.
LEFT: Robert Knox, from the frontispiece of his journal.
RIGHT: the pious British were horrified by elephant execution, as depicted in this engraving by someone who had never even seen an elephant.

OVERCROWDING

At one stage, when 600 Dutch were caught trying to steal a herd of the king's tame elephants, there were no fewer than 1,000 foreign captives in Kandy.

They have a sharp iron which they put on their teeth at such times."

Although women were spared corporal punishment, the king frequently lost patience with the lot of them: "He gives command to expel all the women out of the city, not one to remain; but, by little and little, when they think his wrath is appeased, they do creep in again."

Rajasinha seems to have been almost unique among Kandyan kings in leading a subdued private life, as Knox's observations on his Indian

CHARACTER STUDY

Robert Knox liked the Kandyan people very much: they were "proper and well-favoured, beyond all people that I have seen in India, active and nimble in their limbs, very ingenious, very hardy, both for diet and weather, very proud, not very malicious one towards another, and their anger does not last long, very few spendthrifts or bad husbands." A modern Sri Lankan would be less happy to acknowledge the accuracy of his assessment of their main failing: a low standard of honour. "They make no account nor conscience of lying, neither is it any shame or disgrace to them, if they be catched in telling lies; it is so customary."

consort showed: "She hath not been with him, as it is known, this twenty year… As he is abstemious in his eating, so in the use of women. If he useth them 'tis unknown and with great secrecy… He allows not in his court whoredom or adultery; and many times when he hears of the misdemeanours of some of his nobles in regard of women, he not only executes them but severely punisheth the women, if known." The king was indifferent to religious matters and sufficiently tolerant to allow Portuguese priests to build a church in the kingdom. He closed it down when he found, or at least suspected, that they were running it as a brothel.

A WHOLE LOT OF KNITTING

Knox turned down the offer of a job at the palace and went into business instead. Once his "black boy" – apparently the inspiration for Robinson Crusoe's Man Friday – had taught him to knit, he and fellow English prisoners started producing caps without knowing when to stop. "Caps began to abound, and Trading grew dead, so that we could not sell them at the former price, which brought several of our Nation to great want." His next venture was more successful; he went into "banking," the currency being not money but grain. He lent at a straight 50 percent. If that sounded high, he added, "so is the trouble of getting it."

Courtly manoeuvres

The king had a variety of costumes, including a towering four-cornered hat with a long upright feather, a doublet with sleeves in a different colour, and ankle-length breeches. Rajasinha might sometimes slip on a disguise and go out at night to spy on his subjects, but his public appearances, even if no more than a few steps from the palace, were an ordeal for the guards.

His royal walk-abouts were accompanied by a full entourage of "Flags and Soldiers, Drummers, Trumpeters, Pipers, Singers and all belongings, such as Elephants, Horses, Falkeners and their Faulkens, and many others, to stand at the Gate in a readiness to attend his pleasure."

His pleasure, unfortunately, was completely unpredictable, so the whole guard might assemble and disperse three or four times before the king deigned to show himself. "And oftentimes," wrote Knox, "he come out when none there are aware of it, with only those that attend on his person within his Palace. And then when it is heard, that his Majesty is come forth, they all run ready to break their necks, and place themselves at a distance to Guard his Person and wait his pleasure."

Knox escapes

In the end, Knox made a run for the Dutch-controlled north with another Englishman, abandoning with some regret his house and estate, an old man who looked after them and, most of all, a girl named Lucea, who was the daughter of a fellow captive. It was on their way north that he came across the ruins of Anuradhapura which, for all his local knowledge, he had never heard of.

In 1698, Knox was back in the East as a ship's captain, and in China he ran into one of his fellow prisoners, who had been released after Rajasinha's death. He learned that other old friends were still in Kandy, so he wrote to let them know that life in England was hard and that he was still a bachelor. He enclosed a picture of himself with the request that it be passed on to Lucea. "You know that I loved the Child & since have no cause to hate her." ❏

LEFT: the Temple of the Tooth, the last in a long line stretching back to Anuradhapura.
RIGHT: Kandy bridges ancient and modern: a 20th-century fresco at Kelaniya depicts the arrival of the Tooth in the 4th century, but its style is Kandyan.

THE NEW MASTERS

Along with coffee, tea and rubber, the Dutch and British

transplanted western institutions into Sri Lankan soil

I t is said that in their ultimate victory over the Portuguese at the siege of Jaffna in 1658, the pragmatic Dutch used Portuguese tombstones as mortar bombs, packed the defeated men off to captivity in Batavia, kept the women, declared a special day of thanksgiving for their victory over "popery and idolatrous

practices" and looked forward to making money. After the Portuguese, the historian Philalethos concluded, "the Dutch did not bend before the grim Moloch of religious bigotry, nor did they worship at the shrine of superstition; but cent per cent was their faith, gold was their object, and Mammon was their god."

In fact, Dutch missionaries did try to convert the island to Calvinism, and the secular administration helped the cause by reserving jobs in the civil service exclusively for Christians. Education was perceived as "work whereby God's glory was promoted and the Company's position is at the same time assured." The subjects taught were Latin, Greek, Hebrew, theology and the control of natural passions. If this seemed a tall order, by 1740 a schools inspector reported his astonishment at the facility "with which little black fellows chatter in Latin and construe Greek."

Austere Calvinism was too much even for those islanders who could comfortably worship Buddha, a pantheon of Hindu gods and the Virgin Mary at more or less the same time. The Dutch did not really care; their main goal was building exports of cinnamon, elephants, pearls, salt and areca or betel nuts. It was to the semi-addictive properties of the juicy nuts that a large part of Asia's population gratefully owed their perennial red teeth and gums.

The odour of cinnamon

Cinnamon grew wild in damp, elephant-infested jungle. Collecting it was hard, dangerous and the exclusive job of the Choliah caste. They used a special knife to strip the bark off branches in long tubes. These were bundled up and taken to "surgeons" who bit off pieces to assess quality, the premium being on milder varieties without an after-taste. A ritual slice of bread between batches was not to cleanse the palate in the wine-tasting sense but to ease pain; repeated mouthfuls of cinnamon were torture on the tongue.

Cinnamon was so valuable that it was made a capital offence to damage any of the plants,

---

PRECIOUS OILS

Islanders traditionally used the acorn-sized fruit of the cinnamon tree to make hair and body oil. Mixed with coconut oil, it burnt brilliantly in lamps. But there was another oil, made in heated tubs from scraps of bark, that proved a bonanza. "Oyle of cinnamon," a contemporary medical report declared, "doe greatlie strengthen all the inward parts, as head, hart, mawe and lyver."

It could only be produced in small quantities and was consequently worth a fortune, bottles being individually sealed and kept under lock and key by the Dutch governor himself until sold by special auction.

which grew up to 3 metres (10 ft) in height, or to sell it on the black market. However, Moorish traders were more familiar with the coastline than Dutch naval patrols, so contraband cinnamon and even elephants went out; Indian rice and textiles came the other way.

The Dutch eventually cultivated cinnamon around Colombo, partly because harvesting in the wild was expensive and resulted in territorial clashes with Kandy, whose kings were by treaty allowed to collect their own supplies for sale to the Dutch. After initial difficulties arising from the kingdom's delay in settling in cinnamon its huge debt to the Dutch for their help

obsequiousness. The Dutch took full advantage of the king's proud spirit by flattering him with an army of ambassadors who told him that they were his ever loyal humble servants and subjects. "It is out of loyalty to him," wrote a disgusted Robert Knox when he witnessed their activities in court, "that they build forts and keep watches round the country to prevent foreign nations and enemies from coming in." Such flattery was lapped up by the king who seemed oblivious to the fact that the Dutch were not just the new invaders but one of those "foreign nations" too.

A Dutch governor produced a memorandum

against the Portuguese, the governor Van Goens left a word of advice for his son, who succeeded him. "It can easily be seen what a mischievous and horrible thing war is... All our efforts should be directed in future to reduce our expenses by a well-regulated establishment and to increase our profits by faithful economy."

Dealings with Kandy

As a matter of company policy in dealings with the king of Kandy, the better part of valour was

LEFT: an 18th-century Dutch gravestone from the Groote Kerk in Galle.
ABOVE: a collection of colonial coins.

listing suitable presents for the king. Nothing too expensive, just "two or three fine Persian horses and Persian goods, some tea, porcelain, Indian preserves, etc would be sufficient." He added that the king had a soft spot, too, for "pictures, paintings, portraits, representations of sea battles, and snuff." Exotic additions to the king's private zoo were always welcome. As a result, relations between the two parties were usually cordial.

The relationship could not be sustained when the Dutch in 1766 sacked Kandy and imposed a mile-wide cordon between the kingdom and the sea. Apart from the physical and perhaps psychological isolation, this cordon denied

Kandy access to precious salt in coastal lagoons. The idea was that the kingdom should buy its salt from the company, paying in cinnamon, but it proved unenforcable. "The inhabitants of this Province do not purchase salt," a Lieutenant Schneider noted, "having sufficient opportunities to steal it from the salt pans – as much as they want, perhaps more."

Dutch Law

Governors sitting in Colombo applied the principles of Roman-Dutch law. Certain matters were judged according to codified Tamil and Moslem law, but the Sinhalese were a passion-

ately litigious people who had developed a legal system so complex that it was beyond any outsider's comprehension. Under Kandyan law, for example, people who failed to pay fines had stones piled on top of them until they complied. Either that or they were made to stand with bare legs apart while a thorn bush was rubbed briskly to and fro.

While the Dutch gave up trying to turn such practices into statutory law, the Sinhalese for their part took to the Dutch system like ducks to water, and the country remains to this day a bottomless pit of extremely able lawyers and barristers. The author Michael Ondaatjie mentions that the power of silky persuasion was in the gift of the *thalagoya*, a cross between an iguana and giant lizard which is common on the island but almost unknown anywhere else. Its prickly tongue – used to snare prey – was removed after knocking the creature senseless, placed between two slices of banana like a sandwich, and swallowed whole. "I am not sure what other side effects there are," he says, "apart from possible death."

By modern standards, Dutch law was ferocious but reasonably impartial, as indeed one of the Dutch governors found out. Petrus Vuyst was as close as the Dutch got to matching the Portuguese crocodile keeper Dom Jeronimo de Azavedo. Disappointed not to have been given a larger country to govern, he landed in 1726 with a hand over one eye, saying he could see quite enough that way. To anyone else, his administration looked like systematic sadism. He was sent home after three years, impeached and executed.

The British move in

The British East India Company began showing an interest in the island because of the natural harbour of Trincomalee and a possible back-up for the company's operations in India. The American War of Independence provided the pretext for its capture, the Dutch fleet having failed to observe the British blockade of American ports. To complicate matters, the French were known to be keen on the island, so when France invaded Holland in 1794, it was time to ask the Dutch whether a protective British presence in Ceylon would give them one less thing to worry about. There was no colonial war between Britain and the Dutch. The issue was settled by British naval

A DUTCH CARICATURE

A satirical description of the typical "Dutchman" was given by Captain Percival of the Royal Irish Regiment: "He rises early, about six, and either goes to walk, or sits down by his door in a loose robe and night-cap to smoke a pipe. This with a glass of gin, which is called a *soupkie*, fills up the interval to seven. A dish of coffee is then handed him by his slaves, and his lounging posture and tobacco-pipe are again resumed." Dutch wives looked upon their menfolk "with the greatest veneration and affection" and made themselves attractive by "cracking their joints, and rubbing them over with oil" which made them "uncommonly supple."

supremacy, although the finale was provided by the secret service with the help of a large Dutch cheese.

British victory

Having landed at Trincomalee against only light opposition, 1,200 British troops and two battalions of sepoys from the British Indian Army began the long trudge along the beach to confront the Dutch garrison at Colombo which, for some years past, had been reinforced by crack Swiss mercenaries under a Comte de

DUTCH REMAINS

Sri Lanka's Dutch heritage is seen today in the characteristic architecture and canals, a cuisine imported from Dutch Indonesia and parts of the law.

Hugh Cleghorn, a professor at St Andrew's University in Scotland. The count confided, probably over a drink, that some of his creditors were pressing. Cleghorn, who by then understood what de Meuron did for a living – he had left the Swiss mercenaries in the charge of his brother Pierre – established that the sum of £4,000 would keep the creditors quiet while the pair of them sailed off to India on an adventurous trip which involved picking up an Arab *dhow* in the Red Sea.

Meuron. The British troops were shadowed on one flank by a Kandyan army eager to join battle with their new ally against an old enemy. They had a written albeit unsigned agreement that, for helping Britain, Kandy would be awarded one of the Dutch ports, thus ending the kingdom's crippling inland isolation.

It was only in the 20th century that the truth about the decisive battle for Colombo came to light. Some months before Britain made its move, it seems, Comte de Meuron had been holidaying in Europe when he bumped into

LEFT: a gateway in Galle, dated 1669.
ABOVE: cannons on Galle Face Green in Colombo.

Cleghorn, it transpired, did odd jobs for the British secret service, and it was in the finest tradition of that institution that brother Pierre, sitting in the Dutch fort in Colombo, was surprised to receive an unsolicited gift from India in the form of a large Dutch cheese. Of course, the cheese contained a secret communication. If, some time later, the British troops and Indian sepoys approaching Colombo wondered what had happened to the Swiss mercenaries – why there was no resistance apart from some Malay mercenaries – they had no way of knowing that the Swiss no longer worked for the Dutch. The cheese had advised Pierre and his men that they were contracted to join the British army and their new posting, with immediate effect, was in Canada. With their services unrequired, the shadowing Kandyan forces never did get a signature on the promise of a port. Instead, the kingdom was allowed access to the sea – but only for the purpose of obtaining fish and salt.

Britain's prime minister, William Pitt, described the island as "the most valuable colonial possession on the globe… giving to our Indian empire a security it had not enjoyed from its first establishment." It was entrusted to the Hon. Frederick North, aged 32, a son of George III's prime minister and a classics scholar with a passionate interest in ancient Greece.

The conquest of Kandy

Shortly after North's appointment, Sri Wikrama Rajasinha was crowned King of Kandy. North paid his respects by presenting him with an elaborate stage coach plus team of horses. The coach had to be delivered in pieces because, apart from a thoroughfare in the capital wide enough to stage elephant fights, there were no proper roads in or to the kingdom. Nothing had changed since the mighty Rajasinha banned bridges and even the widening of paths through the jungle. Its impenetrability was the kingdom's defence against European armies.

When the young king demonstrated in no uncertain manner that he was not to be bought

with gifts, North was inclined to depose him by force. To do so required some sort of pretext. It wasn't much, but it was enough, when an army officer at a remote outpost reported that Kandyan officials had snatched some betel nuts from Moorish traders and refused to pay for them or give them back. Bugles echoed round the army base in Colombo and a battalion of the 51st Foot marched out "with the countenances of the soldiers full of cheerfulness and joy," the rear brought up by a long baggage train of elephants, mules and coolies carrying, among other things, large drums of arrack. Four miles out of town, a halt was called so that the officers could join friends for supper at the Cocoa-Nut Club overlooking the Kelani river.

Reality took on a sterner complexion when the column entered the jungle. Leeches got in everywhere so that it was quite likely that at the end of a day's march, and without feeling a thing, their uniforms were covered in blood. At no time was there any protection against mosquitoes, jungle fever or the debilitating combination of roasting heat and torrential rain. If their rations ran out, beri-beri caused limbs to swell agonisingly to elephantine proportions. The jungle was Kandy's defence in depth – draw the enemy in and let nature kill them off.

The Kandyan army

In contrast, the bulk of the Kandyan army were conscripts from the royal estates. Not more than a third of the available men were mobilised at a time, and then for a maximum of 15 days. They reported for duty with an assortment of ancient muskets or in some cases bow and arrows. Other equipment consisted of an umbrella-cum-sunshade made of palm leaves, a cooking pot and enough rice, cakes and coconuts to last the prescribed 15 days. On being relieved by a fresh intake, they returned to their villages.

The army also had Malabar regulars smartly turned out in turbans, red jackets and blue trousers. Malays, who had usually come over from the Dutch, served as the king's bodyguard. They were not only fearless but, as outsiders, had none of the blood-ties that would otherwise make them susceptible to plots against the crown. They trusted the kriss, a knife known affectionately as *swammy*, or "little god." No king of Kandy was ever killed by his Malay guard.

A hollow victory

The British troops found the capital abandoned and in ashes, the Kandyans having evaporated into the jungle. The city had been sacked so often by the Portuguese and Dutch that Kandyans no longer built for posterity. Most of the smouldering houses were no more than mud huts. The only building that had not been put to the torch before the tactical withdrawal was the Dalada Maligawa, the Temple of the Tooth. On the other hand, British officers recognised the charred remains of North's presentation stagecoach: someone had at least gone to the trouble of assembling it. North installed Muttusamy,

grimness was relieved by the intervention of the king to save the life of the last surviving patient, a Sergeant Theon. He was invited to live in the kingdom on a royal pension. Theon accepted and over the course of the next 12 years married a local girl and had a son. Muttusamy bravely surrendered himself to save the lives of his guards and was executed. The guards were also executed, although a corporal somehow survived a blow that did not quite take off his head. He made a miraculous return to Colombo still supporting his head with his hands and survived to tell the tale.

Three wars were fought before the kingdom

the forlorn but not undignified puppet he had selected to be king, in the blackened palace. While the main force returned to Colombo, a detachment was left behind to look after him. Most of them were soon sick. "God only knows what will become of us here," one of them wrote, "for if we are ordered to evacuate the place, there is scarce a single European that could walk a mile."

The bed-ridden soldiers were butchered as the Kandyans regained their capital, but the

finally fell in 1815 when the famous Kandy Convention ceding the island to Britain was signed. Rajasinha went off to spend the rest of his life in comfortable exile in Madras, leaving the most striking of his legacies to Kandy: the artificial lake near the Temple of the Tooth. Built for aesthetic rather than irrigational purposes, in the tradition of Anuradhapura and Polonnaruwa, the former mosquito-infested swamp was, in earlier times, ironically the city's last line of defence.

While Buddhist chroniclers shed few tears over the departure of the last of the Malabar kings – whose exploits included the impaling of hundreds of people in a "merciless death" –

LEFT: the last Kandyan king in effigy at Dambulla. **ABOVE:** no more hiding in the shrubbery once the Colombo to Kandy railway was built.

he won over his British captors, reminding one of them of Henry VIII of England. It was not only his bearded corpulence but the fact that an island in the middle of his lake served as a harem. The British turned his love-nest into a powder magazine.

British control

Thereafter, Britain's control of the island was never seriously tested. Once the British had pushed roads through the jungle, it could no longer hide a clandestine independent state. A more accurate gauge of the new situation was that in 1821 Kandy staged its first horse-race

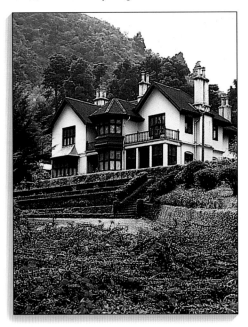

meeting. The last of the royal pretenders made his bid in 1848, which coincided with unrest triggered by a rumour that women were about to be taxed according to the size of their breasts, a feature of local anatomy that seems never to have escaped colonial officers when they wrote their memoirs. On the whole, Ceylon was a peaceful place until the communal rioting that led to civil war after independence.

Plantations

Profound changes came on the economic front. With new roads criss-crossing the highlands, which were ideal for growing coffee, word flew round England that fortunes were to be made.

"The first ardent adventurers," wrote Sir Emerson Tennent of the inevitable rush, "pioneered the way through pathless woods, and lived for months in log huts." The new life in the jungle was full of excitement and romance. So dazzling was the prospect that expenditure was unlimited, and its profusion was only equalled by the ignorance and inexperience of those to whom it was entrusted.

Transplanted Tamils

Planters thought the reluctance of local peasants to provide labour was innate indolence; they failed to appreciate that virtually all had plots of their own that kept them fully occupied. Sinhalese kings of old had imported labourers from India to peel cinnamon, and Britain followed their example. With south India then teetering on famine, the prospects in Ceylon sounded like Eldorado. Indians swarmed across the narrow straits in catamarans and on rafts in order to set out on the long walk to the plantations. A quarter of them never made it, dying at the roadside to await burial by the police. Moreover, the harvest was seasonal, so they went home afterwards with whatever they had managed to save and ran the gauntlet all over again the following year.

The coffee planters were hit by the rising popularity of tea lowering demand for coffee, and the so-called Coffee Bug finished them off. Tea was both their ruin and salvation. "The new generation of tea planters," a contemporary wrote, "have only to step into the poor collapsed coffee planter's shoes and comfortable and accessible quarters."

The transition for the Indian labourers was more problematic. Unlike coffee, tea was picked all-year round and therefore required a permanent labour force. In the space of 15 years, nearly a million men, women and children arrived. They lived in plantation compounds, as many as 10 people cooking, eating and sleeping in a compartment measuring 4 sq. meters (144 sq. ft). They were landless aliens, which put an unbridgeable gulf between them and Tamils who had settled, mainly in the north, from the 3rd century BC as hangers-on of repeated invasions. The British government was alarmed: "Every attempt must be made to secure protection for the immigrant, not only as a matter of humanity, but also as one of public interest."

The planation economy became a ladder of

opportunity not only for the Sinhalese but also for long established Tamils and descendants of colonists or "Burghers" who were already part of the cosmopolitan *milieu*. The familiar route was to use working capital made out of selling drink to buy into tea or rubber plantations or the mining of graphite. The de Soysa family, genuine tycoons, prided themselves on managing their estates with no Europeans whatever on the payroll.

In general administration and education, the British colonial authorities built on the Dutch foundation. Formal recognition was given to "the religion of Boodhoo" and the Tooth, which had fallen by accident into British hands, was given back. Sinhalese, Tamils and Europeans went to separate schools in Colombo, although the theory was that they would emerge with the ability to compete on equal terms and, no less importantly, with ingrained respect for "order and the present government." Right from the start, North had urged that the brightest pupils go on to universities in England and two sons of the Mudaliyar de Saram thus left for Cambridge University in 1811, leading the way for many distinguished successors.

Political advancement

The prickly imperial question of how much political representation should be given to the indigenous population resulted in a divergence between the authorities in London, who were inclined to be liberal, and officials on the spot who spluttered about their subjects being "utterly deficient of the requisite elements." Effective political representation was a long time coming. The Ceylon National Congress was formed in the aftermath of World War I as an amalgam of all the main communities, although there was an omen of divisions ahead when the Tamils broke away to form a separate organisation.

Meanwhile, Ceylon became the first colonial dependency in Asia to be given universal suffrage without literacy, property, income or gender qualifications. Further consideration was suspended by the outbreak of World War II.

LEFT: under British rule the uplands sprouted incongruous Edwardian villas and equally incongruous suburban gardens.
RIGHT: the rediscovery of Pali script enabled Sri Lanka's written history to be read again.

World War II

To the ordinary people of Ceylon, World War II began as a dispute on the other side of the world about things that did not concern them. This changed in early 1942, when Singapore, Rangoon and the Dutch East Indies fell to Japan and the assumption that India was the next target put Ceylon in the front line. If Calcutta were put out of commission, Britain had no other ports closer than East Africa or Australia. Ceylon's air defences against the Japanese carrier fleet that had attacked Pearl Harbor amounted to a few Catalina flying boats and some antiquated Wildebeeste bombers known

CEYLON'S ROSETTA STONE

In 1826 a provincial agent named George Turnour was burrowing in a temple on top of a 200-metre (600-ft) rock called Mulgirigala on the south coast, and came across a stack of palm-leaf parchments that provided the clues that enabled him to decipher the archaic Pali script of the *Mahavamsa.* "From the native chroniclers," wrote an electrified Major Forbes, "we find that the ancestors of a people whom Britons long regarded as savages, and for some time treated as slaves, existed as a numerous and comparatively civilised nation at a period antecedent to the discovery of Great Britain and its semi-barbarous inhabitants."

to their crews, with some understatement, as "flying coffins." As more airworthy reinforcements were rushed out, followers of the turf saw their beloved Colombo racecourse turned into an aerodrome. The hot-weather exodus from Colombo to the hill stations seemed to start a little earlier that year.

On Sunday, 5 April, aircraft from the Japanese carriers bombed Colombo, although not before their approach was spotted by Squadron Leader L. J. Birchall of the Canadian Royal Air Force in one of the Catalinas. He managed to get off a signal before being shot down and taken prisoner. Two merchant ships in the har-

bour were hit and a bomb landed on a mental hospital a little way out of town. Sirens wailed in Trincomalee four days later, and a number of British warships in nearby waters were sunk, including the carrier Hermes.

An invasion was not on Japan's immediate agenda, however; the main objective was to destroy Britain's Eastern fleet. Thanks to the one-sided advantage of radar, however, the fleet was able to keep out of the way in the Maldives.

By the end of the year Ceylon became the springboard for offensive operations eastward. Lord Louis Mountbatten set up his South East Asia Command headquarters at Peradeniya in Kandy, Trincomalee was the base for the "advanced operations school" of the British Special Operations Executive, who infiltrated saboteurs and resistance organisers behind Japanese lines, and as one of many new airstrips all over the island happened to be at the foot of the Sigiriya rock fortress, the saucy murals were swathed in bamboo and cotton wool, although against the vibrations of heavy engines rather than longing eyes.

Preparing for independence

As the war drew to a close, the Tamils proposed a "Fifty-fifty Scheme" that would give half the seats in a future legislature to the Sinhalese (roughly 70 percent of the population) and reserve the other half for all minorities combined but excluding the Indian immigrant labourers, who would lose the vote they had under existing British rules. It was stated in London in July 1945 that "His Majesty's Government are in sympathy with the desire of the people of Ceylon to advance towards dominion status..."

London made no secret of its preference for the United National Party (UNP), a moderate organisation which, under the stewardship of D.S. Senanayake, cut across ethnic and religious lines. The opposition represented specific sectional groups and an eclectic range of Bolshevik-Leninist, Trotskyist and Stalinist communists. Senanayake's party won an overwhelming victory and, in British eyes, all bode well for a seamless transition to independence. ❏

THE CEYLON DAILY NEWS, TUESDAY, M

[...]R, G. C. S. CUREA Ceylon's Ambassador in Washington, looks on while Mr. Hume-Wrong, Canadian Ambassador to the United States, presents the Order of the British Empire and the Distinguished Flying Cross to Group Captain L. J. Birchall (right) of the Royal Canadian Air Force at Washington on April 29.

BROTHERS IN ARMS

Allied troops swarming all over the island had nothing but praise for local hospitality. "They were much made of," says E.F.C. Ludowyk in her *Story of Ceylon*, "not because they were regarded as defenders of the island, but as interesting people with whom there was much in common... For the first time Ceylonese came in contact with the white man as an ordinary human being, a person like themselves in fact, stripped to the waist in tropical heat and working on the same laborious tasks they knew only too well – road-making, clearing the jungle and moving heavy loads from place to place."

LEFT: Captain L. J. Birchall's heroism was recognised in 1949, and made the news in Ceylon.
RIGHT: the restoration of ancient monuments, such as the Rankot Vihara at Polonnaruwa, is symbolic to many Sri Lankans of the restoration of national parks.

INDEPENDENCE

In five decades of independence, Sri Lanka has struggled to build a future.
But it has found itself beset by demons from the past

Ceylon embarked on independence on 4 February 1948 in good shape. War-time demand for rubber had put plenty of money in the bank and the military presence on the island had created jobs and opportunities for keen-eyed entrepreneurs. The military had also launched a blitz on mosquitoes, lifting Ceylon to the threshold of becoming the first country in Asia to eradicate malaria.

As minister of agriculture in the pre-war government, D.S. Senanayake had devoted himself to restoring the derelict irrigation systems of ancient Anuradhapura and Polonnaruwa. As the first prime minister of independent Ceylon, he outdid Parakrama the Great, the 12th-century king who had famously ordained that not a drop of water should reach the sea without serving man. The Gal Oya project on the Mahaweli river would create an inland sea four times larger than the Parakrama Sumadra, the Senanayake Sumudra.

Unfortunately, the boom was deceptive. The economy was unable to weather volatile international demand for its narrow range of natural products, and even the eradication of malaria had a dark side, slashing the rate of infant mortality and creating a baby boom that would challenge the weakened economy. The prime minister's persuasive charm, too, showed signs of succumbing to a Ceylonese phenomenon noted by the historian Sir Ivor Jennings, that anyone in public office "is given an enthusiastic welcome and has at least a year before the ants begin swarming over him."

The Tamil question

Senanayake entered negotiations with his Indian counterpart, Pandit Nehru, over an issue that would tarnish relations between the neighbours for years to come. He insisted that the Indian or "New Tamil" plantation workers, even if some had been living on the island for two or more

generations and had been recognised as residents by Britain, were foreign – specifically Indian – nationals. It would not have escaped his notice that they used the franchise given to some of them by Britain to vote for their own sectarian candidates, not the prime minister's UNP. For its part, India was concerned about

Indian émigré populations in East Africa and elsewhere and had drawn up its own rules of citizenship, which among others did not cover the workers in Ceylon.

The multi-racial fabric of the UNP was then threatened when S.W.R.D. Bandaranaike defected to form the Sri Lanka Freedom Party (SLFP). Ostensibly it represented a more radical but still multi-racial departure from the UNP's "neo-colonial" outlook. Bandaranaike was a member of the Kandyan nobility torn between a Westernised upbringing – he had taken the well-trodden road to Oxford University – and Kandyan pride in their tradition of championing the combined cause of Sinhalese Buddhism. He

LEFT: a new dawn for a nation with a long memory.
RIGHT: D.S. Senanayake, the first prime minister of independent Ceylon.

had given an early hint of his political direction when, on returning from Oxford before the war, he shed both Western clothing and Christianity and pronounced himself "Sinhalese to the core". Before long, that just about summed up the SLFP. The audience it addressed were the rising generation of Sinhalese who had been educated in Sinhalese, wondered why the official language was still English, and were disappointed, economically, by independence.

The Sinhalese find their tongue

D.S. Senanayake died in 1952 after a fall while exercising his mount on Galle Face in Colombo.

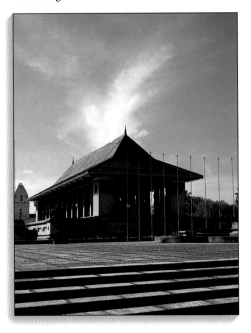

In being succeeded by his son, Dudley Senanayake, the pattern was set for an extraordinary demonstration of dynastic tennis: Senanayake and the UNP in one court; opposite them, a succession of Bandaranaikes in various permutations of the SLFP.

Sir Ivor Jennings' ants were waiting for Dudley Senanayake. With soaring inflation and unemployment, he turned to organisations like the International Bank for Reconstruction and Development and took their advice to cut the subsidy on imported rice. The result was an explosion that was settled only by a full-scale state of emergency to restore order. He resigned with tail between his legs. There was a brief

interregnum before Bandaranaike stormed into office on a platform of making Sinhalese the official language. The formal introduction of his cabinet was an echo of his gesture on returning from Oxford: they wore a length of white cloth draped from the waist and loose, long-sleeved white shirts. It was of course a political statement, akin to Chairman Mao's buttoned tunic, but it bemused the population at large who had never seen anything like it except on Indian politicians. Subsequent presidents stuck to the innovation, bravely ignoring sniggers.

The language campaign catapulted Bandaranaike into office with a huge majority, but when the appropriate bill was read in parliament, delighted Sinhalese and resentful Tamils – who communicated with one another in English – came to blows in the streets. Neither the prospect of a new official language nor nationalisation of key industries like transport and ports made any difference to a deepening economic crisis, and Tamils demonstrated their lack of confidence by deserting en masse to their ancestral lands in the north and raising the cry for an independent Tamil state as of old.

The implications were not lost on Bandaranaike, but his swift dialogue with the Tamil leadership served only to whip up extremists in both camps. An orgy of looting, murder and savagery broke out.

In what would later be called "ethnic cleansing", Tamils were driven out of Colombo and other areas where they had lived among Sinhalese, while Sinhalese ran for their lives from Tamil areas in the north and east. Bandaranaike had hoped to stop the haemorrhage, and it was because he was willing to explore possibilities with the Tamils that a Buddhist monk walked up to him and, at point blank-range, emptied a revolver.

Relations worsen

After a brief interlude occupied by Dudley Senanayake, Mrs Sirimavo Bandaranaike, the assassinated prime minister's widow, was ushered into office, on a wave of sympathy, as the world's first woman prime minister. She began by picking on the one group that could hardly fight back: 500,000 "Indian" plantation workers were deported to India, the *quid pro quo* being that 300,000 would be allowed to stay. Although winning considerable stature abroad, not merely as a woman prime minister but as a beacon of the Third World's new order, Mrs Bandaranaike's stumbling record at home elicited an attempted coup by army officers and, soon afterwards, a heavy defeat at the polls. Dudley Senanayake lasted five years as her successor but fared little better, abandoning an attempt to run the country according to the Buddhist lunar year. Mrs Bandaranaike came in again, but if she had any new ideas they didn't work. Something had to give.

In his book *Running in the Family*, Michael Ondaatjie describes an uprising of thousands of young people who took to the streets in tennis shoes and trousers with a stripe down the side protesting that they were hungry. They were well organised and might have realised a plan simultaneously to invade every police station, army barracks and radio station in the country but for a mix-up over the day in question. They had got hold of official records listing the whereabouts of every registered weapon in the country and went off to collect them.

A gang of about 20 arrived at the Ondaatjie home demanding two weapons they knew were there, but they were local youths and recalled a past kindness by Ondaatjie's father. Piling their collected weapons on the lawn, they borrowed a cricket bat and ball and played for most of the afternoon.

Organised by the ultra-left *Janata Vimuktu Peramuna* (JVP), the rebellion was not just spontaneous games of cricket. A frenzy of bomb attacks struck government installations and an attempt was made to kidnap the prime minister herself. More than 10,000 rebels were arrested and a number of the leaders killed.

Mrs Bandaranaike redoubled her nationalisation programme, expropriating all private agriculture and the tea estates, the two areas of the economy that were still functioning. At the same time, she pushed through constitutional amendments turning Ceylon into the Republic of Sri Lanka and giving herself, with dubious legality, two extra years in office. The response, orchestrated by disaffected members of the ruling coalition, was the worst wave of strikes in 20 years. Jaffna demanded a wholly independent Tamil state to be known as *Eelam*. Mrs Bandaranaike went to the polls – the one tradition from which no island politician has ever

deviated – and received thumbs-down from 86.7 percent of the electorate.

Junius Richard ("J.R.") Jayewardene broke new ground in two respects. He was someone other than a Senanayake running the UNP and his economic theories were the antithesis of Mrs Bandaranaike's loose-cannon socialism. His model was Singapore; the flagship of his economic initiative was a free trade zone north of Colombo. Tamil and English were elevated to the status of "national" – less than "official" – languages, and a system of proportional representation guaranteed parliamentary seats to minority parties who gained a certain percent-

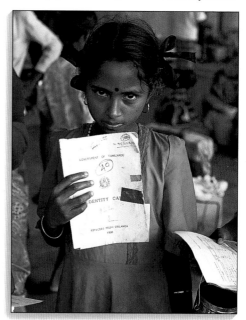

age of the overall vote. If Jayewardene made a mistake, it was to introduce an executive presidency along French lines but with modifications that guaranteed chaos if the president and prime minister, standing in separate elections, were from different parties.

The Tamil Tigers

With the economy back on track and an influx of foreign investment and tourism, growing optimism was shattered when Jaffna secessionists, soon to be known as "Tamil Tigers", ambushed an army patrol, killing an officer and 12 soldiers. Racial violence erupted in a "Black July" that left 387 dead and saw 90,000 Tamils

LEFT: Independence Memorial Hall in Colombo.
RIGHT: a Tamil refugee.

packed into refugee camps. A bill was rushed through parliament to outlaw all separatist movements; 16 Tamil MPs baulked at some of the implications, refused to swear loyalty to parliament, and were expelled. Their departure made the SLFP the largest opposition party again but not under Mrs Bandaranaike. She had been impeached for abusing her powers as prime minister and had been stripped of all civic rights. The new party leader was her son, Anura Bandaranaike.

Indian peacekeepers

Violence escalated throughout 1985, and punitive operations by the armed forces accelerated the exodus of Tamil refugees to India, the total climbing towards 100,000. Ostensibly to stem the flow, the Indian air force began dropping food parcels over northern towns. Supplies by sea led to clashes between the Indian and Sri Lankan navies. In July 1987, it was announced that by mutual agreement 45,000 Indian troops would land with strict orders to disarm the Tamil Tigers.

To Sinhalese extremists, especially the JVP group in the south, this was not peace-keeping but an intolerable resurrection of medieval invasions from the mainland. More rioting left thousands dead and brought the economy to a wincing halt. Before the Indian army was finally withdrawn in 1990, its numbers had grown to 120,000, its losses to 1,000 dead.

President Jayewardene stepped down in December 1988 to make way, by prior arrangement, for a completely different revolution. Ranasinghe Premadasa was no Kandyan aristocrat. He was from a low-rung *Hinaya* or "washerman's" caste, born in a shack in a run-down area of Colombo. He kept the property although the house got better as he advanced from the labour movement through municipal politics and eventually became prime minister.

The small garden was adorned by an unusual ornament: under a glass case was an exhausted Morris Minor, the president's first motor car and proudest possession. Colombo's upper castes, or for that matter those in Delhi with whom the president had to deal, hardly bothered to conceal their contempt for his origins or, even worse, the way he boasted about them. Jayewardene had promised him the presidency in exchange for dropping his virulent campaign against the presence of Indian peace-keepers.

It was said – and he never attempted to deny it – that, as prime minister, he had slipped arms to the Tamil Tigers.

Premadasa vowed to rejuvenate the economy and to end both the Tamil Tiger war and the continuing rebellion by JVP underground extremists in the south. The economy did in fact respond, and to begin with it looked as if he might succeed on the military fronts as well. JVP leaders were tracked down and summarily executed without too many tears being shed, but the "disappearance" of thousands of their sympathisers caused an international outcry. The Tamil Tigers appeared to be contained in

the Jaffna peninsula, and Tamils living among Sinhalese elsewhere were encouraged to use their language and show off their cultural identity in any way they liked. The economy was doing well enough to subsidise generous aid programmes, including cash handouts to farmers, and the Indian peace-keepers decided it was time to go.

The Indians had scarcely left when Tamil Tigers hit police stations and introduced a virtually unstoppable weapon, the suicide bomber. In 1991, MPs led by opposition leader Lalith Athulathmudali drew up an impeachment motion accusing the president of "abuse

of power, incompetence and corruption".

The president, who almost enjoyed making enemies, had Athulathmudali flung out of parliament. Both were dead in the space of a week: Athulathmudali was shot while addressing a rally and the president was blown up by a 14-year-old with a bomb strapped to his body. A broken cyanide capsule was found in the bomber's neck. No matter that their own leader had been assassinated; opposition supporters greeted the president's death with fireworks and wild celebration.

ABOVE: Prime Minister Sirimavo Bandaranaike (left) and President J.R. Jayewardene meet in 1980.

A change of government brought a new face, an old name and an unrecognisable SLFP into the political arena. The incoming prime minister was Chandrika Bandaranaike Kumaratunga, daughter of S.W.R.D Bandaranaike and his widow Sirimavo and, at 49, herself a widow. Her husband, a popular actor turned politician, had been assassinated in 1988, probably because he had gone to the north – with his wife – to communicate with the Tamil Tigers. The party had now exchanged rabid Sinhalese nationalism and Third World socialism for market economics and national reconciliation, especially with the Tamils.

The ill-conceived executive presidency pitted Chandrika Bandaranaike, as prime minister, against a president from a rival party who could choose any cabinet portfolio he liked in her government and, in practice, sit in on her party's policy decisions. The easiest way for the prime minister to resolve this nonsense was to stand herself when the next presidential election came round and, assuming victory and the necessary parliamentary majority, to change the system back to a presidency with just ceremonial duties. To do so required someone to keep her prime minister's seat warm while she nipped off to become a temporary president. Logic suggested that she and the seat-warmer could then change places. Her choice to play the role of her alter ego was her mother, Mrs Sirimavo Bandaranaike, then 78 and just rehabilitated after the loss of her civic rights.

These machinations, however, were purely cosmetic. The government's real substance was to put forward a plan that would make the Tamil communities in Jaffna and the east virtually self-governing but not quite fully independent. A huge military offensive, "Operation Leap Forward", was aimed at silencing the Tigers while a massive injection of aid rebuilt the region's infrastructure. Tamil and Muslim parliamentary parties in parliament liked the idea of a federation of states, but the reactionary Buddhist clergy and Sinhalese extremists condemned it as a sell-out. The Tamil Tigers sent suicide bombers into the heart of Colombo. As Sri Lanka approached the 50th anniversary of its independence, a leading article in *The Times* of London offered cold comfort: "There is no democratically elected leader anywhere in the world who has a less enviable task than Chandrika Bandaranaike Kumaratunga." ❏

CIVIL WAR

Tamil Tiger atrocities make regular appearances on television news bulletins around the world. What keeps Sri Lanka's enduring conflict alive?

No simple reason could ever explain a civil war that runs for more than a decade and claims over 30,000 lives. Straightforward certainties are even more elusive when, as happened in the 1980s, there were actually two wars going on in Sri Lanka; and while the huddled masses in the middle might have had

certain sympathies, they would rather have had nothing to do with either of them. For the record, the lesser of these two wars, the fundamentally economic rebellion of unemployed Sinhalese youth, might be said to have ended when the JVP leadership took seats in parliament as the representatives of a legitimate political party. That leaves the more familiar war synonomous with the Tamil Tigers.

The opening shots

The war surfaced in 1983 when guerrillas – identified to begin with as "Jaffna secessionists" – ambushed an army patrol, killing an officer and 12 men. The incident provoked a Sinhalese backlash against Tamil civilians that resulted in scenes of communal savagery. The Tamil Tigers emerged under the leadership of Velupillai Prabhakaran, whose involvement traces back to when, as a youngster, he saw his uncle burned alive by soldiers after riots triggered by government moves to make Sinhalese the national language.

In 1971, when he was 17, the government pushed Sinhalese preferment policies a step further by, for example, setting higher entry requirements for Tamils wishing to enter university. Prabhakaran got together with 30 likeminded Tamil teenagers, who knew him as Thamby ("little brother"), and formed the Tamil Tigers. While their Sinhalese contemporaries took inspiration from Anuradhapura, the young Tigers could look back to their ancestral hold on the north, and in particular to the precolonial independent Tamil kingdom of Jaffna.

Their idea of secession from Sinhalese-dominated Ceylon and the creation of some kind of separate Tamil state on the peninsula therefore had a considerable historical precedent, even if the economic viability of an independent state in modern times would be, to say the least, questionable.

A ruthless leader

Prabhakaran was born into the lowly *Karaiar* (fisherman) caste, and although he married into the higher *Vellala* caste – having saved his future wife, then at Jaffna university, from starving herself to death in a protest against Sinhalese discrimination – the upper echelons of the Tiger movement remained firmly rooted among fellow *Karaiars*. Not that the upper echelons were stable, because from quite early on he was unsentimentally predisposed to kill any serious rivals for his leadership.

Prabhakaran claimed to have immersed himself in sacks of chillis so that he could withstand pain in the event of being captured and tortured. Later, as the most wanted man in the country not only for countless atrocities at home but also complicity in the assassination of Rajiv

Gandhi, the Indian premier, he took to carrying round his neck – as indeed did many of the Tigers, some still children – a capsule containing a fatal dose of cyanide. One way or another, no one ever expected him to be taken alive.

Tactics of terror

Disregarding some of their tactics, like strapping explosives around the bodies of children and sending them into public places as suicide bombers, the Tigers proved themselves to be tenacious fighters. Probably never more than 10,000 strong, they tied down an Indian "peace-keeping" army of 110,000, and forced Sri

of independent *Eelam* (Precious Land) – and in particular a bunker on the northern outskirts of Jaffna city, Prabhakaran's command post. Government troops engaged in "Operation Leap Forward" fought their way into Jaffna in November 1995 to find that the Tamil Tigers, just like the Khmer Rouge in Phnom Penh in 1975, had ordered the entire civilian population of 150,000 out of the area at gunpoint rather than let them submit to government administration. Nearly every house was booby-trapped to prevent their return, and among the rubble of a shattered city were the ashes of a priceless Tamil library.

Lanka to increase its national forces to around 100,000. Although the jungle was their natural terrain, they did not shrink from mounting head-on attacks on government military bases or sending suicide vessels into action against naval warships.

There were terrorist attacks in, for example, the heart of Colombo, but by and large the war was contained in the northern and eastern parts where most Tamils live. The epicentre was always the Jaffna peninsula – the proposed site

LEFT: a monument to the first female martyr to the Tamil separatist cause.
ABOVE: a checkpoint operated by female soldiers.

A hard fight

As the Tigers retreated in true guerrilla fashion to the jungle, many of the civilian population did return, their hopes pinned to President Chandrika Bandaranaike Kumaratunga's proposal of a semi-independent Tamil state within a kind of Sri Lankan federation. The prospect of permanent peace, however, depended on the Tigers settling for less than total independence and on Sinhalese die-hards, notably elements of the Buddhist clergy, who were inclined to regard any compromise with Tamils as a sell-out. The saddest episode in Sri Lanka's long history is still not concluded, though even the rebels are weary of this bloody chapter. ❏

ISLAND OF MANY FACES

The diverse peoples that make up Sri Lanka have produced
a kaleidoscopic variety of cultures

The smiling face on a tourist poster may be a cliché, but in Sri Lanka it is no misrepresentation. Sri Lankans are profligate smilers, indiscriminately scattering their priceless good cheer to any passing stranger. The unprepared traveller gets showered with an inundation of smiles. The accumulative effect of receiving so many unsolicited grins is one of the best reasons to go back.

This island is entangled in a mass of florid vegetation teeming with strange animals, but most exotic of all is the human population. Sri Lankans seem incapable of producing anything bland, whether they are making history or just making lunch. Something of the island's tropical abundance gets into everything they do. The way they play politics is sometimes deadly, but certainly not dull, their cricketers play the one-day game with the prolific flamboyance that won them the world championship, which in turn was a cause for uproarious celebrations that apparently haven't yet finished. The numerous festivals that pepper the calendar are enjoyed with the same energy and flair.

The fertile Sri Lankan soil has to support not one population but many. Whilst this racial diversity has been the cause of much strife, it compensates with a diversity of culture and skills. Unbelievably, despite the civil war which has raged for so long, there is a remarkable degree of mutual respect between the different races, who all seem to share an inexhaustible optimism.

Away from the trouble hotspots interracial rivalry is fought out with games of "we got here first" in which claims of long occupation of the land are pitted against each other. The **Sinhalese** have an exact date for their arrival by boat from Northern Bengal but the **Tamils** claim that their Dravidian ancestors got to the island before that date, walking across when there was a land link to their homeland in Southern India. The **Muslims** in turn can date the first Arab sailors to very ancient times. These claims and counter-claims may seem surprising since the people who are the undisputed winners of this backward race through history, the **Veddhas**, beat their nearest rivals by thousands of years. It is a shame that their victory should have been rewarded by persecution and eviction. Sitting out of the contest are the **Burghers**, descended from Portuguese and Dutch colonists, who, apparently ashamed of the brevity of their sojourn, mimic their more established neighbours in dress and language.

This ethnic diversity has brought great richness to the island. It is not a cause for war and hate but a cause for celebration and smiles. At least the Sri Lankans haven't forgotten how to do that.   ❑

PRECEDING PAGES: Australian-born painter Donald Friend found his muse in this teeming island; a serene procession of Buddhist monks, who have an enormous influence on the social and political life of the country.
LEFT: fruit sellers at Kandy market.

VEDDHAS

These people are the only inhabitants today whose ancestors were in
Sri Lanka before the Aryan migration began

A ll Sri Lankan peoples have arrived on the island from somewhere else: the earliest literally walked over from India when sea levels were low enough to join up the dots of Adam's Bridge. Many of the later settlers – Arabs, Portuguese, Dutch and others – arrived in a little more style by sea. The Veddhas have

halese who found the jungle impenetrable.

Alternatively there is a legend that the Veddha race was actually founded by Prince Vijaya, known as the founder of the Sinhalese nation in around the 6th century BC. The tale goes that he married a woman of the *Yaksa* tribe who produced a son and a daughter. These two went

the edge on them all as the descendants of the earliest-known inhabitants. These Stone Age hunter-gatherers were Lanka's "first people" and had more racial affinities with African Bushmen and Australian Aborigines than with any of the island's other Aryan settlers.

Spirit peoples

The Buddhist chronicles of the *Mahavamsa* identify the Veddhas as *Yaksa* and *Naga* tribes, who are descibed as spirits or ghosts. This is a tribute to how little impact they made on the environment that they inhabited. They flitted through the thick jungle leaving no trace of their presence, to the consternation of the Sin-

forth to the Ratnapura District, near Adam's Peak, and multiplied, allegedly producing the Veddha race. Whether or not this story has any foundation in fact, the Veddhas and Sinhalese have certainly lived in close proximity over many centuries, and intermarriages have led to their decline in numbers. The languages of the two races are similar and Robert Knox even described 17th-century Veddhas as speaking Sinhalese.

The term Veddha comes from the Sanskrit word meaning "hunter with bow and arrow", although they prefer to call themselves the "people of the forest" or *Vanniyalaetto*. Their lush habitat allows them to maintain a rich diet including venison, rabbit, turtle, monitor lizard, wild boar and monkey, a delicacy being dried meat preserved in honey.

Women are socially equal to the men and descent passes matrilineally. In the wedding ceremony the bride ties a bark rope, which she has twisted herself, around the waist of her husband to be. Wives are faithful and caring and bring up their children with a great deal of love. Traditionally, when a death occurred in a cave dwelling, it was the practice to cover the body with dried leaves and for the whole community to move to a new dwelling. But, perhaps as consolation for bereavement and for having to

ditional lifestyle. Far from happy, they soon abandoned these so called sanctuaries, which they claimed were not big enough to sustain them, and returned to their original habitations. They have recently given up the worship of ancestral spirits and those who intermarry with Sinhalese now embrace Buddhism. The tribal social codes are sadly disappearing with their way of life.

The two last remaining pockets of Veddha settlements are in Dambana and Nilgala, in a mountainous region in the Uva district. The aged chieftain Tissahami still wages a debate against the government, claiming the right of

move house, a widow was permitted to marry her husband's brother.

Modern age hunters

Today's Veddha no longer lives by his bow and arrow; in fact his tools are more likely to be the chainsaw and gun. Since the 1960s these proud people's way of life has been under siege, and the government has been herding them into settlements without any consideration for their tra-

FAR LEFT: a Dutch engraving of a "noble savage".
LEFT: Veddha rights have been championed by their chief Tissahami.
ABOVE: a Veddha boy with a home-made gun.

the Veddha to remain in ancestral land. But, sadly, all too many of today's descendants of the Neolithic Sri Lankans are reduced to dressing up and putting on a show for curious tourists.

At the end of the 19th century there were more than 5,000 members of this indigenous tribe scattered in several locations in the eastern and north central provinces. The 20th century closed in on them, and as a result only 200 or 300 of these Stone Age people still maintain a Stone Age lifestyle. The outside world is slowly learning to respect their rights, and even begining to learn from them – but only just in time. ❑

THE SINHALESE

The majority population of Sri Lanka has an ancestry that reaches back through Buddhist history to their origins in Northern India

A love of dancing and singing, and a belief in the influence of the stars and planets are characteristics that most Sinhalese will admit to, but how many would attribute them to the ancient Minoans or else Phoenicians, who stumbled on the island in search of trade? Legend has it that small bands of Mediterranean seafarers found themselves washed ashore on a lush island they called *Heladipe* and integrated with the aboriginal tribes there. They were soon joined by some more castaways; this time the Sinhala people who came from the Indus valley, in Bengal.

A peoples' story

Here we enter recorded history thanks to the *Mahavamsa,* the Great Chronicle. The chronicles claim that the exiled Prince Vijaya and 700 of his followers reached the island on the day the Buddha gave up his mortal body, signifying that the Sinhala race was anointed with the task of preserving the teachings of the Buddha. Even though they were not converted to Buddhism until much later, the Sinhala race and the Buddhist religion were inextricably linked and still are.

The Mediterranean settlers and the Sinhalese met and mingled. How else could the western influences that were prevalent on the island be explained? The Hellenic people brought with them the legend of the sun and the worship of nature and the Sinhalese brought the traditions of a Lion race. They were united under one King Pandukhabhaya, the son of a Hellenic prince who married a descendant of Vijaya. He was the builder of Anuradhapura.

The Sinhalese have grown accustomed to taking on cultural influences from visitors and traders. Their willing acceptance of cross-pollination of ideas and people was further strengthened by the large-scale emigration to the island of people from South and North India. Many of the Sinhalese dynasties were supplemented by imported royal stock from Indian coastal kingdoms. Their retinues, mercenaries and artisans provided a wealth of knowledge and expertise which helped develop the culture. Poetry, dance, drama, painting and sculpture all thrived in such favourable circumstances.

National preservation

The foreign domination of the past five centuries brought other stimulating influences, many of which enriched Sinhalese culture; the national dish, rice and curry, for example is derived from the Dutch; and the British education system transplanted well. However all this was at a terrible price. The level of exploitation and the divisive methods used to control the populace struck deep. Sinhalese nationalism is an understandable but negative reaction to earlier suppression.

Despite being rooted in many cultures and enduring 500 years of foreign control, the Sinhalese have carried through their turbulent his-

LEFT: a Hill Country man on *poya day.*
RIGHT: a shopkeeper with a moment to spare.

Boy Monks

At birth, a male child is considered a veritable treasure by the adoring Sinhalese mother. One salient fact is that the male child can be responsible for vesting large quantities of blessed merit on the mother, beneficial to her spiritual development. The course of action required by the child is to indicate an interest in entering the Buddhist monkhood. The parents generally consult with the astrologer who cast the child's horoscope and the senior Buddhist monk in the temple where they worship. If it is considered

auspicious by the astrologer, and the senior monk agrees to undertake the training, the parents prepare to offer the child to the monkhood. During the initial years of childhood the parents are asked to arrange for the child to work in the temple as an aide, when he will receive preliminary instruction on the undertakings of a monk.

INITIATION

Around the boy's 10th birthday the family members prepare to sever all ties with him. When the boy is admitted to the order of monks the ordination ceremony is moving and eventful, with the whole village participating in the ceremony. The boy is purified by dousing with water, dressed in

princely robes and taken in procession on a palanquin or an elephant. Along the route the boy receives veneration from the community.

On his return to the temple, the family is cast aside and he is dressed in the simple saffron robe of a Buddhist monk. The boy becomes a novice and education and virtuous living are his normal daily practice. Higher education in a Buddhist university enables the novice to gain the station of a practising Bhikkhu. During the remaining years of his life a Bhikkhu may be called upon to participate in the administration of the temple and welfare of the community members worshipping it.

A BUDDHIST TEMPLE

The sacred land on which a temple is built houses an array of buildings and structures. A Bo tree is the main landmark, besides the *dagoba* (relic chamber), which is a symmetrical half-moon shaped solid structure with a spire on the highest point. The image chamber contains images of the Buddha and his disciples. In most temples, this chamber contains artistic depictions of the life of the Buddha in his various incarnations. A simple preaching hall, which contains a belfry, is situated in the same compound. The living quarters of the monks are adjacent to the other structures. Temple premises contain an image chamber of Hindu gods, most giving credence to the fact that Buddhism and Hinduism enjoy a spiritual unity. Hindus believe that the Buddha is an avatar (human guise) of Lord Vishnu, one of the major gods of the Hindu triumvirate.

Devotees have the opportunity to worship in the temple premises at all times. Special days are marked by the quarterly lunar cycle, when activities of worship within the temple are intensified. On a rotating basis, the meals of the monks are offered by the lay members of the temple. Other offerings, which are placed around each of the sacred structures, are flowers, incense, oil lamps, camphor and fruit. Each offering has a specific spiritual significance and is accompanied by audible chants.

The Bhikkhus are active in the community, as spiritual and family advisors. Some practice the healing arts and astrology. In the contemporary context, Bhikkhus participate in the economic and political life of the country.   ❑

LEFT: a boy monk has a childhood experience that separates him from his old school friends.

tory an intensely felt sense of their unique identity, pointing to the purity of the form of Buddhism practised on the island and on the long history of their kings.

The Sinhalese are proud of their dynasty of kings reaching back 2,300 years, an unbroken chain of 167 monarchs, who reigned in various parts of the island, ending with the capture of Kandy in 1815. Throughout the centuries, one feature that endured was the balance of influence maintained between the rulers, the Buddhist monks and village society.

The monks provided the spiritual glue which maintained the cooperative spirit and serenity of village life. To this day the Buddhist temple doubles as a place of learning where young and old are taught history and culture of the Sinhala race and the Buddhist tenets of practical living.

The caste system

The early Sinhalese monarchs nurtured the intricate caste system which originated in India. This divided society into four major castes – wise men, kings, merchants and farmers – plus a large number of minor castes. Each caste had its own occupation ordained by royal decree. The various castes, some 150 altogether, ensured the orderly progress of economic and social life.

The Sinhalese monarchs developed a more humane caste system by closely aligning themselves to the farmers. Hence, the king became the Head Farmer. The farming community was the predominant social force in the country, and it gave birth to the senior statesmen and provincial governors who formed the king's council. Consequently, an elite caste of decision-makers was born.

Each caste stood in a pre-ordained hierarchical position, and when both the Portuguese and Dutch imported labour from the south of India to work on the spice plantations, the descendants of these workers were absorbed by the community and accorded a special caste.

The setting up of a pecking order and the intrepid jostling for social position is a modern phenomenon, which did not exist in the feudal system of Sinhalese kings. The caste structure was pre-ordained for social stability. Consequently, the people in each caste maintained their boundaries, avoiding friendship, social intercourse or social and communal activities outside.

Arranged marriages

To maintain caste integrity, freedom in choosing a mate is severely curtailed. Family and caste community determine the choice of partner. Even when arrangements are apparently casual, amounting to tea parties for friends or acquaintances with a son or daughter the appropriate age, the intention is the same. The phrase "arranged marriage" should not be equated with forced or loveless marriages.

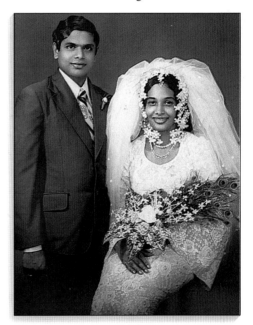

RIGHT: the English way of marriage was adopted, and just as quickly dropped.

Planetary and magical influences

The Sinhalese take their superstitions very seriously. Marriages, births and any major social events are planned with great consideration on the advice of astrologers and gurus, backed up by the whole pantheon of Hindu deities and a lower order of demonic beings. Astrologists prescribe the specific types of rituals and chart auspicious occasions right down to days and times. These rituals are then carried out by demon priests or exorcists.

A life under the stars

Every Sinhalese child has a horoscope based on the time of birth. The position of the stars and planets is carefully analysed by an astrologer to determine the flow of the child's early life, usually the first five years. Thereafter, five year horoscopes are cast in detail and predict good times and bad, wealth, job and marriage prospects and their effect on family members.

Auspicious hours, days and months are carefully considered before conducting any individual or family business or social activity. Negative influences can be countered by devotion to the Buddha, and propitiation ceremonies, several thousand in number, can be prescribed to forestall danger or earn favours at work or in any other area.

The horoscope is based on a mixture of planetary influence, religion, legend and folklore and provides the backdrop for the construction and execution of a Propitiation Ceremony. The ceremony consists of narratives, recitations, bell-ringing, drumming and dancing, complete with appropriate masks depicting the mischievous deity or demon.

Some ceremonies have been known to last for three days during which large amounts of food and drink are consumed

The life of Buddha

Buddha was born into a royal family in a kingdom in North India bordering Nepal. Prince Siddhartha Gautama was the name by which he was known prior to achieving the state of "spiritual enlightenment". The court astrologer had warned his father that Siddhartha would be either a model illustrious king or an ascetic whose teachings would influence the world. Heeding those words, the king provided the young prince with every comfort.

Siddhartha was 16 when he married. He lived in the palace for 12 years but then rejected the trappings of luxury and pondered instead on the cruel realities of life and how to escape them. "There is a getting born and a growing old, a dying and a being re-born," he said, "and from this suffering alas, an escape is not known. When shall such escape be revealed?" Soon after his son was born, he left the palace and his wife and family, donned a simple yellow robe, shaved his head and accepted a begging bowl in preparation for a journey which was to find the key to human existence. He was just 29 years old.

For 16 years he practised the teaching of ascetics and religious teachers. Not satisfied, he cried in desperation; "Let my skin and flesh shrivel up, let the blood in my body dry up, but I shall not stir from this meditative stance until I have experienced the supreme joy and wisdom of enlightenment." The ascetic Prince had adopted the lotus position under a large ficus tree (*Ficus riligiosa*), later to be known around the world as the Bo tree, at Buddhagaya in

Northern India. On the night of the full moon during the month of May, on the very same lunar calendar day he was born, Prince Siddhartha attained the state of enlightenment. He was privy to the understanding of all human existence, and freed himself from the cycle of birth, death and rebirth.

During the 50 years following his enlightenment, the Buddha taught in many parts of India and South East Asia. He is believed to have visited Sri Lanka three times and taught the concepts of his philosophy to the islanders. The three locations, Sri Pada (Adam's Peak), Mahiyangana and Kelaniya, are now sacred to all Buddhists.

Today Buddhism plays a vital part in the lives of the Sinhalese and the most important elements in the make-up of their character are the teachings of Buddha, the Buddhist monkhood and the Buddha as a spiritual role model.

Buddhism in Sri Lanka

Two-and-a-half centuries after the landing of Vijaya, King Asoka, the ruler of all of India, sent his son Mahinda to hasten the introduction of Buddhist thought to Sri Lanka. The legend pursues the reigning King Devanampiya Tissa who was on a hunting trip and encountered a stately deer browsing in a thicket. The sport of kings at the time denied the taking of an animal's life if it was stationary. The king's followers disturbed the animal and he pursued it up a steep incline. The king was on horseback and easily out-paced the deer. However, when he finally reached within bow shot distance, instead of a deer he encountered a Buddhist monk complete in ascetic garb.

The monk was the sage Mahinda who preached the first Buddhist sermon on the spot. The king reached a state of divine understanding and ordained that the Buddhist tenets be shared amongst his followers. The ascetic Mahinda undertook the teaching of the first group of Sri Lankan Buddhist monks.

The Sinhala community

All Sinhalese people are bound together by their shared love for parents, extended family, friends and children. This is mutually expressed through gestures, body language, looks and obeisance instead of words. The placing together of the palms and fingers of both hands indicates a wholesome acknowledgment of another individual.

Today the Sinhalese are renowned for their hospitality, as well as their natural good looks and strong cultural heritage. Visitors to the country, particularly those who have the time to tour rural Sri Lanka and communicate with the local people, will encounter a proud and traditional but fun-loving race who genuinely treasure human contact. ❑

LEFT: an exorcist prepares to out-stare the demons.
RIGHT: travellers have remarked on the physical attractiveness of the Sinhalese for centuries. The evidence is all around you.

THE FOUR NOBLE TRUTHS

After spending his allotted sojourn beneath the Bo tree, the Buddha proclaimed the Four Noble Truths which designate man's problem of existence:

1: Living from birth to death is full of suffering.
2: Selfish desire and attachment are the causes of suffering.
3: Extinguish selfish desire and attachment and suffering will cease.
4: Adopt the Middle Path to forsake desire in easy steps. The Middle Path was to be steered between the extremes of sad and useless asceticism and ignoble hedonism.

MUSLIMS, MOORS AND MALAYS

The Islamic communities of Sri Lanka unite people from various backgrounds,

with each contributing their particular traditions and stories

Pagan Arabs first visited Lanka millennia before Christ. By 1000 BC the pearl divers of Mantota (Mannar) were Arabs and Persians, and the pearl necklace which adorned the neck of the Queen of Sheba is said to have come from here. In the time of the ancient Sinhalese kings, Anuradhapura had an Arab street where stallions were traded for spices. However, the main influx of Arabs arrived post-Islam, and large settlements grew around Jaffna and all the way along the western coast to Galle. The Muslims had a virtual monopoly on trade on the island until the Portuguese conquered the Maritime Provinces. The Muslims sought protection from the King of Kandy, who hid them in places like Gampola, Mawanella, Welimada and Akuressa.

The British, busily classifying everything and everyone, put the Ceylon Moors in a separate category from the later Muslim arrivals; the Malays who descended from Malay regiments brought over by the Dutch, and the Indian Muslims (Bohras and Memons – a distinct Indian Shia sect hailing mainly from a Gujarat village named Kutch) the British had brought over themselves. Today's Muslim community constitutes 7 percent of the population. The Moors account for 95 percent of the total number.

Muslim leaders played a prominent and distinguished role in the struggle for the country's independence. S.W.R.D Bandaranaike said "The Ceylon Moors have been in Ceylon as long as we Sinhalese. A close bond of friendship exists between the communities." Perhaps the reason they integrated with ease was intermarriage. The Malays and Moors arrived here without womenfolk of their own. They married with Sinhalese and Tamils.

LEFT: Muslim men gather for conversation after morning prayers at the Jami-ul-Alfar Mosque in Colombo's Pettah district.

MUSLIM FOOD

Islamic foods, typically using saffron and rosewater, are popular with all Sri Lankans. Along with mutton curry and *buriani* are *godumba roti* (elastic pancakes), *wattalappan* (a rich custard of Malay origin) and *Kahuwa* (thick spiced milk coffee).

Muslim weddings

A well-known saying from the prophet goes:

If anyone dies, bury him promptly.

If marriage is discussed, finish it quickly.

The month of the Prophet's birthday (*Sal*) is a good month for weddings, which take place at night in the bride's home. The family compound is decorated with plantain stalks and crêpe paper but not usually flowers. The groom and his party arrive and the bride's brother washes the groom's feet, while the bride remains inside.

A leader of the community, usually a priest, asks whether the father consents to the marriage. On the father's consent, the groom is asked if he is willing to marry the bride and assume responsibility for her. The question and answer are repeated three times in the presence of two witnesses. The groom has then to announce the quantum of *mahar* (bride price) that he is to give to the bride.

After this the *Sura Fatiha* from the Quran is recited to solemnise the marriage and a *baithe* (religious song) enumerates various blessed unions between the prophets and their wives. Next a young male member of the bride's household leads the groom by his right hand to the bride. The groom's elder sister prepares the bride for the groom and gives him the *thali* (a ceremonial necklace adopted from Tamil custom) to put around the bride's neck. The groom takes his place alongside the bride on the throne (akin to the Sinhala *poruwa*) and they share a cup of milk fed to them by the groom's elder sister. The groom finally joins the male company and they dine whilst the bride and the other women dine separately.

The first week is spent at the bride's house, but there is a reciprocated visit, the *mapala shapada,* to celebrate the consummation of the marriage. Traditionally, the groom hosts this feast to announce to the world that he accepts the girl as his wife. ❑

THE TAMILS OF SRI LANKA

The diverse groups of people with common origins in Southern India have, over time, acquired separate identities under the label "Tamil"

U ntil recently it was thought that the Tamils arrived in Sri Lanka by boat across the Palk from South India about 2,000 years ago – shortly after the arrival of the Sinhalese, also from India. However, Dravidians probably emigrated much earlier – that is, well before 500 BC when a rise in sea-level separated Sri Lanka from the sub-continent. Pre-Stone Age dwellings have been found around Anuradhapura, as well as Tantric shrines which pre-date Hinduism.

The Jaffna Tamils

Sri Lankan Tamils fall into five groups. All but the "up-country Tamils" have their roots in the northern peninsula of Jaffna which was taken over by the Tamil Tiger terrorists, ethnically cleansed of non-Tamils and Tamil-speaking Muslims.

Jaffna was a 20-year battle-ground until government troops recently liberated it in 1996. This once large, peaceful community is now a settlement of weary war-victims trying to re-establish community life.

Everyone who visited the area before the conflict describes being enchanted by its hospitable and straightforward people.

Urban Tamils of Colombo

Some of the country's leading politicians, professionals and businessmen are Tamils, and most have university degrees from abroad. They seem above the racial conflict in Colombo where, except for the occasional Tiger bombs, it is difficult to believe the country is at war. In private, however, urban Tamils do reach deep to help their war victims.

They are so culturally mellow that Tamil-Sinhalese or Tamil-foreigner love-marriages nowadays receive parental approval. In this group it is impossible to tell Tamil from Sin-

halese for the stereotype that one is a sensual dark serious Dravidian with curly-hair and the other a doe-eyed lighter skinned smiling Aryan with straight-hair, does not run true. There has been blending for a long time and history shows it was the custom of the Kandyan kings to prefer South Indian brides.

LEFT: Tamil girls in their finery watch Jaffna's Nallur Temple festival.

RIGHT: pleating their saris, devotees prepare for the southern festival of Kataragama.

A STUBBORN STREAK

The Tamils have a fiercely independent character, just as the Sinhalese are fiercely proud. This trait is described by Bertha Daniel, a doctor who, back in 1927, was engaged in setting up a free medical clinic in Jaffna which also distributed government-sponsored free milk to the poor for two weeks. At first not one Tamil would accept the handout. Bertha Daniel eventually placed a tin on the counter and to it taped a note in Tamil saying that donations towards the cost of the milk could be placed inside. Almost immediately a queue formed and the milk was solemnly accepted, although not one penny was ever found in the tin.

Up-country Tamils

About a third of the Tamils are, or have come from, a labour-force once conscripted mostly for tea and rubber estates directly from South India. Some families go back nearly 200 years. No travel brochure seems complete without a beautiful Tamil tea-plucker wearing a colourful sari and some combination of earrings, nose rings, bracelets, necklaces, anklets and toe rings – always gold and often studded with real gems. She wears a small round (usually black) *pottu* mark mid-forehead, both as a decoration and to denote her race. The men wear simple *saarams* (sarongs) either ankle or thigh-length.

Liberation Tamil Tigers of Ealam

Unfortunately, there is a tendency abroad to think that all Sri Lankan Tamils are members of the notorious Tamil Tigers led by the megalomaniac genius of Velupillai V. Prabhakaran, who as a teenager, rumour has it, watched an uncle being burned in oil by soldiers and announced, "I will make you sorry."

The United States credits him with creating the most deadly guerrilla force in the world. Though he lives in the jungle with about 5,000 followers, he has used the Internet to help finance his cause by claiming to represent all Tamils. Now the truth is out, the Tigers have

A HEALTHY PROFIT

Victor Heiser, a physician with the US Public Health Service, visited Sri Lanka in 1915, bringing "the gospel of health, to let in knowledge so that the teeming millions.... should also benefit by the discoveries of science."

He told the English Planters Association that their labourers, then dying by the thousand from smallpox and hookworm, could be saved. They refused, saying the cost was too high. Angrily, he produced figures to show it was cheaper to keep labour alive than import replacements. Cheaper! That was different.

Immunisation became compulsory and the life-expectancy of the Tamil estate labour soared.

become an illegal organisation in the USA and Canada. Their income, once said to exceed $1 million a month, has shrunk.

The Tigers use village children as young as 11 for the front-lines. Rows of little bodies riddled with bullets after each major battle are a heart-breaking sight. Their Black Tiger suicide bombers are fearsome and fearless. A lottery chooses who will dine with their leader before departing to end his or her life as a hero. The boy chosen to blow up President Premadasa spent more than a year developing enough trust to get close enough on a bicycle. When Prabhakaran violated President Kumaratunga's election promise of a cease-fire in 1995, she decided to push for full military victory and has been achieving it.

The Tamil diaspora

Tamils left the country in droves during the Jayewardene and Premadasa regimes. They have continued to gain top places in western universities and professions. However, many gladly supported the Tigers with their earnings – until it was evident Prabhakaran was out of control.

When support isn't forthcoming, Tiger organisations may put pressure upon exiles. A few years ago, a Tamil family man in America was visited twice by members of the Tigers, who listed his assets and demanded US$800 a month. He explained he did not have the money as he had just purchased a house. The Tigers' response was: "You have two sons. You will pay." Fortunately, he has heard no more from them but he remains terrified of their return. One young Tamil with an unlisted personal telephone number will not even give it to his mother in Sri Lanka.

To avoid being suspected terrorists, too, some have completely changed their names or dropped the Tamil endings.

The religious tradition

Some Tamils credit their work ethic to the fact that South India and Jaffna are riverless areas of drought which required creativity and persistence to tame. Most also give credit to their Hinduism which emphasises order (the caste system), disciplined behaviour (instilled in childhood), right behaviour (good *karma*) and respect for all life (vegetarianism).

Hinduism is behind their tradition of quickly creating a community wherever they find themselves, for the castes ensure each person knows his role. A child may not go to school without breakfast and a visit to the prayer-room. He may not enter the prayer-room without bathing and putting on freshly washed clothes. He must eat with his right hand and wash with his left. Prayer, cleanliness and routine become second nature. Hindus have no required rites (as in the Catholic religion), but individual households

always develop their own, as do the Temples. God is personified with infinite variety. There are 1,008 names for Siva, 1,000 for Vishnu, and Kali is one of many mother images. Hindus accept Jesus as an avatar (a god in human form) and depict him sitting on a fish.

Unlike strict Muslims, Hindus don't ostracise those who defect. When Catholic missionaries preached equality in God's eyes, many of the lower castes converted to Christianity. The missionaries benefited from these hard-working newcomers who did not consider any job too menial, were eager for education and were used to elaborate religious festivals. ❑

LEFT: tea pluckers are a distinct group untouched by the Tamil-Sinhalese conflict.

RIGHT: a siva devotee in Jaffna untouched by the physical world.

CASTES IN SRI LANKA	
HIGH CASTE:	*Brahman* – priest
Vellala – landowner	*Chettiya* – merchant
MIDDLE CASTE:	*Kollar* – blacksmith
Koviar – domestic servant	*Nattuvar* – musician
Thachchar – carpenter	*Thattar* – goldsmith
Karaiyar – trader, fisherman	*Kusayar* – potter
Mukkiyar & Thimilar – fisherman	*Acari* – wood carver
LOW CASTE:	*Ampattar* – barber
Vannar – Dhobi (washerman)	
Pallar & Nalavar – toddy tapper, day labourer	
Paraiya – sweeper, funeral drummer	

SHRINES AND OFFERINGS

Effigies of evil spirits and shrines by the roadside are just two of the many indications of how vital a role belief plays in Sri Lankans' everyday life

The evidence of the invisible can be seen everywhere in Sri Lanka. No matter which religion occupies their minds, Sri Lankans express their devotion with objects, sometimes valuable, sometimes worthless, but always colourful.

Shrines sprout up almost anywhere, literally in the case of a Bo tree, which will be revered by Buddhists no matter where it grows.

The most popular Hindu deities on the island include Skanda, venerated at Kataragama, Pattini, bringing health, and Ganesh, the remover of obstacles. There are also Hindu deities to be found in Buddhist temples, and Hindus reciprocate by declaring Buddha to be an avatar or incarnation of Vishnu. Catholic saints are easily accepted as further additions to the accumulated clutter of religious images.

Many of these religious images are crudely made and sloppily painted, but that only adds to their charm. They are everyday objects expressing the spiritual side of daily life. The offerings presented are frequently just as modest; a few petals or some small coins.

The belief in demons or evil spirits is another source of inspiration for Sri Lankans. The supernatural is part of the daily routine, and plays an important part in the great ceremonies of birth, marriage and death.

▷ **GANESH SHRINE**
Hindus ask the elephant-headed Ganesh to bring them success, especially in intellectual pursuits.

△ **ROAD WATCH**
A colourful family of effigies is set up at the roadside to scare away evil spirits, in particular those that appear as wild elephants.

△ **SKANDA'S *VEL* (TRIDENT)**
Skanda, the chief deity of Kataragama, has six heads and 12 arms. His trident is decorated with ribbons and coins tied in cloth.

△ **FOOD FOR THE GODS**
As well as toys and soft drinks, the stalls on the road to Kataragama sell offerings for the gods. Pilgrims can choose between painted earthenware aubergines and outlandishly garish gourds.

ALMS-GIVING AND BUDDHA *PUJAS*

▽ **PAUSE FOR THOUGHT**
Numerous wayside shrines to Buddha attract passers-by to break their journey and leave an offering of money or, failing that, coconut.

▽ **ST SEBASTIAN SHRINE**
Many of the Catholic saints introduced by the Portuguese have become the object of veneration, even by non-Christians.

Buddhist monks and nuns are forbidden to prepare their own food, and they are not supposed to eat after midday, a form of fasting that is a daily discipline. But there's no danger of going hungry thanks to the practice of *dana* or alms-giving.

Providing food for monks is a religious duty for lay Buddhists by which they earn merit. Its ancient origins are shown by the vast "rice boats" found in the ruins of Mihintale, which were filled with donated food. Today a monk is likely to have a regular lunch appointment with a devout family who are honoured to lay an extra place at table. Others go from door to door to beg for their morning meal. The meritorious act of giving assures the donor of a more advanced rebirth on the spiritual ladder.

Food is also offered in temples – usually a tray of rice and curry placed before an image of the Buddha.

◁ **FLORAL TRIBUTES**
The lotus is a sacred flower to Buddhists: seven of them bloomed as Buddha took his first steps, and again at the moment when he reached enlightenment. This woman also holds a small bag of fragrant jasmine petals.

▷ **DAGOBA FLOWERS**
The stamen of sal flowers are shaped like a tiny *dagoba* surrounded by a crowd of tiny filaments that symbolise people.

BEHIND THE SNAPSHOTS

Sri Lankans love having their pictures taken, but the portraits do not reveal their identity crisis as they choose between traditional and modern values

Since it is impossible to stop taking pictures of this absurdly photogenic island, nearly everyone will have video or photographic mementoes to take home with them, each accompanied by a story and a few random associations imprinted on the memory. Once the stories are told and the prints are imprisoned in their album, the only pictures of Sri Lanka they are likely to see are gruesome news shots of the ongoing civil war. Somehow the news pictures and the postcard views both fail to convey the ordinary lives carried on in spite of the tourists and the terrorists.

Bombs explode, there is mourning, but despite the international publicity tourists keep on coming, in search of paradise. In defiance of the maxim that a picture is worth a thousand words, some explanation seems to be in order.

Smile for the camera

It is not hard to meet the ordinary Sri Lankans. Accustomed to washing out of doors, sharing a crowded island and even more crowded buses, they do not demand much privacy. You may feel invasive as you point your camera at a scene of picturesque poverty, but whilst your curiosity is reciprocated, your embarrassment is not. Sri Lankans like being photographed. Outside big towns you will find villagers, peasants, fishermen or tea pluckers who will drop everything to stand in front of your viewfinder. Stop to snap a mother and child, and within minutes uncle, auntie, grandfather and many a cousin will have gathered, flashing the most perfect teeth (kept clean by a mixture of coal grit and salt). You need not be suspicious of their intentions: some have never seen a photograph of themselves.

If this fails to bring a smile to your own face, whatever you do, don't scowl. Rather than send

PRECEDING PAGES: Galle road scene at evening.
LEFT: sunbeds and semtex; bomb damage viewed from the roof of the Intercontinental Hotel, Colombo.
RIGHT: umbrellas can be used as protection from gaudy movie posters.

them in the opposite direction, this will cause amusement. You will be noted as mad or wicked and a friendly mob will gather to inspect you. It's far easier to grin back.

Harder to capture on film are the rich Sri Lankans, although they may have a picture of you on their security cameras. This elusive breed

can be found in restaurants or at smart hotels for after-dinner ice-creams. They are always immaculately dressed and cool, living in an air-conditioned world, but they are not aloof. Whilst they won't crowd around the minute you remove your lens cap, they have their own more subtle form of posing.

Class distinctions

Despite several periods of socialist government, there is not much hope that Sri Lanka will ever become a classless society. Recent governments have switched from state intervention to stimulating self-improvement. Experiments in public ownership were halted, and then reversed in a

A TALENT TO DECEIVE

While making Joseph Conrad's *Outcast of the Islands* in the 1950s, the film director Sir Carol Reed described Sri Lanka as "the most natural and complete outdoor film set." A starlet was born. Other foreign film makers were quick to get the fledgling on her way. *Elephant Walk*, with Elizabeth Taylor and Peter Finch, was one of the early black and white movies which used the magnificent backdrop of Polonnaruwa. But the big break came in 1955, when David Lean shot *Bridge over the River Kwai* using various parts of the Mahaweli Ganga to pose as Burma. The film won seven Academy Awards.

It looked as if a lucrative career beckoned, but just as things were shaping up nicely – with *Purple Plain* starring Gregory Peck – Hollywood, it seemed, went cold. However, since the 1980s, the starlet has made her comeback as a serious international film location. Local film maker Lester James Peries produced critically acclaimed films which drew attention to the island as the perfect movie backdrop. The moment John Derek began shooting *Tarzan the Apeman* (having unsuccessfully combed Africa for a spot) the jungle drums were out. While Kandy was being made to look like Calcutta for *Mountbatten – the last Viceroy,* Colombo was put through its paces as a lookalike, improbably, for Melbourne in *Light Over the Water.* John Derek could hardly wait to come back and shoot *Ghosts Can't Do It* and Kandy gave a convincing performance as New Guinea for *The Further Adventures of Tennessee Buck.* There was no looking back now. Everywhere you turned, a foreign film crew was slapping a clapper board or focusing a light meter or snorting annoyance at the documentary makers of nature programmes who had been here all the while. Colombo brushed up its act to play frantic Madras for *Caught.* Then *Indiana Jones: the Temple of Doom* treated Kandy as if it was northern India and made it look convincing, and *Shadows of the Cobra*, a six-hour TV movie, brought in even more dollars.

Currently, foreign film makers spend an average of US$10 million a year in Sri Lanka. This spending persuaded a local company, Film Location Services, to invest in post-production facilities to enable film makers to avoid the cost of shipping equipment into Sri Lanka (while benefitting in the process). Also, locals are getting experience as "extras". The island's lush flora helped the island simulate Vietnam for *The Iron Triangle,* while the fishermen of Puttalam doubled as black American GIs and Lankans of Malay blood were convincing as Vietcong soldiers. The Sri Lankan's penchant for posing might have found its use.

process of privatisation, called "people-isation". Now capitalism is encouraged, within limits and within free trade zones.

No matter what economic models are followed, it seems, the "haves" and "have-nots" remain chasms apart. Whilst the "haves" pay Rs250 for a glass of beer, across the country there are thousands who would run the water out of their rice fields if there was hope of finding a 10-rupee note in them.

Climbing the lower rungs of the economic ladder are the country's second largest "export", the thousands of domestic workers that leave their families at home to work in menial jobs in

the UAE and elsewhere. Mainly women, they bring in US$2 billion a year between them, but many suffer terrible abuse by their employers. It seems these vulnerable people can be raped or treated like low-paid slaves with impunity.

If that wasn't bad enough, they are further exploited by the agents who take a slice of their earnings. It is a sign of the economic times that there are seemingly endless supplies of new recruits. Many have never seen a microwave or dishwasher before, so there are training academies that offer courses in operating electric gadgetry. Of course, the students must pay for their education in mechanical drudgery from their future earnings.

Money talks

The whole island wants to be rich, like Singapore or Hong Kong. Unfortunately one of their greatest assets in achieving this ambition, an education system in the English language, has been thrown away. Instead of speaking the language of international trade the country has two languages, neither of which is of any use.

The economic rivals that are cited either had no history of colonialism (Thailand, Japan) or comparatively little history at all (Hong Kong, Singapore). Sri Lanka has both, which is why there is a government ministerial department dedicated to promoting the Sinhalese identity. This work involves finding long-fangled words in classical Sinhala and injecting them into gormless soap operas on television. Even graduates in Sinhalese cannot follow the plot. Needless to say, the work of this department undermines the efforts of the Ministry for Economic Development.

It is easy to see why having English as the national language was intolerable to national pride, but not only has English ceased to be the language in which children are taught, it has also been struck off the curriculum altogether, and is not even offered as a foreign language. Ambitious parents have no choice but to go private and send their children to so-called "International Schools".

Sensing a profit to be made, unscrupulous entrepreneurs have moved in, taking advantage of lax monitoring to set up schools where the teachers owe their meagre learning to a career in taxi driving. It is more important to have a school bus emblazoned with a logo than to have trained teachers. Both the government and the people are eager for economic improvement, but sometimes it looks like they are at odds.

> ### YES AND NO
>
> Posing a simple question is not easy in Sri Lanka, since they try to give the answer you want to hear. The resulting head waggle can either be interpreted as "yes" or "no", whichever you please.

For richer, for poorer

After independence the best educated Sri Lankans emigrated to Australia, Canada or England in search of top-dollar jobs, but recently the brain-drain has started backing up, with Sri Lankan yuppies (often with foreign spouses) returning to take up residency in the chic districts of Colombo or Galle in architect-built villas.

LEFT: boys on the beach at Polhena.
ABOVE: a couple strolling on Galle Face Green.

Unlike the tea planters and colonial officers who washed up here a century or two ago, these western types are eager to go native. They may be international players during the week but they rediscover their roots at the weekend when they rush out of town on Friday afternoon in air-conditioned Range-Rovers to designer mud huts in the jungle.

For three nights each month they sleep on mats, live on red rice and lentils and wear sarongs to practise yoga. They are just another manifestation of the national identity crisis; how to be modern and traditional, Sri Lankan and international, all at the same time.

Happy to meet you

As a foreigner you will be beset by the "have nots", but you may also be propelled into the company of the "haves". Friendly newcomers get quickly invited to the round of parties which is so much a part of Colombo society. You will be moving among generous and quite often blue-blooded Sinhalese, but equally quickly dropped if you appear to be free-loading or if you are unwashed; bathe, wear clean clothes and give gifts according to your means. If you accept an invitation to stay in someone's house, expect him to show up at yours in a year or two. In return, if you talk about your travel plans,

FROM MUD HUT TO LOW-RISE ECO-FRIENDLY LIVING MODULE

A style of architecture that combines luxury and simplicity, old and new, is uniquely Sri Lankan and yet bears inter-national comparison, is an island success story. The dilemma faced by a newly self-ruling nation is expressed by the Independence Hall, which was built in traditional style, but out of concrete, not wood. So, it was Sinhalese, and yet it was modern. (It was paid for by a foreign power, but never mind that.)

One Danish architect irrevocably changed the design of buildings on the island. Until Ulric Plesner arrived in the early 1960s, the local architecture remained in a colonial time warp. Plesner brought the outdoors indoors. Ferocious monsoon rains, once watched through closed windows, now poured into living room ponds full of water lilies and goldfish. He and Geoffrey Bawa (considered one the best architects in Asia) revolutionised local design.

The resulting creations sometimes seem inspired by a kind of Miami-Bali chic, and even the tourist hotels have been affected by this adventurous spirit. Some are masterpieces, whether simple huts in the jungle or pure swagger, with pools that merge into the sea. The smart houses are cool and airy even when, as in Colombo, they are very densely packed. They are decorated with a sort of ethnic minimalism and lots of houseplants.

someone might take you where you want to go.

If you have to fall back on more mundane tourist transport such as a chauffeur-driven van or car, there's no problem. This could turn out to be an adventure in itself as your driver detours 100 km (60 miles) to visit his family – who will, of course, be thrilled to meet you, and will grin tirelessly for your camera and press you with home-made sweetmeats to take back with you. These drivers are constantly in touch with their roots, both familial and historical, and they have daily dealings with foreigners. The combination seems to do them no harm.

Behind the smiles

Despite their gregariousness, there are things that Sri Lankans would prefer you not to see. For example, Sri Lanka has the highest suicide rate in the world, according to a study conducted by Harvard University. This is one national record that no one is likely to boast about. The problem is grave and gets aired in the local press. Social stress is one of the many excuses offered, 15 years of civil strife might be another; but no one mentions mental illness. In a land where any form of mental disorder bears a heavy social stigma, a suicide due to clinical depression is brushed beneath the statisticians' carpet as "disappointment in love".

Looking into the national character, you cannot fail to see a very strong sense of pride. Personal dignity is so important that loss of face is sufficient to provoke suicide. A young man caught out in some trivial misdemeanor might throw himself in front of a train rather than face the shame of disappointing his elders, whom he has been taught to respect with a reverence long since forgotten in the West.

National shame

If personal pride bestows dignity at a cost that can sometimes be fatal, so does national pride. Sinhalese and Tamils have much to be proud of, but their pride has turned into nationalism, or separatism, which threatens to destroy the country altogether.

Apart from anything else, the civil war is

economically crippling, as the government sinks 46 billion rupees in defence rather than development, whilst the poor are sickened by violence and desperate to improve their lot.

Sri Lanka is poised between different options. The political choices seem clear: Do you want to be modern or ancient? Do you want to be national or international? Do you want to be rich or poor? Do you want peace or war?

The answer you will get is always the same, it may be wordless but it contains more wisdom than you may think. In fact, it is the only truthful answer anybody can ever give; the Sri Lankan head waggle. ❑

LEFT: living in a billboard. Curd sellers' houses in Hambantota have been turned into inhabited adverts by Lever Bros. In return, the huts are weatherproof.
RIGHT: an example of the colourful fabrics designed by Barbara Sansoni.

FROM SWEATSHOP TO CATWALK

Look inside your underwear and you may well find a label bearing the words "*Made in Sri Lanka*", a tiny flag of international trade that the island has attracted with low wages and poor conditions. Your cool and colourful boxer shorts may have emanated from a hot and noisy workplace, but with its skilled craftspeople and sophisticated designers, Sri Lanka has no need to go for the cut-price market.

The top designers such as Ena de Silva, Yolande, and Barbara Sansoni produce work that is both modern and traditional. And their workers enjoy better pay and more comfortable surroundings, too.

FESTIVALS

Elephants in drag, fireworks, pageantry and frenzied worship
are all part of a land with a surfeit of celebrations

Sri Lanka has more festival days than anywhere on earth. There is so much here to enjoy it's no wonder the Lankans love to party. They have such a plethora of celebrations demanding ritual, religion, razzmatazz and pageantry, and enough elephants, drummers, dancers and temples as exotic backdrops.

The current calendar lists 29 public holidays for the year but that only takes care of the elaborate religious holidays and feast days celebrated by the Buddhists, Hindus, Christians and Muslims. There are other causes to celebrate if you are born on this island; the first cutting of the sod before mining for gems; moving to a new home; laying foundations for a building; the first day at school; or the complex ritual practised by farmers after harvesting the grain and giving thanks to the guardian of all treasures of the earth, are just some events taken very seriously. Add to that the secular holidays of May Day, Independence Day, National Heroes Day and the *Poya* holiday which occurs every full moon and you will see why most tourists are delighted by this overkill on festivities. Anyone visiting on business, however, needs to consider the impact on their schedule.

Sinhalese New Year

Sinhala and Tamil New Year is called *Sinhala Avurudu* despite being celebrated by both Hindus and Buddhists alike. It marks the completion of the solar circuit and has to be astrologically determined. So the *Sinhala Avurudu* may begin at 3pm somewhere between 13 and 15 April, depending on the sages. No business worth its salt will stay open for this orthodox time of great rejoicing. To complicate matters even more, there is an astrological conclusion

to the old year and the few hours beyond the new are the neutral period which is reserved for religious activity, regardless of the religion one might practise.

The New Year customs are highly complex and the rituals are carried out between members of one's family, business associates, local

tradesmen and even beggars. New clothes are worn, horoscopes are foretold, money is given and special foods are made, served and offered to the gods.

Vesak

Vesak is celebrated on the day of the full moon in May. It is the most hallowed of Buddhist festivals, almost a Christmas, Easter and Whitsun rolled into one as it commemorates the birth of the Buddha, his enlightenment and his death. Perhaps Buddhists feel short-changed that their spiritual leader chose to attain the light and die all on the day he was born or they would have attained the light and razzmatazz of yet another

PRECEDING PAGES: at the *Nallur* festival, Jaffna Hindus draw the temple chariot with enormous ropes.
LEFT: Raja, a tusker elephant, is dressed in finery to carry the relic casket on his back.
RIGHT: a Sinhalese woman lights the traditional oil lamp to celebrate the start of the New Year.

couple of feast days. But for the tourist this festival is a good time to be here. Myriad paper lanterns in every colour and shape under the sun deck out the streets, shops and temples. Tiny clay coconut oil lamps are lit in every street and village and in the cities electrically illuminated *pandals* are put up depicting events in the Buddha's life. Buses and cars are dressed in streamers and garlands.

Because it is considered meritorious to offer gifts of food and drink during the festival, you will find specially constructed roadside booths called *dansal* where food and drink are offered free. The fare on offer ranges from rice and

Mihintale you get to see the works. The temples are crowded with white-garbed devotees, the streets are illuminated and decorated. It is second only to *Vesak* itself.

Kandy's *Perahera*

Robert Knox described Kandy's *Perahera* in detail in his journals in 1681: "The Perahar at Cande is ordered after this manner… first some forty of fifty elephants, with brass Bells hanging on each side of them, which tingle as they go. Next, follow men dressed up like Gyants, which go dancing along agreeable to a tradition they have, that anciently there were huge

curry to *Vesak* sweetmeats. The devout, a steady stream of white-clad *sil* takers, can be seen waiting to pass through the temples. Obtaining spiritual purity for them means consuming only coriander or ginger tea from 12 noon until they give up the fast and observing the Buddhist precepts.

Poson

To experience the full impact of the advent of Buddhism, the visitor should see Mihintale. It was here that the reigning monarch first encountered Mahinda, the son of Emperor Asoka who brought Buddhism from India. The June *Poson* is celebrated all around the island but at

men, that could carry vast burthens, and pull up trees by the roots. After them go a great multitude of Drummers, and Trumpetters and Pipers which make such a great and loud noise, that nothing else beside them can be heard."

Although August is a month for festivals and *Peraheras* all around the island, the Kandy *Perahera* today is more magnificent and mindblasting than any. The entire town comes to a standstill for this "most spectacular event in all of Asia" which lasts for 12 days. So if you are agoraphobic or averse to dressed-up elephants, whip-cracking acrobats, frenzied drumming, decorous and devilish dancers, each group more shimmering and stupefying than the next, then head out of town fast. But you may never see anything quite like this again.

Vel

Vel is the Hindu festival held in Colombo during July or sometimes August to venerate the trident of Skanda, the god of war. The main event is a great gilded temple chariot which contains the *ayudha* (weapons) of this fierce god, headed by two humped black bulls but actually drawn by hundreds of devotees dressed in the egalitarian white waist cloth and shawl and smeared with holy ash. It's quite impossible to recognise some of Colombo's wealthiest Hindus amongst them.

Every year the *vel* of Skanda is carried in a procession that starts at the Sea Street *kovil* in the Pettah district of Colombo and moves onto the Bambalapitiya *kovil* 5 km (3 miles) away and alternatively each year to the Wellawatta *kovil*. The temple whose turn it is goes to town with gaudy stalls selling souvenirs, sugar cane and sugary sweets of many hues. Don't worry if you are late to catch the *vel* procession; the 6.5-

LEFT: street dancers during Colombo's *Vel* Festival.
ABOVE: the best view of the Kandy *Perahera* is from the back of an elephant.
RIGHT: a hindu devotee at Kataragama pierces his cheeks to fulfil a vow.

km (4-mile) journey proceeds at a snail's pace and takes a whole day, which makes it fabulous for the curious and a hideous slog for the Hindus dragging the cart.

Hindu festivities are at their most vibrant in the Jaffna area during this same season; the Nagapooshani Ammal on the island of Nainativu, the Perumal and the Sellasannathi at Thondamannar, where you can see some eye-popping firewalking by devotees, are just some of a host of extraordinarily colourful festivals. For the time being at least, the visitor to Lanka will miss these. But a smaller one, the *Kali* Festival at Munneswaram near Chilaw is enter-

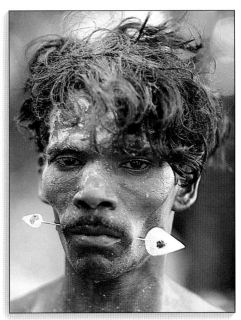

taining and the Uddapu and Mundel festivals in July has some mean firewalking.

Kataragama

Kataragama is not so much a festival, more a way of life for the thousands of pilgrims who make the journey by foot, some from as far as Batticaloa. Without its throng of flailing sado-masochists in action this most holy spot on the island has remarkably little of interest to the traveller. Indeed, visit it outside the two-week period of festivities and you will wonder what brought you here. But during the festival self-mortification is the password. There is scorching sand to roll naked on and searing hot coals to walk barefoot over. Some participants prefer to poke a spear through one cheek, skewering the tongue in the process as it passes through the other side.

For many the acts of penance don't just start on arrival since they have carried a *kavadi,* a decorated arched yoke, for up to 160 km (100 miles) without putting it down.

The chanting of the pilgrims, the writhing bodies, the gruesome sounds of the blowing on conch shells, the frenzied beating of drums, the myriad shrines and deities all

GOT THE TIME?

Ask a pilgrim to Kataragama what time he plans to get there and he will reply: "In God's good time." He will not presume to have any control over his plans.

For the Muslim community, the Id-ul-Fitr marks the end of Ramadan, a month's fasting from dawn till dusk when the devout will not swallow anything – even their own spittle.

Adam's Peak

The pilgrimage to this holy mountain begins in December and carries right through to mid-April. A sophisticated Muslim from Tangier, Ibn Batuta, described his ascent of 1344: "On the mountain are two paths leading to the Foot of Adam. The one is known

decked out in profuse garlands and the gaudiest offerings combine to make this festival an unforgettable experience. It brings together Christians, Buddhists, Hindus, Muslims and even the Veddhas to worship here and be part of the throng.

Deepavali

Deepavali is a festival of lights celebrated by Hindus and usually held at the end of October or the beginning of November. Thousands of flickering oil lamps are lit to denote the triumph of good over evil as Rama returned after his period of exile and to welcome Lakshmi, the goddess of prosperity.

by the name of 'the Father's path' and the other of 'The Mother's Path'. By these terms are Adam and Eve designated. The Mother's route is an easy one, and by it the pilgrims return; but anyone who took it for the ascent would be regarded as not having done the pilgrimage. The Father's Path is rough and difficult of ascent."

Pilgrims of Christian, Buddhist, Muslim and Hindu faiths have been venerating this footprint of Adam, Buddha or the Prophet Mohammed since the 11th century.

Unique traditions have mushroomed: first time climbers pile turbans of white cloth on their heads; the *Indikatupana* or "place of the needle" is where the devout stop and fling a threaded needle into a bush beside the path marking the spot where Buddha paused to mend his robe. At the summit you may clang the bell to say you have completed the pilgrimage of Sri Pada.

Duruthu *Perahera*

The Duruthu *Perahera,* held at the Raja Maha Vihara temple in Kelaniya, 8 km (5 miles) outside Colombo, is second only to the Kandy *perahera* in spectacle. Held annually in January, it commemorates the first visit of the Buddha to Sri Lanka.

Thai *Pongal*

Here at least is one festival you can count on being on the same day every year, as Hindus celebrate 14 January in honour of the sun god. The word *ponggol* means boiling over and, after worship at the *kovil,* a huge pot of rice is ceremoniously cooked in spicy sweetened milk and left to boil over. The direction of the spilling will indicate good or bad luck in the coming year. And the rest makes a delicious sacramental feast. ❑

LEFT: dancers carrying *Kavadi* at Kataragama.
ABOVE: a conch shell is blown to announce the start of a ceremony.

POYA DAYS

The Buddha urged his disciples to undertake special spiritual practices on every full moon (*poya*) day, and the practice has stood the test of time. Buddhists still venerate each *poya* day, spending it in meditation and worship in the temple. In Sri Lanka, every *poya* day is a public holiday, the one in May being of particular significance.

Sri Lankans take *poya* days very seriously, particularly if they fall on a Friday or Monday. People often travel around the island at this time, so be warned that hotels and buses and trains are likely to be busy. In addition, no alcohol is supposed to be on sale, but some tourist hotels will not deprive foreign guests.

May (VESAK)
Commemorates the triple anniversary in the Buddha's life: birth, death and the day he attained enlightenment. The third and final visit of the Buddha to Sri Lanka was on a Vesak Poya Day.
June (POSON)
Marks the introduction of Buddhism to Sri Lanka by the sage Mahinda in the 2nd century BC.
July (ESALA)
Celebrates the arrival of the tooth relic in Sri Lanka and delivery of the first sermon by the Buddha.
August (NIKINI)
Marks the three-month retreat of the Bhikkhus, which was held soon after the Buddha passed away.
September (BINARA)
Remembers Buddha's trip to heaven to preach to his mother and celebrates the Bhikkhuni (Nuns' Order).
October (VAP)
Marks the return of Buddha to earth.
November (IL)
Celebrates the ordination of 60 disciples by the Buddha to spread his teachings.
December (UNDUVAP)
Marks the arrival of a Bo tree sapling in Sri Lanka 2,300 years ago.
January (DURUTHU)
Honours the Buddha's first visit to Sri Lanka.
February (NAVAM)
Marks Buddha's declaration at the age of 80 that his own life would end in three months.
March (MEDIN)
Celebrates the first visit of the enlightened Buddha to his father's palace.
April (BAK)
Commemorates the second visit of the Buddha to Sri Lanka five years after enlightenment.

FOOD AND DRINK

Sri Lanka's food is as colourful as its festivals. Look out for tropical fruits, fine spices, unrecognisable vegetables, oversized fish and gargantuan prawns

Food in Sri Lanka is treated with very great respect. It is thought of so highly that people offer it to their gods. Indeed, if you are invited into a Lankan home to enjoy a meal with a family, however humble the location and whatever caste or creed your host, the array of dishes will be a feast for the eyes and far from anything encountered in a tourist hotel. It will invariably be the very best your host can afford. The choicest Sri Lankan food is to be had *en famille* and each family will horde favourite recipes handed down from generations of cooks.

Rice and curry (not curry and rice)

Sri Lankan cooking has evolved around the staple rice. The national meal is not referred to as "curry" but as "rice and curry" which gives credit in descending order, for a Sri Lankan will sit in front of a mountainous plate of rice to which is added small spoonfuls of curries, meat or vegetable, along with spoonfuls of various pickles or *sambols*.

More than 15 varieties of rice are grown on the island, from the tiny white, translucent pearl shapes to long-grained *basmati* and the red *kakuluhaal*, a nutty strain with as much flavour as the Camargue red rice so much in demand in Europe. The fully cooked (not *al dente*) rice has the highly spiced accompaniments rubbed into it and each mouthful is gently massaged to mix the flavours. A proper curry would not be swimming in sauce (*isma*), as this would be too messy.

A Sri Lankan curry served in western proportions would have an explosive effect, testing the most asbestos throat. Help yourself to small portions, beware the tell-tale red flecks denoting chilli and be sure to include plenty of rice, which, as the locals know, cools the mouth far quicker than water or beer.

LEFT: harvesting rice, a Sri Lankan staple. More than 15 varieties are grown on the island
RIGHT: a mouth-watering crop of fruit on display at Kandy market.

Appetising vegetables

You have only to pause at a market or vegetable stall to appreciate the baffling variety of gourds, greens, garnishes and entirely unrecognisable vegetation to see that when nature is this wildly abundant, how can you expect your chef to restrain himself? This astonishing selection of

FINGER FOOD

There is nothing that gets in the way of a Sri Lankan and his *kame* (meal) – not even 20th-century utensils. Everyone from President Chandrika to the poorest pauper will partake of their cherished plates of food using their nimble fingers to eat with. For the westerner, this is an art as difficult to master gracefully as eating with chopsticks. There is required etiquette: you must not mess your fingers any further than the first knuckle (and don't answer the phone with the same hand). But while your clumsy efforts might provide gentle hilarity for those watching, your hosts will not be offended if they can sense your appreciation.

vegetables and fruit produced by this fertile land will ensure that most of the food you experience will be a revelation. Have you ever devoured a deep-fried snake gourd with a side dish of ash plantain? These vegetables have only one thing in common: they are all extremely appetising, especially when cooked in the local dishes. You will find it is no loss to go vegetarian in Sri Lanka. Indeed, Sri Lanka may possibly turn you into one.

Much of the Tamil food, like *thosai, ulundu vade, marsala vade,* and *idlis*, savoury cakes of dal and rice flour, are perfect for herbivores. You will also always find something for a

vegetarian palate in any Muslim restaurant, where watching the cooking is a cabaret in itself. *Godumba roti* lends itself to all manner of culinary contortions: simply folded over into a translucent envelope stuffed with mildly spiced vegetables; ripped to shreds to be stir-fried with practically any ingredient of your choice to make *kottaroti;* or flipped into an egg *goddamba. Mallung* is a healthy melange of shredded green vegetables with herbs, spices and grated coconut.

The great Sri Lankan breakfast

The traditional Sinhalese breakfast is a serious contender to the great British, Irish or American version. In fact, the variety and special focus of a Sri Lankan's breakfast goes some way to explain what made the locals rub along with the Brits for so long. In the days when English planters ruled the tea slopes, the rigour of rising at dawn to ride out on horseback to supervise one's army of *kanganies* was somewhat softened by the prospect of returning to one's bungalow at 10 o'clock sharp. It was part of a planter's daily ritual to come home to a hearty breakfast.

String hoppers, egg hoppers, *pittu, Kiribath* (*see below*) and the full accompaniment of creamy coconut sauces and *sambols* were enough to make any planter eager to leave his tea factory for a respite. These days, the great Sri Lankan breakfast has evolved into something even grander and is served by sophisticated hostesses at dinner parties.

Pittu, a rice flour and shredded coconut preparation which is similar to a coarser type of cous-cous, is steamed inside a bamboo and eaten with a hot *sambol* and an anointment of subtly spiced *pol hoddi.* In its after-eight guise at an upmarket restaurant you are likely to find this same breakfast staple dolled up with crisply fried onions, spices and prawns in a *pittu fish biriani.*

The *appa* is another classic example of a humble food that has achieved gourmet status. The hopper, as it is known in English, has a delicate, puffy, crêpe-like texture combined with the taste of a crumpet. Made from a batter containing coconut milk and palm toddy (*see page 107*), it is left to sit for a whole night to give it time to ferment.

Its cousin, the egg-hopper, shows off its *décolletage* by having an egg broken into the centre, making it even more mouth-watering. Experienced hopper fans will break off the crisp lacy outer rim of an ordinary hopper and dip it into the runny egg yolk of the more glamorous one. Novices might find it easier to deal with one at a time.

Indiappa, or string hopper, is a mound of rice vermicelli steamed over a low fire. It is another social climber which has popped into polite society and now, rubbing shoulders with some favourites of Sinhalese cooking – like meat dishes with cashews and spices – palms itself off as string-hopper *biriani*, which can leave a Chinese chow mein sitting in a corner looking like something the Shi'itsu dragged in.

International influences

The Dutch, who had already cut their teeth on Indonesian cooking when they arrived here, took one taste of the local cuisine and decided it was good enough to wrap up and take home; they came up with *lamprais*, an unfortunate sounding name derived from *lomprijst*, which is nothing to do with lumpy-rice. Far from it: the lightest basmati rice is cooked to perfection in stock, placed in a wrapping of plantain leaf (which lends a delicate flavour) and piled high with a medley of different flavours; perhaps a

How Do You Do?

The traditional greeting in Sinhalese means literally: "Have you eaten rice?"

sour/spicy aubergine concoction; a prawn paste; a portion of curried chicken or mutton; sambol, and perhaps a meatball. Tied up and then gently baked, the result is a prized party dish, and if you want a gourmet's picnic, it travels particularly well, too.

Add to this the many dishes brought to these shores by the Arabs, Portuguese, Malays and South Indians and you begin to see what a culinary beauty contest you are in for.

LEFT: preparing hoppers for breakfast takes skill and devotion, but they are worth it.
ABOVE: eyes down, a family tucking in to a traditional lunch of rice and curry.

Favourite fish

All fish and seafood is freshly caught and available in abundant variety. Crab is cooked in a dozen different ways; lobster is far tastier than its Mediterranean relations; seer, amberjack, skipjack, herring, pomfret, bonito, shark and mullet are at their best from Jaffna or Negombo; tiger prawns are big brutes which flex their muscles as if eager to leave their shells. The smaller shrimp and many other mollusc should not be discounted just because of their size, as their flavour is always excellent.

Drying fish in the sun began as a method of preservation, but the intense flavours produced soon inspired Sri Lankan cooks to use it in unexpected ways. A teaspoon or more of tiny dried shrimps or Maldive Fish is used in all sorts of dishes.

Puddings from paradise

Pure ambrosia can be had in the form of buffalo curd with a thick, dark brown treacle made from the *kithul* palm. Try it and the taste will put a supermarket yogurt in perspective. You will be offered this as "desert", a frequent mispronunciation of dessert, but it makes an ideal light breakfast and a perfect foil to spicy food.

Know Your Spices

Spices are unavoidable in Sri Lanka, and make very good souvenirs to take home. But how well do you know your way along the spice rack? Here are all the spicy details, along with the Sri Lankan names:

Abba – *Mustard*
Black mustard seed is very pungent and acrid. It is used whole, powdered or finely ground, in everything from pickles and chutneys to meat, fish and vegetable dishes.

Enasal – *Cardamom*
One of the most expensive spices available, this plump, three-sided pod contains three clusters of dark seeds which have an aromatic fragrance. An exotic addition to rice dishes and confection, especially in the Sri Lankan national pudding, *watalappam* (*see opposite*).

Goraka – *Gamboge*
The colour of liquorice, its sharp, sour taste is used to flavour and thicken fish, meat and vegetable sauces. A good substitute for this spice is tamarind paste.

Kabarunatti – *Cloves*
The better quality cloves are rich, reddish-brown and large. They are really undilated flower buds.

Use with discretion. An aid to digestion, while clove oil does wonders for toothache.

Kurundu – *Cinnamon*
Once used for embalming Egyptian royalty and to scent the funeral pyres of emperors. The finest quality cinnamon for cooking is pale in colour with a pleasing fragrance. Use whole or broken cinnamon sticks.

Kaha – *Turmeric*
Commonly confused with saffron in some Asian cookbooks, this tropical spice is cheap enough to be used in an unadulterated form if bought already ground.

Karapincha – *Curry leaves*
Always used fresh throughout Sri Lanka, but you can also buy them dried to take home. Bay is a good alternative.

Kottamalli – *Coriander*
The ripe seeds are basic to the curry spices. The green bunches of leaves, also known as *cilantro*, have a very different flavour and are not often used in local food.

Sera – *Lemon Grass*
Also sold as *sereh* powder, this is a vital ingredient in Sri Lankan, Thai and Mexican cooking to flavour meat and fish.

Sadikka – *Nutmeg*
The fruits of the nutmeg tree have single-seed berries which produce two different spices, mace and nutmeg. Though not commonly used in Sri Lanka, they greatly improve the flavour of a curry. Mace is the lacy membrane covering the nutmeg that has been ground to a powder.

Suduru – *Cumin*
One of the pungent and distinctive flavours that make a curry. Best bought whole and ground before use.

Maduru – *Sweet Cumin*
Used in sweet dishes and various alcoholic liqueurs and sometimes called *star anise*.

Uluhal – *Fenugreek*
This hard brown, square-shaped seed with an unpleasant scent needs only a small pinch to flavour curries.

Velliche Misis – *Chillis*
Ripe chillis may be cream, yellow, orange or even purple-black and are easy to dry in the sun or in a slow oven. Used whole, powdered and freshly chopped in the same dish. ❑

LEFT: Sri Lankan cooking would be unthinkable without chillis, but finger them with caution and wash your hands before touching your eyes or mouth.

The Malay-inspired *wattalapam,* a rich coconut crème caramel with *jaggery* (*see information panel, opposite*) and cashew nuts, has practically turned itself into the national pudding. But, apart from this, there may not be a lot of choice on the sweet menu.

Favourite fruits

But who's complaining? There is a cornucopia of pineapple, passion fruit, pomegranate, papaya, avocados which come with sugar and cream, as well as Jaffna's undisputed king of mangoes such as the *gir-amba, pol-amba, ambalavi, vellaicolomban, betti-amba, dilpassand, peterpassand* or *willard.*

Quite apart from exotic fruits you may have had back home, look out for the red, cherry-like *lovi-lovi* fruit, mangosteens with flesh that tastes like lychee or woodapple – good as a rich truffle pudding and a knockout drink too. Or try the sweet-tasting star apples and rambutan – red and hairy on the outside but similar to lychee on the inside. Go for custard apples, cherimoyer or bullock's heart, which are a happy trio of relatives packed with white pulp and black seeds.

Then there's the honey-sweet ripe *jak,* several kinds of guava which make divine jelly, and that maverick monster, the *durian,* whose reputation usually precedes it. There are two vital warnings about this most delicious nougat-tasting fruit. One: when ripe, its flesh stinks like hell. Two: it's strongly but improbably rumoured to be an aphrodisiac.

Drinking notes

Even before you reach your hotel, you will notice fruit-sellers along the way exhibiting golden bunches of young coconut by the roadside. This is the *thambili,* nature's bounty to all who thirst. Its juice is a safe bet when you are dubious about the drinking water, as it comes sealed in the heart of the coconut.

It can also be an effective pick-me-up for a hangover. The balance of glucose and potassium makes it a delicious health drink for convalescents and in medical emergencies it can even be used as a drip.

Another local beverage made from the coconut palm is toddy. This is tapped from the flower of the coconut and left to ferment. New toddy is light and refreshing; fermented, it can be as alcoholic as cider.

A distilled spirit made from the toddy becomes *arrack,* the nation's favourite tipple which is widely used in punches and cocktails but also drunk neat. Ceylon Breweries also makes a very palatable beer using imported hops and water brought from the highlands of Nuwara Eliya.

All these local drinks are inexpensive and are very good alternatives to the many imported lagers, juices and spirits which are readily available but which carry an extortionate 100 percent tax. ❑

RIGHT: sweet-tasting fruits in Galle.

A WEALTH OF CRAFTSMANSHIP

The variety of crafts on offer would shame a Middle Eastern souk.

The good news is that the quality is remarkably high

From the moment you set foot on the island the marvellous crafts of Sri Lanka will have you surrounded. A delicate, rather snooty silver anklet and sleek leopard carved in ebony might team up with some rugged pottery and follow you wherever you roam as part of your baggage.

It's all too easy to let your defences down as you laze in a quiet beach café, browse through bazaars, or drive by an understated but intriguing workshop. The crafts will jump out and relieve you of a rupee or more or wrap themselves up in a batik sarong to become stowaways in your suitcase.

This island has something for every pocket – even high quality jewellery and furniture is reasonably priced. Catering to the top end of the market, several contemporary designers have tailored and augmented traditional craftsmanship into high quality sophisticated wares.

Buying crafts

The government emporium **Laksala** and its countless clones around Colombo are handy if somewhat sterile one-stop shops displaying the full range of crafts with the air of a traditional museum. Many of the more specialised crafts are still made and sold only in faraway towns and villages and, unless you happen to visit one of these, you may miss them completely. The showrooms, however, cream off quality goods from the entire country into a convenient, air-conditioned shop and also have the added attraction of fixed prices, rarely found outside Colombo.

You can buy crafts directly from the producer although the quality, unless you know what you are looking for, can be variable. Most people are happy to buy souvenirs from road stalls

PRECEDING PAGES: a "Sigiriya Maiden" finds her way onto a low-relief chipwork plaque.
LEFT: baskets proliferate at roadside stalls – they are usually made from woven split bamboo or cane.
RIGHT: a Kelaniya potter incises decorative patterns to a pot before firing.

where intricate brass and silverware and varied woodcarving jostle alongside delicate lacquer, leatherware, batik and lace.

Naththarapotha, literally meaning "craft village", only 6 km (3½ miles) from Kandy, contains a far more interesting round-up of arts and crafts. The village was artificially

created by the government in the 1950s to restore fading craft traditions and in half a day you can see potters, wood-carvers, silversmiths and many other artisans working from within small workshops.

As part of a nationwide programme, it is the largest of several centres established all over the country and provides training for craftsmen whose professions were threatened by machinery and assembly lines. But you will still find craftsmen at work in villages all around the island, sitting on the floor hammering away or smelting metal in primitive furnaces. Their remoteness from modern life has kept the purity of their work intact.

Weavers of Sri Lanka

Stalls all over Lanka are laden with textiles as tempting as the fruit on the stall next door. From gaudy batik sarongs to delicate lace, the variety in style is astounding. The ubiquitous batiks vary enormously in quality and colour – from two-toned sarongs ideal for the beach, to detailed works of art.

Whichever end of the scale, they are all made through the same time-consuming process of carefully applying wax to the areas not to be dyed. After each dying, the fabric must be fixed, washed of the old wax, and then more wax is reapplied for the next dying. In this way,

the pictures gradually develop in colour washes as they work from light to dark

For Picasso-inspired batik masterpieces that have been exhibited at galleries in Europe, visit Dudley Silva at his home-cum-workshop, 53 Elpitiya Road, Ambalangoda. High quality handlooms are produced at the **Menikdiwela Weaving Centre** near Kandy, and closer to Colombo is the **Nayakakanda**, known for its artful use of colour.

Hand-loom weaving has inevitably become almost entirely a victim to fast machines, but a few contemporary designers keep a small cottage industry alive with stunning results.

Barefoot, 704 Galle Road, Colombo 3, is Barbara Sansoni's classy, not-to-be-missed outlet. Inside this Aladdin's cave bursting with jewel-coloured fabrics are Tabasco-hot clothes, traditional soft-furnishings in vibrant hues, and toys and gifts unlike any others you will find on the island. Her traditionally woven cotton and silk fabrics are hand-made for a sophisticated modern market, but she is chiefly famed as a colourist and her colour combinations are remarkably bold.

The **Matale Heritage Centre**, in Aluvihare 15 km (9 miles) north of Kandy, is the brainchild of another renowned designer, Ena de Silva. Created in 1984, it was known initially for fine, hand-woven tapestries and batiks, but has also become respected for wood, brasswork and other handicrafts.

Within minutes of entering Galle fort, you will discover what the town is known for. An army of hawkers will descend, bearing armloads of intricate hand-made lace and displaying an unexpected tenacity.

Introduced by the Portuguese, pillow-lace is also made in Colombo and Jaffna, but only by the octogenerians, who seem to have the patience for such time-consuming work. Lace-making involves hours of painstaking work to produce just a few centimetres of lace. The younger generation prefer the speed of machinery to the laborious art of drawing and knotting threads – and who can blame them?

Mats and baskets

Weaving is not restricted to textiles and extends to transforming almost any variety of local palm leaf into an array of colourful mats and baskets. Mats were traditionally functional items, covering floors and beds, and the most famous ones, *dumburra,* are woven in the village of **Henawela** near Kandy.

The *dumburra* weavers are a secluded clan whose weaving patterns are based on geometric designs and do not traditionally depict plants, animals or human form. Given the history of the area, it is probable that their designs have their origin in Islamic art, which also bars depictions of animate forms.

The tapestry is made from hemp that grows wild on the hills and is woven on a narrow loom. The results make attractive wall hangings, cushion covers and table cloths which can look particularly stunning when put together with stark, modern interiors.

Locating good *dumburra* weaving is difficult as pieces take a long time to produce and are snapped up. To see the best designs, visit the Barefoot Galleries in Galle Road, Colombo.

Induruwa, south of Bentota, is also known for a particular type of flat basketware, and its Tuesday market attracts buyers from Colombo. **Kalutara** is famous for its colourful, soft basketry and at the Basket Hall you can see how the weavers tame the unyielding palm fronds, turning them into purses, coasters, hats, and other items.

Silver and silver-plated jewellery is also common and ranges from very simple designs to chunky Indian-style work to delicate filigree necklaces. Kandyan artisans are renowned for their gem setting and intricate workmanship of silver candelabra, trays, tea sets and tableware.

The ceremonial lamps which are used in temples, at weddings and on Sinhala New Year are made from brass laboriously indented with a large nail and hammer to create a delicate design in relief on the surface.

> **HEARTWOOD**
>
> Heartwood ebony is softer than the sapwood and patches of honey-coloured undertones can be seen in the pitch-black wood.

Precious metalwork

Jewellery, traditionally considered to be a Sri Lankan woman's portable wealth, is found in towns all over the island. Gold rings, earrings and chains are bought when times are good as a badge of success, and as a form of insurance in case fortunes change. Sri Lankans demand very pure, high-carat gold imported from India, so you won't find any 9-carat trinkets or gold-plated jewellery.

LEFT: handloom weaving is a labour intensive process, but the results are often strikingly original.
ABOVE: silver and brassware displayed in a metal worker's shop in Kandy.

It grows on trees

On the west coast near **Aluthgama**, you will see what happens to the rest of the palm tree – stalls selling coir matting, brooms and other objects made from coconut fibre line the roads. Coconut shells are polished up and fashioned into spoons and other trinkets. Palm wood is the basis for a diverse carving industry, in which different regions of Sri Lanka are associated with different woods or techniques; **Kandy** for intricate relief work, **Kurunegala** for mahogany and **Ambalangoda** for fine furniture and devil-dancing masks.

Most crafts have interesting histories behind them, but none as gripping as the expressive devil masks which were traditionally used in place of medicine to scare away diseases. When you get to see them at close range – their maniacal gaze, ghastly tangle of hair and raucous expression – you will understand why they worked. Ask questions when you buy and you will come away with a little arcane knowledge from the Sri Lankan occult to go with your purchase. You can also ensure that you don't unwittingly present your mother-in-law with the mask of the Demon of Boils.

The masks are carved from soft *kaduru* wood from the evocatively named *Nux vomica* tree, which is soaked to soften it before carving. Early examples grace the collections of ethnological museums around the world, but today they are no longer painted with vegetable-based dyes. The gaudier designs are popular with magpie tourists; but you will find more authentic examples if you search. The best places to try in Ambalangoda are the well-known **Mask Museum** and the workshop at **Southlands** (at 353 Main Road) where the quality is exceptionally high.

Lacquer crafts

Lacquer bowls, containers and other objects originate from Matale near Kandy but are now found everywhere. Many of these are just painted and coated with varnish but you can find work finished with lac. This is a resinous substance which is secreted by the lac insect when it punctures the bark of certain trees. The resin is removed, melted down and strained through muslin and worked while it is still soft with the pigment.

The two techniques used in Lankan lac ware are *biraluvada* or spool work which is used to decorate objects that will spin on a lathe; the second method is called *niyapotuvada* in which the artisan's thumbnail is used to guide the filament of lac in application. You may find *biraluvada* lac ware being produced near **Tangalla**, while **Matale** is famous for its *niyapotuvada* work.

A country of craftspeople

Whatever your interest, be it pottery, intricately carved spoons, exquisite lace, weaving, lacquer, or sinewy silver chains, you are likely to find your luggage considerably heavier when you leave the island than when you arrived. The only consolation is that, unlike the majority of souvenirs available in other tourist destinations, the crafts in Sri Lanka are of a high standard and are unlikely to be consigned to the rubbish bin when you arrive home. ❏

LEFT: scare away diseases with a devil-dancing mask as sold in Ambalangoda.
RIGHT: brasswork at a Sigiriya souvenir stand.

GEMS

The precious stones found in Sri Lanka have been attracting covetous and open-mouthed admiration for thousands of years

"When you leave the Island of Angamanain and sail about a thousand miles in a direction a little south west, you come to the Island of Seilan, which is in good sooth the best Island of its size in the world...

Now I will quit these particulars, and tell you of the most precious article that exists in the world. You must know that rubies are found in this Island and in no other country in the world but this. They find there also sapphires and topazes and amethysts, and many other stones of price. And the King of this Island possesses a ruby which is the finest and biggest in the world; I will tell you what it is like. It is about a palm in length, and as thick as a man's arm; to look at, it is the most resplendent object upon earth; it is quite free from flaw and as red as fire. Its value is so great that a price for it in money could hardly be named at all."

—Marco Polo, *The Travels*

The gems of Sri Lanka have been famous since Biblical times. It was to Ratnapura, the City of Gems, that King Solomon sent emissaries to procure the jewel which won him the heart of Queen Sheba. In the book *1001 Arabian Nights*, Sinbad tipped off his master, Haroun Al Raschid, that the best gems were to be found in *Serendib*, as the Arabs called Sri Lanka.

More recently British royals have been struck by Lanka's exquisite stones. A cat's eye discovered in a rice paddy and weighing 105 carats had the distinction of being admired and caressed by four British royals in turn – Edward VII, George V, Edward VIII and Elizabeth II – when they visited the island. Indeed, the largest sapphire in the British crown is the Blue Belle of Asia, found in a village near Ratnapura. The famous Panther Brooch made by Cartier in the 1930s for the Duchess of Windsor, Wallis Simpson, holds another Sri Lankan sapphire of 152.35 carats.

A curious phenomenon about the Sri Lankan gem pits is that a variety of gems are usually found together. There always seems to be an assorted collection of spinels, corundums (sapphire and ruby) and star stones. Aquamarines, tourmalines, topaz, garnets, amethyst, cats' eyes and zircons are also found here. Their names in the Sinhala language are even more melodious: *pushparaga, vairodi, nila, rathu keta, mola neero, padmaraga*. But the most outstanding

GEM LEGENDS

Gems have been put into legendary settings as elaborate as the filigree goldwork that holds a ruby. They are believed to confer magical powers and are often used as talismans. For instance, a moonstone is believed to give its wearers the power of prophecy if they put the stone on their tongue at the time of the full moon. Sceptics should be wary of scoffing at the magical power of gems. According to one story a young prince of ancient Lanka wore a large cat's eye to protect him against the assassin's blade or phial of poison. He survived seven attempts made on his life and in the end succeeded to the throne.

of all are the glistening rubies and sapphires for which Sri Lanka has been one of the oldest sources in the world.

The methods used today are as primitive as when the first precious stones were mined. All that is required is patience, excellent eyesight, a tolerance of damp working conditions, and a great deal of luck. It is to ensure the latter that an elaborate series of superstitious rituals has been developed.

A male astrologer is always used to investigate the horoscopes of diviners – women are

> **MISNOMER**
>
> The famous Star of India belonging to the Queen of England is in fact a Sri Lankan sapphire.

will bring him good luck as some pits can be as much as 10 metres (30 ft) deep. The astrologer no doubt shares his anxiety, as do the various other people whose livelihoods depend on finding a glint or sparkle in the coarse water-borne gravel called *illam.*

The first in line to share the spoils is the financier of the pit along with the licensee who pays the Sri Lankan government for the mineral rights; next comes the pump operator followed by the gemmer, a connoisseur of the true gem, who both get a share. Last of all to gain from

never used for this task. He not only calculates their chances of finding a gem but also advises on the most auspicious moment for a ritual known as the "sod-cutting ceremony". This takes a full day and starts with the offering of a venerable *puja* to the guardian gods and ending exactly 24 hours later when a *kapurala* or priest blesses the chosen diviner at the exact time that the sod is cut.

A miner, clad only in a loin cloth or *amudes,* then sinks into the pit, praying that the gods

PRECEDING PAGES: sapphires and rubies in Ratnapura.
LEFT: the arduous and muddy search for gems.
ABOVE: a gem-studded armlet in a gold setting.

the find is the supposedly star-blessed man who toils in the mud.

Buying gems

Beware a friendly Sri Lankan with a "relation" in the gem trade. The unwary tourist can be fooled by some convincing talk and a handful of glinting gems which turn out to be worth a lot less than he or she paid. The first rule is not to buy gems unless you are prepared to do a lot of homework to protect yourself from confidence tricksters. Choose a dealer or a shop who is a member of the Sri Lanka Gem Traders Association or the International Coloured Gemstone Association. The words "Tourist Board

Approved" sometimes displayed in shops have no offical backing. If you are serious about buying, obtain a list of gem dealers from the Export Development Board.

Remember you are the buyer. Don't be pressured into making a snap decision. View the stone in both natural and artificial light. When buying jewellery, ask for a receipt that details the weight of the gold and the stones. Ask for the price of the stone alone, then calculate the gold. The remainder is the dealer's profit, plus a charge for workmanship.

CAT'S EYES

The silky flash that crosses the gem following its every movement recalls the gleam of a cat's eyes. It is called *Chatoyancy*, derived from the french word *chat*.

If you are spending a large amount or have a suspicion about authenticity, go with the stone to the State Gem Corporation to get it tested – that is, if you can persuade the jeweller to let you borrow it. Some Colombo jewellers might be willing to accompany you. This organisation is located at 310 Galle Road, Colombo 3. On the floor below the Gem Corporation is the Colombo Gem Exchange where most of the best Sri Lankan stones are sold to foreign jewel merchants for export. ❏

WHAT TO LOOK FOR

Although people are often interested primarily in cut and clarity where diamonds are concerned, Sri Lankan gems have a distinctive colour which is the first priority in assessing their quality. The best stones to look for are:

◆ **Sapphire:** all colours, but blue/pink and yellow are the best.

◆ **Spinel:** look out for bright pastel attractive colours.

◆ **Chrysoberyl:** an abundance of low-quality cat's eyes are coming in from India. For the best Sri Lankan stones, look for faceted chrysoberyl, occasionally found in very attractive green/yellow, and green colours.

◆ **Garnet:** found in every colour except blue, the most

popular are the *pyrope* or "firey garnet". Those with a purplish overtone are the most prized, and large good quality stones are often readily available.

◆ **Aquamarine:** the majority are pale and overpriced.

◆ **Blue Topaz:** any blue examples you see have been irradiated abroad using white topaz found locally.

◆ **Moonstone:** world's best blue flash, but large pieces (over 3 carats) are rare. The only gem found in lode form, in the village of Mitiyagoda.

◆ **Alexandrite:** a rare gem named after Tsar Alexander II who came of age the day it was first discovered. It is green in daylight but raspberry red in artificial light.

Pearl Lottery

Prehistoric man had only to develop a liking for shellfish in order to acquire a nugget of scientific knowledge that oysters which somehow go wrong produce a pretty object, the pearl.

Pearls were responsible for a spectacular tumult on the shores of the gulf of Mannar, a kind of lottery which amounted to bets on how many – and which – among tens of millions of oysters had gone wrong. Speculators bought mountains of the things, laid them out in the sun to rot, and then gently prised the shells open to see what they had won. In a good season, between 1 and 2 percent revealed something, if only a meagre consolation prize. In 1797, however, a poor coolie who had scraped together enough to buy just three shells squatted over them while they rotted, opened them up, and hit the jackpot with the most valuable pearl anyone could remember.

The oysters, like any gems found below ground, belonged to the king (farmers owned the surface but that's all). Tissa, for example, who ruled at the time of the conversion to Buddhism, styled himself "Lord of the Pearl Fields". The oysters returned annually to their feeding grounds on banks about 30 km (20 miles) out to sea, their numbers varied, and only a proportion of them were of the right age, between five and seven years old; "if left too long, the pearl gets so large and so disagreeable to the fish that it vomits and throws it out of the shell". An official inspector went out by boat to see if the oysters were ready for fishing. Timing was critical and hostage to the possibility that the oysters might be swept away by exceptional currents. The big day was announced four or five months in advance, so there were always smugglers planning to jump the gun.

In normal times, the village of Marichchukadi was a motley clump of huts, but with the approach of the big day hundreds of overloaded boats arrived from India to join a roaring bedlam attended by an army of snake-charmers, conjurors, astrologers, betel-sellers, harlots and "dancing boys". Lots were drawn to decide which of the boats would form the official fishing fleet. The winners were at once importuned by "shark-binders" who, for a daily rate, offered to protect divers from shark attack with a combination of incantations, magic potions, con-

tortionism and dancing about on the beach. Options to buy hauls from various boats changed hands in what would now be recognised, on the stock market, as trading in futures. Bizet was sufficiently impressed by the drama to write "*Les Pecheurs de Perles*" for the opera *Leila*, which opened in London in 1887.

The banks were at depths between 6 and 20 metres (19–65 ft). Divers jumped in with two ropes: one tied to a heavy stone and themselves to accelerate descent, the other to a basket or string bag. Although the record was reputed to be six minutes, they generally stayed down for between 40 seconds and a minute, wrenching the shells off the seabed

and filling the bag. They gave a tug when their lungs gave out, and both ropes were yanked to the surface. Bleeding from the ears and nose, divers repeated the exercise up to 50 times per day. The boats then raced back to the shore to auction their haul, keeping a commission of about 20 percent.

There were 36 successful seasons in the 19th century, and 1905 was the best year ever, when 5,000 divers brought up 80 million oysters. The village of Marichchukadi has seen nothing like it since, although conch divers still congregate from January to March each year. With a growing understanding of the reasons for the decline of the pearl oysters, there are hopes that the exciting days of the pearl season may yet return. ❑

LEFT: shopping for gems in a Sri Lankan jewellers.
RIGHT: the risky business of pearl diving.

SANCTUARY

With habitats that range from rainforest to hilltop plains, the wild places of Sri Lanka are teeming with fascinating flora and fauna

To stand on a mountain, with the trees about you alive with the twinkling lights of a galaxy of fireflies, and gaze on villages thousands of feet below, is to experience the spirit of this island. The visual spectacle is often paralleled by the hauntingly sweet perfumes of the Queen of the Night or the large, white, pendulous Angels Trumpets and all around the silver bell sounds of tree frogs tinkle a mysterious melody.

Travelling through the mountains of Sri Lanka is always a rewarding experience. The high country combines with the monsoons to give the island at least four distinct types of forest, each with its own peculiar complement of plants and animals. There are wildlife sanctuaries in each area and all are irresistible, and quite accessible. Sri Lankans have always taken conservation seriously, perhaps due to their Buddhist principles, with records of animal protection found even in the ancient text of the *Mahavamsa*. This tradition continues today and some regions have restricted access.

In other areas, you may be prevented from seeing leopards because of the activity of human big cats. Unfortunately some parks are in no-go areas, such as Gal Oya, Wilpattu, and some parts of Yala are currently being used as a hide-out for Tamil Tigers. This situation changes so frequently that you will need to check on arrival which parks are open.

Mammals

The fauna of Sri Lanka is exceedingly rich for such a small island. Of the large mammals there are the elephant, buffalo, elk, spotted deer, leopard and sloth bear. The elephants of Sri Lanka do not sport large tusks as a rule, and when they do ("tuskers") it is only in the males. Once the elephant was found all over the coun-

PRECEDING PAGES: a leopard caught napping at Wilpattu National Park.
LEFT: charging cross-tusked elephant at Yala.
RIGHT: a black-faced grey langur sits on the fence at Tissamaharama.

try, much like the leopard, elk and spotted deer. Today they are generally confined to the lowland dry zone, the leopard and elk still maintaining their presence in the mountain forests. Sri Lanka has two smaller deer, the mouse deer and barking deer, both shy creatures that can sometimes be seen at dawn and dusk. The wild

boar is widespread and is often encountered during night drives through the country. Three small cats – the fishing cat, the jungle cat and the rusty spotted cat are all secretive by nature, nocturnal and most often seen crossing the road at night. The mongoose is another widely distributed animal: there are four species on the island, the largest being the rare badger mongoose with a badger-like marking on its neck.

There are three species of monkey. The two most common species are the red-faced macaque and the grey langur. The grey langur has a black face and grey body and is usually shy of humans. The red-faced macaque on the other hand is bold: it approaches people in search of food and can be very aggressive and quick-tempered. The third type is the rare purple-faced leaf monkey or bear monkey, so named for its robust body and shaggy fur. It is usually encountered in mountain forests.

Reptiles

Many large reptiles are found in Sri Lanka, the largest being the saltwater crocodile, a true giant attaining sizes exceeding 8 metres (25 ft). Others include the massive leather-back turtles, which come to Sri Lanka to lay eggs, the rock python which grows to 9 metres (30 ft) and water monitor measuring 2 metres (7 ft).

plain. Here, the forests are dry thorn scrub, interspersed with small dusty glades – the ideal habitat to view elephants, Sri Lanka's largest mammal. Other large animals such as the leopard, elk and the enigmatic sloth bear also frequent this area.

Bundala National Park, just west of Ruhuna, is a special bird habitat housing 149 species, including the only resident flamingo population in the south. More accessible than Yala, in a four-hour jeep ride, the park is home to a great deal of wildlife, including elephants and crocodiles (evening visits in the dry season are best for spotting elephants). A little fur-

It is not unusual to see large land monitors or *cabaragoyas* lizards crossing the road and holding up all traffic, as buses and cars wait patiently for them to cross.

The sanctuaries

The largest and most famous of the Sri Lankan national parks is Ruhuna, better known as **Yala**, in the southeastern corner of the island. This region, known as the "dry zone", is dramatically different from the lush rice paddies and palm trees of the south coast. In the hour's drive from Tangalla to Hambantota, the gateway to the "dry zone", you would be forgiven for thinking you had stumbled onto an African

ther south, **Kalmateiya Bird Sanctuary** possesses a mature mangrove swamp with an extraordinary collection of waterbirds. The best time to see birds is from November to March (the migrant species conveniently follow the tourist season although for slightly different reasons). This is also the calving season for many animals when you can see families of elephants with their young.

The southern region has three other major parks – Gal Oya, Uda Walawe and Lahugala. The **Gal Oya Park** surrounds the first "modern" reservoir in an island famous for well over 10,000 massive reservoirs built by ancient kings. These tanks were the arteries for agricultural activity over the past 3,000 years. Today these gigantic reservoirs offer travel by boat as an alternative to the more usual vehicle trek. Although tame elephants, accompanied by their *mahout*, are a common sight, the experience of watching wild ones a short distance away while silently gliding past in a boat is a heart-stopping experience.

The **Uda Walawe** is another park that surrounds a modern reservoir and is perhaps one of the easiest to get to and probably one of the most heavily populated with elephants. The Lanugala National Park near the east coast is another where large herds of up to 100 ele-

rainforest – **Sinharajah** and **Kanneliya** – easily reached from Galle, just 30 km (20 miles) away. Dominated by the tall majestic *hora* and *kina* trees, these forests are often over 40 metres (130 ft) high and close-galleried, thus providing a shrub-free, easily traversed forest floor. Visiting Sinharajah requires permission from the Wildlife Department and visiting Kanneliya requires permission from the Forestry Department.

Kanneliya contains the last of the rainforest elephants and has been nominated for a Rainforest Elephant Rehabilitation programme. It is also the habitat of leopard, elk and many rare,

phants can be seen feeding on the abundant elephant grass. The elephant is rapidly becoming a symbol of the conflict between conservation and development. The eastern part of the island, in which the sugar plantations are cultivated in the middle of Elephant Country, provides some classic examples.

Jungles in jeopardy

North in the western quarter are the two last pockets of Sri Lanka's once extensive cover of

LEFT: a large crocodile senses an unwary intruder at his jungle pool in Wilpattu Park.
ABOVE: a spotted deer stag makes a rapid getaway.

TALKING TO THE ELEPHANTS

Elephants have a vocabulary of noises. A low stomach rumble denotes pleasure as when greeting an old elephant acquaintance. A series of louder rumbles means the animal is cornered and unable to get out of trouble. A "woosh" made by blowing air through the trunk shows the elephant is surprised or wants to warn an intruder of its presence. The shrill, piercing sound described as trumpeting can mean two things: a mild, shriek-like trumpet warns of danger, a loud, blood-curdling trumpet followed by a deep-throated roar as the elephant stamps his forelegs and swings his ears forward means he is about to charge.

endemic birds, reptiles, fish and butterflies. When visiting Kanneliya, a swim in the crystal clear streams is like swimming in a tropical aquarium. Many of the multi-coloured fish are the same species as the popular aquarium fish that you see back home.

Colombo was once ringed with a vast mangrove swamp and riverine wetlands. Some of it still remains, inhabited by many species of birds, mammals, reptiles and fish. The **Panadura Wildlife Resource Centre** runs canoe safaris providing a tantalising glimpse of these unique wetlands. To see them at closer range, take the turning off the Colombo–Kandy

road onto the Warakpola–Mirigama road. Just before you reach Mirigama town is a last patch of remnant rainforest, guarded by the Boy Scouts of Sri Lanka. It provides wonderful photo opportunities of the trip to Kandy and the trees of Bedi Del with their hard, scalloped leaves making a striking canopy.

Just 2 km (1¼ miles) from the centre of Kandy, you encounter a sight listed among the 138 wonders of the world: **Uduwattekelle**. This deep forest has many endemic birds, butterflies and plants. It is also home to the bizarre "lyre-headed lizard", a colourful, large creature found only in the rainforests of Sri Lanka. Around dusk, the awakening and flight of fruit bats leaving the forest on their twilight jaunts beats any Indiana Jones movie.

Cloud forests

From Kandy to Nuwara Eliya the landscape changes from lowland forest to the cloud forests of the mountains. These cloud forests "comb" the passing clouds for moisture and channel it through their roots to the soil where they feed small streams that flow even in times of no rain. Examples of cloud forests are easily seen in the **Galways Land Sanctuary** at Nuwara Eliya or on a leisurely stroll to watch the mountain birdlife at the **Hakkgala Reserve**.

Below this is the **Hakkgala Botanic Gardens**, which are well worth a visit, not only for the wonderful collection of plants but also to view the bear, monkey and blue magpie which visit from the adjoining forest.

Highland peaks and plains

No visit to the mountains would be complete without seeing the breathtaking **Horton Plains**, an hour away from Nuwara Eliya. These plains, formed by millions of years of erosion, lie right on top of Sri Lanka's mountains. Here large herds of elk, silhouetted against the clouds of the lowlands, move among scarlet rhododendrons. This is also the home of the rhino-horned lizard, a rare relic species from Sri Lanka's prehistoric land connection with Africa. The crystal-clear pools still run with trout, a legacy from colonial times.

The forests also contain an extraordinary shrub called *nillu* that flowers once every five to 10 years. But as there are many populations of varying ages, there are always some in bloom during the season. The sight and smells

CORAL REEFS

The offshore wildlife of Sri Lanka is no less exotic than the denizens of its jungles.

A visit to the Coral Sanctuary of Hikkaduwa provides a complete change of pace. The first marine sanctuary, it was created just in time to preserve the rapidly disappearing reef of Hikkaduwa. Many coral reef organisms can be seen when snorkelling around the shallow bay.

For a different experience, the proposed Reef Sanctuary at Unawatuna, near Galle, is well worth seeing. This reef contains a higher number of fish species than the Great Barrier Reef and can be seen with ease.

of a large *nillu* flowering and fruiting attract an amazing diversity of animals to the area, from birds to bears.

South from Nuwara Eliya lies the Uva valley. The picturesque town of Bandarawela, within the valley, was once hailed as possessing one of the healthiest climates in the world. This is also the centre of the "flavoury tea" district and produces some of the finest tea on the island. Between the towns of Bandarawela and Welimada, lies the **Uva Herbarium**, a garden dedicated to growing

> **MANEATER OF PUNANI**
>
> A man-eating leopard was shot in 1923 after killing 20 people. Her stuffed carcass is preserved in the National Museum in Colombo.

Peak Wilderness, so-called as it lies on the same mountain ridge as the famed "Adam's Peak", is a montane cloud forest and home to large herds of elk; and the leopards of these hills possess a thicker coat than their lowland relatives.

The other exciting mountain reserve lies on the Knuckles range. To get there, first go to Kandy and then travel on to Matale and proceed along the Illukubura road. The views en route are spectacular and the forests contain many plant and animal species which can be found nowhere else in the world.

herbs and re-establishing indigenous forests. Here, many species of birds can be easily sighted and photographed.

Just west of Nuwara Eliya is the Hatton Valley, gateway to the great **Peak Wilderness Forest**. Travelling through a striking landscape of tea plantations, waterfalls and lakes you pass the town of Norton Bridge and then take the Balangoda road.

This road continues through the wilderness, rises to the crest of the hills and descends dizzily to the small town of Balangoda. The

LEFT: the breathtaking Horton Plains.
ABOVE: a safari jeep in pursuit of pachyderm.

The road winds through the mountains and drops onto rock-based wet meadows where interesting eco-systems catch cloud water and percolate it through its many streams. This area is also the only place where you can see the flat horn-nosed lizard.

Between the Knuckles range and the central mountains of Kandy and Nuwara Eliya lies the **Randenigala National Park**. The park was artificially created to protect the hydro-electric reservoir of Randenigala, but it has since attracted a large herd of elephants.

You can also view these mammals by boat, with the mountains providing a wonderfully dramatic backdrop. ❑

Birds

Sri Lanka has more than 400 species of birds, of which 21 are unique to the island, and many more are only found in south India. Travelling through the country, it is easy to see them at fairly close quarters. Many perch conveniently on telephone wires, displaying their colourful plumage at the roadside.

BIRDS IN TOWN AND GARDEN
There are many birds that seem to be as much at home in the city as in the country. At first it seems

that the ever-present crows, of which there are two species, are the only birds in town, rooting through dustbins and dodging traffic, but a dawn walk will provide a fair bird list. There are the sweet-songed black and white magpie robin, the green barbet, the golden oriole, which migrates from India, and the noisy, chattering grey Indian babbler, as well as bulbuls, noisy flocks of parakeets and the chocolate-coloured mynah. Viharamahadevi Park in Colombo will give the city-bound twitcher a swift fix.

WETLAND BIRDS
Both coastal and inland wetlands provide great opportunities for the birdwatcher, and if you're not a birdwatcher you soon will be after observing the

spectacular show that is put on daily at any tank or lagoon. Cormorants and snake birds are the diving champions, whilst plovers and waders keep to the muddy banks. The painted stork ventures further in search of crabs, frogs and water snakes and with luck you may spot a kingfisher waiting to pounce. One bird even the most amateurish ornithologist will be able to identify is the spoonbill, swishing the water from side to side, like a diner searching for something in his soup. Another strange creature is the pheasant-tailed jacana, which has developed elongated toes for walking across lily pads.

FOREST DWELLERS
The rarer rainforest and mountain birds are not at all difficult to spot if you visit any of the parks or sanctuaries. In contradiction of the proverb, birds of a different feather do flock together, including leafbirds, flycatchers and babblers. The brilliant blue magpie lives in groups in the hill forests, feeding on insects. The pied ground thrush got its name because it has pied markings on its wings and is often found foraging through leaf litter. The Malabar trogon is widespread in Sri Lanka, the male easily identifiable by his bright red breast and black head. Others to look for are the yellow-green Ceylon iora, the wedge-tailed drongo, as well as barbets, parrots and minivets in the original forests of the wet zone mountains.

An infamous bird of the forests is the "devil bird", so named for the horrifying sound of its call that is uttered in the middle of the night. Although it is not difficult to hear, no one has positively identified the maker of these sounds. The raucous call of the bizarre Malabar pied hornbill in the dry zone will guide you to the flocks that live on the tallest tree tops.

BIRDS OF PREY
Other birds regularly seen on drives around the island are raptors, in particular hawks and eagles. Most of the reservoirs have the fishing tank eagle or the white-bellied sea eagle. Mountains with cliffs are frequented by the black eagle and the mountain hawk eagle, the brahiminy kite, and the serpent eagle, which are all predators who prey on small mammals and birds. ❑

LEFT: a green bee eater, one of three types of bee eater in Sri Lanka, waits to snap up a passing insect. **RIGHT:** clockwise from top left: malabar pied hornbill; serpent eagle; bar-tailed godwit; red-wattled lapwing; spoonbill.

EXPLORING THE ISLAND

Intrepid spirits can choose between diving in coral reefs, snorkelling with turtles, trekking through tea estates or whistling through white water

Exploring the island with your own private transport is the best way to sample the secrets of Sri Lanka's interior. As soon as you get away from the main tourist routes the traffic on the island is generally light and you will be able to explore the real, untouched Sri Lanka at your leisure.

You could hire a vehicle but you may find it more rewarding (and cheaper) to use a car complete with chauffeur and thus avoid the stress of driving on Sri Lanka's roads (the movements of other road-users, whether vehicles, pedestrians, carts or roaming animals, are unpredictable). Many drivers can turn out to be a mine of local information and you may find you've forged a friendship by the end of your journey.

Bike it

To get a closer look at a slower pace, you can adopt the most widely used form of transport in Sri Lanka, the bicycle. The great thing about cycling is that it allows you to get right to the heart of an area, and cycling in Sri Lanka is no exception. There are extensive well-maintained trails through the lowland tea, rubber and spice plantations which are a joy to cycle along, while those in the Hill Country can provide more of a challenge, right up to the seriously steep tracks suitable for only experienced cyclists.

Cycling doesn't have to take you far. Once you get off the main routes, such as the terrifying Galle Road, you can ride through small, friendly villages to experience all the sights, sounds and smells unimpeded by windscreens or air-conditioning.

Hike it

For an even more intimate view of the countryside you have to rely on your own two feet.

PRECEDING PAGES: a shoal of silver sardinella.
LEFT: where can you windsurf whilst admiring Buddhist architecture? In Unawatuna.
RIGHT: keeping old cars going is not just an exercise in nostalgia, as new ones carry huge import duties.

Trekking through the countryside and villages enables you to enjoy and interact with the environment and people better than any other activity. You will learn first-hand about the character and spirit of the land and its people and probably find it a much more rewarding experience than simply stopping off at tourist attractions

for a quick-fire photo shoot. You will probably also be amazed by the huge range of faces in the countryside.

The main trekking centre on the island is Kittulgala, the starting point for a variety of treks into the Hill Country. Decent hiking maps are hard to come by in Kittulgala itself, though there is a good four-piece country map available from the Survey Department in Colombo, if you can find it. Local villagers, however, are more than willing to help you navigate, though try to be patient. Also, it is not a good idea to ask for directions by pointing, as the locals, being polite, will invariably agree to whichever way you point.

Canoeing

For the footsore, canoe and boat trips allow quiet and enjoyable exploration of the many miles of sedate rivers and canals which traverse the low country of the island. Previous canoeing experience is not usually necessary if you are going with a guide, but advisable if you want to take a canoe or kayak expedition on your own.

If that sounds too peaceful and you are looking for a more action packed adventure, then white-water rafting could be for you. There are an increasing number of travel companies offering first time thrill-seekers and experts alike

careful of the strong currents that make much of this beach unsuitable for recreational swimming. Midigama is a quieter, more remote surfing beach further down the west coast while Polhenha beach, just before Dikwella, has an in-shore reef as well as great waves.

The waves are too rough on the coast for windsurfers but there is ample provision for them inland, as Sri Lanka generally has consistent winds throughout the year, making sailing and wind-surfing a pleasure. The Bentota River behind Bentota and Aluthgama is an ideal place for water-skiing, windsurfing and sailing, with a wealth of facilities and beautiful

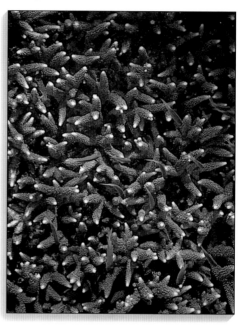

the chance to ride the island's turbulent rivers, such as the Kelani.

Sea sports

Beaches are not just for sunbathing on, as any surfer will tell you. The best surfing beach is at Arugam Bay on the east coast but this is a long way off the tourist trail and often off-limits in any case because of ethnic troubles. The beach resort of Hikkaduwa has good surfing and traditionally attracts surfers from all over the world. The best break is just south of the Coral Sanctuary in front of Wewala and Narigama. Waves for body surfing can be found further down the strip, though you should be

calm waters. Hotels and travel agents will hire out equipment and organise guides or tuition if necessary. A range of sailing boats (Laser, Hobby Cat or traditional catamarans) can be hired for anything from an afternoon to a couple of weeks with various recognised courses also on offer. The Colombo Sailing Club can be found on the Bologoda Lake at Moratuwa. There is also good windsurfing to be found on Bologoda Lake.

Diving and snorkelling

There's a wide choice of opportunities here. The diving season runs from November to April when the sea is very calm, around 27°C

(80°F), and offers clear visibility of, on average, 20 metres (65 ft). Diving is still possible out of season, but the visibility is a lot lower and there are strong swells which can make the sport too dangerous at times.

Scuba diving focuses mainly around wrecks and rocks, though there are also some deep reefs and reef walls. There are many shipwrecks dotted around the coast, some dating from the 19th century, and they provide an ideal habitat with plenty of hiding places and growing surfaces for all kinds of marine life. Night dives are also offered by the watersports companies.

Snorkelling is very popular in these parts, as

Coral Sanctuary at Hikkaduwa offering the best variety (*see page 128*). Snorkellers should always take a boat out to the rocks.

Swimming with turtles

There is always a good chance of seeing turtles at Hikkaduwa, where they come in at high tide or in the afternoon to feed in the still lagoon about 15 metres (50 ft) offshore between two converging breaks. Swimming with the turtles as they feed and glide gracefully through the water is a wonderful experience.

Another coral sanctuary is being planned for the reef at Unawatuna and further along the

there is a vast variety of brightly coloured fish. The best times to go snorkelling are in the early morning and late afternoon, when the fish come out to feed.

The on-shore coral reefs are ideal for snorkelling, though a large majority have suffered irreversible change by dynamite fishing, unauthorised removal of coral and the increase of water-based pleasure sports. There are still some good patches surviving, though, with the

FAR LEFT: Dendrophyllia coral.
LEFT: Staghorn Acropora coral.
ABOVE: a butterfly fish in the reef at Hikkaduwa.
ABOVE RIGHT: Goniopora coral.

south coast Polhenha beach has a reef that you can walk out to from the shore.

Deep-water fishing

If you are looking for a slightly calmer watersport, many local fishermen will jump at the chance of taking you fishing with them – even more so if you buy some of their catch. They will also want to chat to you.

Deep-water fishing is growing in popularity, and local tour companies, hotels and even some entrepreneurial individuals are organising special trips. Tuna, seer, para, ray fish or shark and marlin are found in great abundance in Sri Lanka's waters. ❑

AYURVEDA – HERBAL HEALING

Sri Lanka's ancient medicines are more popular than ever today,
whether in treating disease or maintaining health and fitness

Increasing numbers of visitors now come to Sri Lanka specifically to experience the ancient healing practice of Ayurveda. Based on an holistic approach to health, Ayurveda has for thousands of years used the island's prolific herb and plant life to cure and revitalise. Though discredited by western colonials

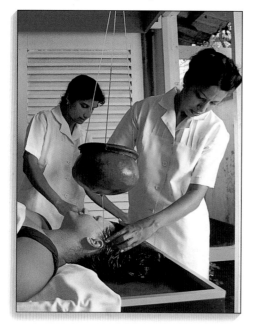

during the 19th century, Ayurvedic practice has always been revered by the Lankan people who have passed its secrets down the generations and kept the art alive through chants, verses and *ola* leaf manuscripts. And now, with the West's awakening to natural health philosophies, Ayurveda is being given the international respect it has always deserved.

If you have doubts about the healing properties of Ayurveda, it is worth noting that, when Lankans are bitten by a snake, they rarely consider any Western-style allopathic treatments, preferring tried and tested Ayurvedic cures. However, while Ayurvedic treatments are widely recognised and readily available, the newly-

arrived traveller needs to be clear that it comes in many different forms and from many different outlets and centres. So, if you are planning a holiday around a course of treatments, it is essential to find out what exactly is on offer at your proposed destination to avoid disappointment. Visitors wanting only to experience herbal baths, massage, de-stressing and toning with cleansing oils will not need to be quite so discerning as someone who is seeking serious cure.

A science of life

Because Ayurveda is such an integral part of the island's culture, you will find its influence in all sorts of places and products. Locally manufactured toiletries, beauty treatments, food, laxatives and supermarket-shelf consumables are all quite likely to contain Ayurvedic ingredients. A mouthwash made from *muna-mal*, for example, will strengthen the gums; lime fruits boiled with dill seed are considered effective for dandruff; and *bombu* sticks are excellent for cleaning teeth.

The ordinary Sinhalese curry contains 13 key herbs and spices: *rampe* (*Pandanul latifolia*), *karapincha* (*Murraya kopenigii*), *sera* (*Cymbopogon citratus*), onions, garlic, chillis, lime, turmeric, cumin, fennel, coriander, fenugreek and ginger. These 13 ingredients not only add flavour but also have digestive and medicinal powers.

If you need specific health treatments quickly, Ayurveda is readily available from a number of sources. You could visit the nearest local clinic, find an Ayurvedic physician or seek out the wise man in every village, who will be familiar with Ayurvedic remedies. In fact, most households in Sri Lanka have some knowledge of this ancient indigenous treatment. Your success at most of these sources, however, will probably depend on your command of the Sinhala language.

LEFT: herbal oil treatment at an Ayurvedic hospital.
RIGHT: a herbal dispensary.

The full treatment

For those who have come to the island for less urgent or longer-term treatments, and perhaps want to pamper themselves at the same time, there are an increasing number of luxury hotels: these include the Kandalama Hotel near Dambulla, on the edge of the Cultural Triangle, where you can expect tip-top attention from trained specialists, doctors and masseurs while surrounded by forests and mountains.

Dr Hettigoda of the Siddhalepa Wellness Centre recommends a course of treatment lasting three weeks, which, he maintains, is enough time to find relief from practically all maladies of the body. But for those who are simply curious, illness is not a prerequisite for trying them. Many hotels have jumped on the bandwagon, and whilst there is no harm in a relaxing massage with herbal oils, some do not do justice to the full range of therapies. See the *Travel Tips* section of this book for a guide to some of the best hotels, health centres and also suppliers – for those who want to take a few pungent bottles home with them.   ❏

> **HOMEGROWN HEALING**
>
> Sri Lanka is a storehouse of healing herbs, the most valuable are called *aralu, bulu* and *nelli*.

> ### HOW AYURVEDA WORKS
>
> Ayurvedic philosophy postulates that the development of each of us from birth is governed by the varied combination of the five basic elements in nature – Air, Fire, Water, Earth and Ether. Add to these three other classifications called *Vatta*, *Pitta*, and *Kapha*, and this is the Ayurvedic practitioner's starting point. Any variations in each of us around these combined eight "modalities" provides a basis for diagnosing and prescribing our individual health needs to balance the overall mind, body and spirit, plus our relationship to the environment.
>
> Revitalisation therapy is a prominent feature of Ayurveda; it is claimed that longevity without senile decay,
>
> heightened memory and improvement in bodily strength are all possible. Illnesses which do not respond readily to allopathic treatment – such as diabetes, arterio-sclerosis, asthma, allergies and mental ailments – also benefit from the system.
>
> Ayurveda is an entire science of life (*Ayur* means life). It is based on the idea that our general well-being is closely related to our choice of lifestyle, habits and nourishment. That doesn't differ much from the tenets of Western medicine, of course, but one of the most significant advantages of Ayurveda is that there are no side-effects or debilitating reactions from this treatment.

ELEPHANTS: LANKA'S FRIENDLY GIANTS

The Sri Lankan elephant, known as "Elephas maximus maximus", is a more majestic sub-species of the Asian elephant, "Elephas maximus"

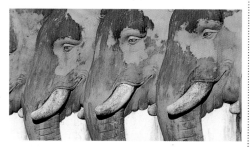

The elephant population is a major feature of Sri Lanka and, although endangered in the 1960s, is now protected and a regular sight on the island.

Elephants in the wild live in tight-knit family herds of no more than 15, headed by an elderly female. Although elephant family ties are strong, it is common for ageing males to exile themselves from the herd so that the females mate only with the virile younger bulls.

Working elephants are controlled by *mahouts*, who bring them to heel by an elephant lore called *Sinhala Hasti Sastraya*. This involves stimulation of 72 pressure points (*anila* and *nila*), activated by the *mahout*'s stick, the *ankussaor goad*.

ELEPHANT DIETS

The trunk is the most important organ for the elephant, capable of gathering up 180 kg (400 lb) of food and 150 litres (40 gallons) of water to drink or to douse with. Surviving on bark, twigs, reeds and leaves, however, takes a toll on the animals' dentistry and elephants go through three sets of molars in their lifetime. When the third set begins to wear down, the ageing elephant moves towards water to live on semi-solid food. Elephant graveyards are, therefore, generally near a waterhole.

△ **ELEPHANT RIDES**
A trip through the countryside on an elephant is an unforgettable part of any trip to the island.

▷ **GOOD VIBRATIONS**
Elephants can pick up vibrations through thei huge legs and by placi their trunks on the gro but are very shortsight

◁ BATH TIME

After romping in the water, fitful lovemaking and a long drink, the elephants then powder themselves with dust to prevent insect bites.

△ ELEPHANT IN ART

A highly decorated elephant is depicted on one of the many beautiful wall paintings in the Kataluwa Temple, near Galle.

DECORATING THE ELEPHANTS

The annual *perahera* (procession) in Kandy (above) is one of Sri Lanka's most spectacular sights and a time when the island's beloved elephants are honoured and decorated in keeping with their revered position.

The procession in Kandy began almost 2,000 years ago to parade the Tooth Relic of Buddha, housed in the Temple of the Tooth, through the town to be honoured by the public.

The procession is led by the "tusker" elephant, which is draped from trunk to tail in a brightly coloured embroidered cloth decorated with tiny electric light bulbs. It is the tusker's role to carry on its back an illuminated *howdah* which holds the gold, *dagoba*-shaped *karanduwa* (reliquary), an exact replica of the casket which holds the sacred tooth within the temple. Behind the tusker is a train of 12 other decorated elephants, followed by a parade of temple officials.

The Kandy Perahera is the most impressive procession but numerous parades throughout Sri Lanka decorate elephants as part of the festivities.

△ HUMAN ELEPHANT

The elephant is honoured in human form in this exquisite gold painting on the ceiling of the Temple of the Tooth in Kandy.

▷ CONTROL

The trained *mahout* is so skilful in controlling an elephant that he can induce its hind-quarters to collapse, unaided by voice.

PLACES

*A detailed guide to the entire island, with principal sites
clearly cross-referenced by number to the maps*

A papal legate six centuries ago wrote that "From Ceylon to Paradise, according to native legend, is forty miles; there may be heard the sound of the fountains of Paradise." For those unable to enter Paradise itself, its neighbour has enough diversity of landscape, people and culture to make one forgive Eve's transgression: mountains, jungles, ruined cities, vast man-made lakes, statues as impressive as anywhere in the world, fertile uplands where tea estates reach as far as the eye can see; elephants, leopard, birds, turtles, coral and other sea life. And then there are the beaches...

Early travellers arrived by boat, eventually turning the harbour in **Colombo** into a thriving and busy port. The entire **Southwest Coast** is now thriving and busy with holiday resorts, but you are never far from history and legend; the old Portuguese port of **Galle** was said to be the location of Tarshish of the Bible. Inland are rubber and cinnamon estates to explore, and the unparalleled Sinharaja rainforest, but venture further afield and you will have even more to take your breath away. **Kandy**, the second largest city, was the last capital of the Sinhalese Kingdom and is still home to culture, religion and traditional arts. It is here, each August, that the stupendous *Perahera* festival takes place, featuring 100 robed elephants, fiendish dancers, acrobats and a procession so ancient it was chronicled by Marco Polo. From Kandy, the sheer beauty of the tea estates punctuated by waterfalls will draw you into the **Hill Country**, which surrounds the town of **Nuwara Eliya**. Or southwards to the fabled **Adam's Peak**, which is a sacred goal to the multitude of pilgrims who scale it every season. At its foot lies the ancient city of gems, **Ratnapura**, one of the five major gem producers of the world.

In the arid North Central Province, in the so-called **Cultural Triangle**, cities dating back to 250 BC have survived the ravages of time. **Anuradhapura** was the capital of the island for over 1,000 years and has ruins that rate not far behind the Egyptian Pyramids. **Polonnaruwa** succeeded it for a short but glorious medieval reign, with impressive ruins in fine fettle. Last but not least, the stupendous monolith of the fortress of **Sigiriya** has been declared the eighth wonder of the world. While northern Sri Lanka remains out of bounds, the **East Coast** is slowly opening up, with **Trincomalee** attracting some adventurous travellers.

The last temptation of Sri Lanka is idleness. It is the land of the Lotus Eaters in which it seems to be always afternoon. All round the coast tourists swoon in the languid air, resting their weary limbs on sunbeds as soft as asphodel. Most visitors succumb. ❑

PRECEDING PAGES: stilt fishermen of Welligama, on the south coast; a tea plucker scours the hillsides for young leaves; the Ruwanelisaya *dagoba* at Anuradhapura.
LEFT: boat trips on traditional outriggers entice tourists off the beach at Negombo.

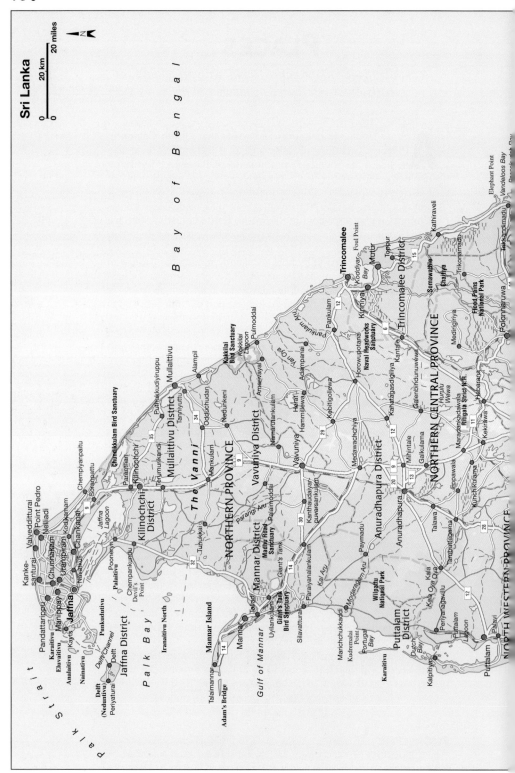

Sri Lanka

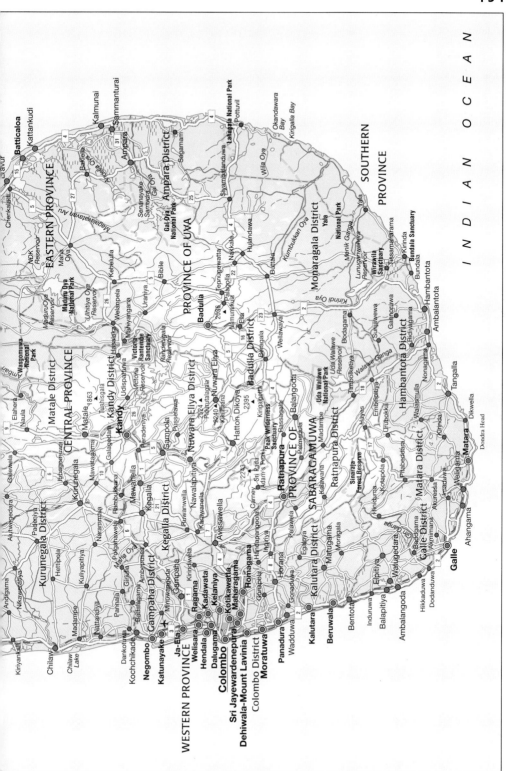

කල

චිතුපට දෙ

දෙසැ. 2 සි

ටිකට්ස්. සැමිස් , ස

ඨනකාර්යාලය වි

වයින පුධාන කාර්

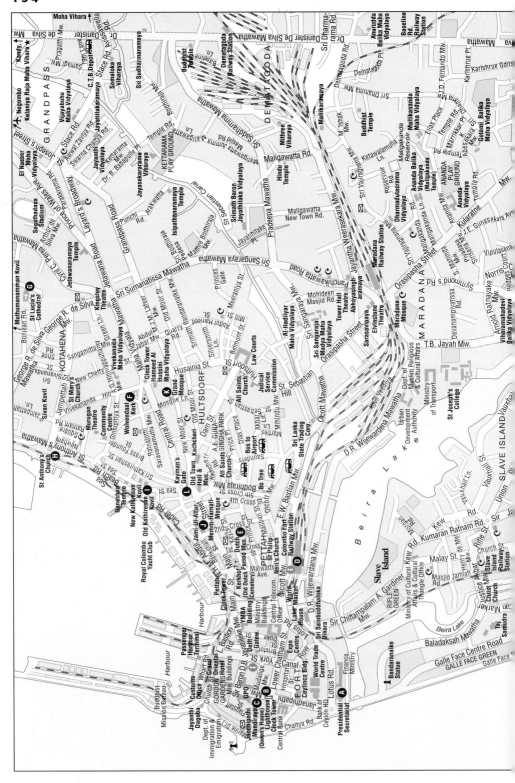

Colombo

CITY OF COLOMBO

*Sri Lanka's hot and bothered capital is shared by
affluent business people, over-persistent market vendors,
ever-present crows, smart shops and street-wise cattle*

Map
on pages
154–5

Colombo is like a once-beautiful woman who has let herself go. A woman with a past, one who has been ill-treated by many men, called many names, known by many faces. A Chinese trader called Wang-Ta-Yuan who visited in the 14th century called her *Kao-lan-Pu*. Another foreigner who dallied with her charms half a century later was an Arab Moor, Ibn Batuta, and he was truly stricken. He named her *Calenbou*, "one of the largest and most beautiful (cities) in the island of Serendib."

Hard on his heels a Portuguese man-of-the-cloth, Father Fernao de Queyroz, was smitten and declared his love in gushing letters which he sent home. When the young and lusty Englishman Robert Knox discovered her ample curves, her fragrant sighs, her long stretches of undiscovered territory he was hungry for her luscious fruit: "Columbo means, in the Chingala language, the leaf of the mango tree," he wrote, too mesmerised to get her name right. The Portuguese spelling of Columbo prevailed until much later when the Dutch, German and French came to prefer the dazzling dame to be spelt with an "o".

These days, many people are inclined to leave the dame well alone. She has been through some hard times. She has been abused and now looks grumpy, tired of flirting with the foreign men who took her for all she was worth.

PRECEDING PAGES:
posters and
poseurs.
LEFT: Pettah market
vendors learn their
trade young.
BELOW: shopping in
the 1850's meant a
trip to Cargills.

Colonial Colombo

Even after she won her independence, Colombo's heart clung to the memory of her departed masters. Her monsoon-soaked ribbons of purple-black road teemed with black Morris Minor taxis, whose drivers spoke impeccable English and (almost) always gave the correct change. Their cargo of fashionable wives continued to visit the English stores Cargills and Millers, which were still stocked with imported English goods. Today the shelves are all but empty. The wooden shop cases can offer only dime store trinkets and limp locally made biscuits. The pavement hawkers outside have more promising wares.

If a traveller who knew Colombo in the early 1900s could return today, at least one aspect of street life would be familiar, the ubiquitous trishaws. These motorised descendants of the man-drawn rickshaws that once plied the streets are irresistible hailing bait. They have grown a third wheel and the sweating coolie has become a seated driver. In the old days the tariff was calculated by time rather than by mileage. A "first class" rickshaw coolie cost 10 cents for 10 minutes, 25 cents for 30 minutes and 50 cents for an hour. Today, you would do better to negotiate the fare before you get in.

A whistle-stop tour aboard one of these three-wheelers, wending your way through the carbon

TIP

Colombo is divided into
various postal areas,
numbered from 1 to
15, which local people
often refer to when
giving addresses.
Colombo 1 is Fort, 2 to
10 spread south, while
11 to 15 spread north.
Colombo 7 means
Cinnamon Gardens
and is the city's posh-
est post code.

BELOW:
1910 street scene.

monoxide cloud amid ancient buses and other traffic, could endanger your health, even if you survive the fun fair ride. But it can be fun. Anyone who has experienced the antics of the Indian three-wheel drivers and their suicidal tendencies take heart; the Sri Lankan version is a much better driver. They may seem as if they are taking you straight into the open jaws of death but very few accidents occur. It is not so much that as Buddhists they are not allowed to kill even insects, but having to ditch everything at short notice to escape terrorist bombs (there are no warnings, ever) has made them skilled at survival. Their flimsy windscreens are hung with a variety of charms to provide accident insurance: Jesus, Buddha, Ganesh and the odd guru, all swaying in unified conviction that it is better to travel in hope. And there is nowhere better to head for than the historical heart of Colombo, once the hub of the city's business, but now torn between a prosperous past, an ambitious future and a disastrous present.

Fort – past and present

Fort should not be referred to as *the* Fort. There are no actual fortifications left, so the definite article has been modestly dropped.

The old fortified harbour was originally built by the Dutch to protect their prosperous trade in sapphires, elephants, cinnamon and ivory. But when the British forces came to attack it, the garrison of Swiss mercenaries had already abandoned the area. Colombo surrendered to its new master without putting up much resistance. So the victorious British tore down the old defences and began transforming the city into a thriving port. Remnants of Dutch colonial architecture can still be glimpsed amongst the British buildings and the building sites which are hastily trying to piece together the scars of recent bombings.

Main Street. Colombo.

If you are undaunted by the litter of makeshift security barriers and military guards (who look about 14 years old), hoisting rifles on their hunched up shoulders, you might find a prowl around Fort worthwhile.

As soon as you turn away from the sandstone colonnaded façade of the former parliament building, now the **Presidential Secretariat Ⓐ**, you will have to go it alone. Photography of government buildings such as the Secretariat is banned, and vehicles are not permitted to pass, but don't be shy to try your luck with the teenage sentry. There is no real reason for him to prevent an innocent tourist from looking around, although he may not know this. These lads are prised from their villages, given a two-week "training" and dumped on the streets with a gun and an ill-fitting uniform. So if they seem unkempt or harassed it is most likely to be culture shock. They duly believe that to prevent terrorism they must hiss at tourists armed with nothing more sinister than a bum bag.

Head for the **Lighthouse Clock Tower Ⓑ** at the top of Lower Chatham Street. This Victorian landmark was designed by the British governor's wife in an attempt to instil punctuality into the notoriously bad timekeepers under her husband's rule. After 10 years a light was attached to the tower, and it successfully functioned as the city's lighthouse until the 1950s, despite being in the middle of a busy road intersection several blocks away from the shore. Its regulating influence on the ever-tardy Sri Lankans has yet to be felt.

Cross over to the white mansion which was once Queen's House. In its new guise as **Jandhipathi Mandiraya Ⓒ**, it is supposed to be the President's official residence. However, President Chandrika prefers the safety of Temple Trees, the Prime Ministerial residence on Galle Road, to this beautiful villa built in the late 18th century by the last Dutch governor. It was home to subsequent British governors including the indefatigable Sir Edward Barnes, who unified the country with a massive road-building effort. A shadow of his former self lurks at the corner.

Behind this is **Gordon Gardens**, once a park and now, alas, barred from vision. The entire government is in the process of transferring to a new parliament complex in Kotte, the site of an ancient capital now officially and longwindedly renamed Sri Jayewardenapura – in honour of the ex-president who was unofficially and succinctly known by his initials J.R. Hopefully, when this equally longwinded process is complete, Gordon Gardens will open as a park once again, and the sentries can relinquish their paranoid guardianship of Fort.

The white giant opposite the President's House is the **General Post Office**, whose Philatelic Bureau in the basement is considered by stamp collectors to be one of the most friendly in the world. If you stroll down the length of Sir Baron Jayatillika and turn left into York Street, you will come face to face with the **Passenger Harbour Terminal**, once a busy post of emigration when P&O liners frequented Colombo. From here the Ceylon Steamship Company operated a weekly service which circumnavigated the island calling at Jaffna, Trincomalee, Galle and Hambantota. It took eight days and cost a total of Rs.100 (£1/US$1.60).

Map on pages 154–5

A trishaw is the quickest and most enjoyable way to get through the congestion of Colombo's chaotic traffic.

BELOW: lighthouse Clock Tower.

The original Thomas Cook offices in York Street have been improbably preserved. The polished wood façade still lists the names of all the defunct shipping lines which had their offices in this same building. Further up, the **Grand Oriental Hotel**, an erstwhile luxury hostelry, is another relic from times when all tourists were called "passengers". In 1890, an unknown Russian writer called Anton Chekhov checked in here. His last book hadn't done too well, hardly surprising since it was entitled *A Dreary Story*, but he perked up after a tour of the island and went home to try his hand at playwriting. One of the best views of Colombo harbour can be enjoyed from the aptly named Harbour Room on the fourth floor. Try it for a drink or the buffet lunch. The tiny bookshop in the foyer downstairs is also worth a browse.

The faded grandeur that still clings to the hotel was a gleaming reality in 1914 when Bella Wolf wrote: "It is said that if you waited long enough in the hall of the Grand Oriental, you would meet everyone worth meeting." Times have changed.

Three of Colombo's more recent hotels sprang up around Echelon Square, as concrete expressions of confidence in the future. Unfortunately, modernisation has had to be put on hold, leaving these towers looking rather fragile as they try to withstand the violent buffeting of events. From the gardens of the Hilton you get a most remarkable view of the elegant **Old Parliament Building**, recently abandoned by the parliamentarians. The plate-glass windows of the Intercontinental were intended to reflect the shimmering sea, but now offer a darker reflection of devastated hopes. Finally, the Galadari has put on a brave face, launching a cyber café, **The Surf Board**, open daily from 10 o'clock to midnight, in a valiant attempt to rebuild some self-esteem.

"The locality presents no single advantage to recommend it... the coast is low and unsheltered and the port is less a harbour than a roadstead."

– SIR JAMES TENNENT

BELOW: the harbour as seen by an 18th-century Dutch engraver.

LA VILLE COLOMBO SUR LE GRAND ISLE DE CEYLON.

Die Stadt Colombo
auf der grösten und Zimmetreichen lustigen Insel Ceylon, welche vor mehr als 200 Jahren von den Portugiesen erbauet, und 1656 von den Holländern erobert worden.

La Ville Colombo
sur le grand et agreable Isle de Ceylon, riche de Caneille la quelle a eté batie par les Portugais il y a plus de 200 ans, et en 1656 elle a eté prise par les Hollandois

Pettah

Fort Railway Station ❶ is the main terminus and departure point for the Hill Country and most destinations apart from the north coast. It separates the Fort area from the Pettah, a colourful bazaar which in Sinhalese is known as *Pita Kottuwa,* meaning "outside the Fort". It is possibly outside most travellers' experience of street markets and will make any souk seem orderly by comparison. But there is some method in its madness, if you can stand the noise and squalor. Entire streets are given over to selling leather goods, household wares, or jewellery. The pavement hawkers are also there if you want to practise your bargaining skills. For electrical or photographic equipment, go to First Cross Street; jewellery and watches are sold at Second Cross Street; hardware at Third Cross Street. Get the picture?

The goldsmiths have enjoyed the less tumultuous atmosphere of Sea Street for more than a century. Some of them are members of the *Chetty* caste of craftsmen who came from India. For fabrics you will be directed to Main Street, although you will find bright pyramids of all manner of materials sold by pavement sellers everywhere.

One other street not to miss is Fifth Cross Street, which is given over to every type of tea, spice and Ayurvedic (herbal) remedy. It's a heaven for nosy shoppers. The smells here are a pleasant surprise after the raw abuse to your olfactory sense that a walk through the Pettah provides. Between the screaming pavement vendors and the perilously rudderless trishaws, you have to be nimble to avoid the small mountains of uncollected garbage that stew malevolently on the roadside, attended by ruffled crows.

Churches, mosques and temples

Amongst the shops and the teeming streetlife of the Pettah district you will find some of the oldest and most interesting buildings in Colombo, each providing a respite from bargain hunting – most of them doing it through religion of one sort or another.

The **Dutch Period Museum ❺** on Second Cross Street, at the corner of Prince Street, is one exception. Housed in a typical Dutch colonial residence dating back to 1780, it was for many years used as a Post Office. Now, its original appearance has been recreated using collected furnishings, household goods and maps. This is an old-style museum which has not learned to keep hours abreast of the modern day traveller. You will have to take pot luck on opening times.

Inevitably, the Dutch brought their religion with them along with their furniture, and the **Wolvendaal Kerk ❻**, begun in 1749, expresses their solid faith in the Dutch Reformation. Within its 1.5-metre (5-feet) thick walls, this staunch work of Doric architecture holds a finely carved wooden font, canopied pulpit, crystal lamps and an illustrated Dutch Bible. Its floor is made from tombstones brought from a Dutch church in Fort. *Wolvendaal* means "Dale of wolves", but since there were never any wolves on the island the Dutch must have mistakenly identified a pack of roaming jackals. Today there are no jackals in Pettah either, except those of the human variety.

Map on pages 154–5

BELOW: the bovine traffic jams of Colombo.

Saint Anthony shines a light of hope, with a little help from some lightbulbs.

BELOW: Colombo panorama looking south from Fort.

Not to be out-done by Protestants, the Catholic Church is most magnificently represented in Pettah by **St Lucia's Cathedral G**, which holds 6,000 worshippers. This enormous domed cathedral with ionic columns is dedicated to the Virgin St Lucy of Sicily. Legend has it that she had such alluring eyes that she pulled them out to present them to an unwelcome suitor who was enamoured of her beauty. The building of the cathedral took 34 years to complete and was finished in 1902. Close to it is another Roman Catholic church dedicated to **St Anthony H**. Every Tuesday, people of various faiths flock to this church to tap into the miraculous powers attributed to the saint; this sort of cross-worship happens a good deal in Sri Lanka. Among the devotees will certainly be Hindus who worship down the road in Kotahena Street, where the **Muthumariamman Kovil** is dedicated to the Goddess Pattini – a very popular goddess of health and chastity, also believed to have curative powers. Whilst all Hindu temples are large, *kovils* come in all sizes.

Of course, this being Sri Lanka and, even more so, this being Pettah, sooner or later religion joins with surrounding street-life. Each year the Vel Festival dedicated to the god Skanda begins at the **Kathiresan Kovil I** on Sea Street. The enormous Vel chariot, intricately carved and brightly painted, is dragged around the city visiting all the *kovils* on Galle Road followed by hundreds of devotees.

There are many other Hindu temples and shrines in Colombo. In Maradana you will find **Captain's Garden Kovil**. Other important places of Hindu worship are **Sivasubramania Temple** on Kew Road, Slave Island, and **Pillaiya Kovil** in Wellawatta.

Perhaps the most striking building in Pettah is at Second Cross Street. Built in 1909, the **Jami-Ul-Alfar Mosque J**, is striped in red and white like a stupen-

dous raspberry layer-cake, with candy minarets and arches shaped like bitemarks. At neighbouring Third Cross Street is the contrastingly dull **Memm Harnafi Mosque**, and Pettah also contains the most important mosque in the city, the **Grand Mosque** on New Moor Street.

Map on pages 154–5

Slave Island

Anyone in search of Buddhist monuments should really leave Colombo altogether; the ancient cities have much better, bigger, older and rarer examples. Besides, until a century ago, Colombo was home to more Muslims, Burghers, and Europeans than Sinhalese. Even multi-faith Pettah can't offer an example of Buddhist architecture. However, in the neighbouring district of Slave Island you will find an outstanding modern example.

Slave Island is so named because the Dutch imprisoned their slaves here at night. At the time it was completely surrounded by **Beira Lake**, which has since been compressed to reclaim more land. The slaves were flogged and branded if they tried to abscond, and to discourage them from swimming to freedom, the lake was stocked with crocodiles. Thankfully, the beasts have gone, preserved only by their Dutch name at one of the boundaries of the area, **Kayman's Gate** .

On three island podiums on Beira Lake, easily visible from Sir James Peiris Mawatha, is the **Seema Malaka** , a Buddhist temple designed by Geoffrey Bawa, one of Asia's most renowned architects. This is an exercise in the Kandyan style, with overhanging tiled roofs held up by walls apparently made from collected spindles and bannisters, affording ample protection from heavy rains but no impediment to the breeze. For those interested in Buddhism, a

BELOW: Seema Malaka temple on Beira lake.

resident monk will explain to anyone the main philosophies, the meaning of the moonstone, and what the different positions of Buddha's hands signify. Its peaceful elegance is a haven from the noisy city and a world away from the large, gaudy and utterly bizarre **Gangaramaya Bhikku**  which it serves. A tour (compulsory "donation" required) will gloss over their collection of ancient Sanskrit *ola* leaf texts, and the temple guide will normally rush you to admire large sapphires in an Aladdin's Cave that is a cross between a kitsch antiques market and a vintage car auction. Feast your eyes on these shelves chock-a-block with sandalwood and ivory carvings, brass gods and even old Parker pens and eye glasses strewn between jade and crystal monstrosities and elephant tusks. The resident guide will be disappointed if your jaw doesn't drop.

The less ostentatious gifts the temple has received have been put to use in a higgledy-piggledy arrangement along the front wall, which is perhaps just as well. Built in the minimalist style of the times, the outside of this temple is hardly inviting. But the head monk here is an amiable chap, with a good command of English, so if you feel like a chat or want to know about Buddhism he won't disappoint. One of the impressive elephants used in a *Perahera* around Beira Lake in January is usually kept here, but don't get too close.

Other Buddhist shrines

The most important Buddhist centre in Colombo is the **Kelaniya Raja Maha Vihara**, 11 km (7 miles) east of Fort, on the way to Kandy. The *Mahavamia* claims that the Buddha himself visited, an event celebrated during a mini *Perahera* in January. Do not confuse the event with the *Navam Perahera* round the Beira Lake (*mentioned above*), which is second only to the *Esala Perahera* in Kandy during August.

Nearer the city centre, in Havelock Town (Colombo 5), the **Isipathanaramaya Temple** is famous for its beautiful frescoes. And close by, on Vajira Road, Bambalapitiya, is the **Vajiramaya Temple**, the centre of Buddhist learning whence monks spread the word of the Buddha to the West.

If you want to see a small temple containing every component – the image house, the refectory, a library and assembly hall – then the **Subodharmaya Temple** at Dehiwela has all of these. It is situated on a small lane after the main Dehiwela junction and contains some wonderful murals too. The **Buddhist Cultural Centre** found at Nedimala, Dehiwela, has a collection of rare books for true Buddha scholars.

Galle Face

If you have managed to see the central districts of Colombo in one day you have certainly earned a drink. The oldest, and still the best place to watch the sun go down whilst sipping a mango cocktail or an arrack and soda is the outsize chessboard beside the bar of **Galle Face Hotel** .

"Here, in the course of time and travel comes sooner, or later, every man born of woman, and every woman interesting or uninteresting to man. Go where you will, go East, go West, you shall hardly avoid landing some day at the Galle Face Hotel. Not even if

BELOW: the colonial atmosphere prevails in some Colombo hotels.

your aim be the Antarctic Pole…" So observed an early travel writer named Reginald Farrer in his book *In Old Ceylon*, published in London in 1908. His enthusiasm was due to one of the splendid concoctions from the verandah bar, or perhaps it was the cossetting from the four liveried retainers allocated to each customer.

Map on pages 154–5

This proud old duchess is more than an elegant landmark; it is the oldest hotel east of Suez, and its Oriental charm and spaciousness have attracted dignitaries from all over the world, and beyond. Three moon men – Charles Conrad, Richard Gordon and Alan Bean – boldly explored its marble halls and cavernous ballroom in search of atmosphere and signs of life. A plaque in the foyer lists further celebrities who have stayed here: Noel Coward, Lawrence Olivier, Gregory Peck… A well preserved car is also on display. It was bought by Prince Philip, who was a naval officer stationed here in 1940. It cost him just £12.

The Galle Face Hotel doesn't face Galle – in fact, it has its back turned towards that distant southern town. The hotel, built in 1864, was actually named after **Galle Face Green**, the lawn that stretches between the hotel and Fort. This lawned esplanade was constructed by Sir Henry Ward as his parting gift to the colony on his retirement as governor of the island in 1859. In its heyday it held race meetings, football, cricket and hockey matches, and was compared to London's Hyde Park. Traditionally, everyone would gather at sunset to stroll beside the sea.

A liveried doorman at the Galle Face Hotel.

A century and a half later, the green has reverted to a patch of dust which locals sniggeringly call "Galle Face Brown". Meeting friends, flying kites or eating the many exotic varieties of fast-food sold from mobile canteens are not such commonplace pastimes now due to security problems, but these innocent pleasures are always resumed at a moment's notice, such is the affection for this place where many Colombo couples first fell in love.

BELOW: old man selling windmills on Galle Face Green.

A handful of brash modern hotels are all within a close distance. The Indian-owned **Taj Samudra**, which overlooks Galle Face Green, has lost some of its lustre; to the left of it is the ubiquitous **Holiday Inn**, and on the Galle Road towards the US and British embassies you will find the **Lanka Oberoi**. The new **Crescat shopping mall**, right in front of the Oberoi, has a collection of glitzy shops all under one roof. The **Tourist Information Centre** is on the opposite side of Galle Road, and further along is the **Colombo Swimming Club**. This is one of the few inexpensive places in the heart of town where you can get large quiet rooms facing the sea. For frequent visitors to Colombo it would be worth becoming a member for this reason alone, but if you simply want to use the pool and club facilities it is fairly easy to become a temporary member.

Cinnamon Gardens

Cinnamon Gardens is probably the one area of central Colombo to preserve its colonial atmosphere and is the reason why Colombo was often called "Garden City". In the 1850s this vast area was given over to plantations of cinnamon, the spice that attracted the Portuguese and Dutch to Sri Lanka. The large mansions and the wide tree-lined streets might be a trifle unkempt in parts, but by and large Colombo 7, as this residential area is more often known in these unromantic days, has a charm and a greenness that even the blinkered town planners of the city find hard to disturb. Large trees drop their fragrant blooms onto the street below.

For a long while now, the massive 18th- and 19th-century houses of the richest Colombo families in Cinnamon Gardens have been occupied by foreign embassies or private schools. With the exodus of businesses and shops out of Fort, many have found alternative locations along Duplication Road (so called because it is parallel with – and therefore duplicates – Galle Road). A few plush architects' offices and clubs appeared first, followed by many of the big banks and gem merchants who had previously done business in Fort. Gradually, more select commerce is spreading into these lush and shady streets whose names – Guildford Crescent, Torrington Square and Horton Place – refuse to budge towards any Sinhala *mawatha* as sternly as the English Viceroys after whom they were named.

One or two of these beautiful houses have even opened up as middle-priced guest houses, but not anything like enough to serve a city the size of Colombo; the capital remains infuriatingly devoid of any hotels or guest houses for the budget traveller, while being ridiculously top heavy with sky-scraping four-star hotels where a guest need never encounter the real world.

Cultural Colombo 7

The Germans, French and British vie for cultural influence through the **German Cultural Institute,** the **Alliance Française** and the **British Council**. Each one

BELOW:
National Museum.

conducts a programme of exhibitions, shows films and hosts home-country musicians, actors and artists. Events at all three are listed in a free magazine called *Linc,* which can be picked up in smarter shops.

Map on pages 154–5

The **National Museum** ⓟ, on Albert Crescent, is a purpose-built colonial structure from 1877 containing regalia of the last Sinhalese king and other treasures. It was built by a Muslim who so thoroughly pleased his British commissioners that they promised to grant him any reward he chose. The devout man replied that he would like to be allowed to praise Allah on Fridays. So to this day the museum is closed every Friday to enable its Muslim workers the freedom to worship at the mosque.

The collection provides an education in Sri Lankan art, beginning with a limestone Buddha from Anuradhapura, meditating in the foyer as if undisturbed by the passage of 16 centuries. Small bronzes depicting Hindu deities, many of which come from Buddhist temples, are a reminder that the two religions overlap. You can easily recognise examples of later Kandyan art by the wavy patterns on the drapery, and by the use of painted wood, a medium that doesn't last as well as stone.

A stone carving of a Hindu goddess in the National Museum.

Devil masks have become just another souvenir, but the ones in the museum still have their magical power intact. These gruesome masks represent 18 diseases, ranging from blindness to speech impediment, and were worn by an exorcist who enticed the demon out of the patient's body by dancing. The extracted demon was then put on his honour never to return. No repeat prescriptions were necessary.

The crown, throne and footstool of the last Kandyan kings were appropriated by the British conquerors of Kandy and shipped back to England where they were housed in Windsor Castle until magnanimously returned in 1934. They are displayed in a special room in the museum.

BELOW:
Velu, "kiteman" of Galle Face Green.

Other museums in the vicinity include the **Natural History Museum** ⓠ and, next door to it, the **National Art Gallery** (106 Ananda Kumaraswamy Mawatha), which has a collection of work by Sri Lankan artists – though most of them are portraits which would hold little interest to an outsider.

If you are able to find your way to it, the **Sapumal Foundation** (32–34 Barnes Place, open Thurs–Sat, 10am–1pm) is one of the most delightful spots in which to while away an hour or two. Here, in a sprawling bungalow – once the home and studio of Harry Pieris – you will encounter a collection of Sri Lankan contemporary art by the so-called 43rd group of artists. Basil, the resident guide, will gladly tell you all about this remarkable group of artists.

One of the main instigators of the 43rd group was the barrister, musician and photographer, Lionel Wendt, who is commemorated by the **Lionel Wendt Theatre** ⓡ, at 18 Guildford Crescent. This is the hub of live entertainment in the capital, but there is an unfortunate lack of information. The newspapers seem to mention shows only when their run is over.

In your wanderings, look out for the **Serendib Galleries**, on Rosmead Place, which sells a selection of old maps and prints of Sri Lanka through the ages.

*Tasty snacks
along the way.*

Further south, along Cambridge Place, you will find two of the country's most august academic institutions, **Colombo University** and **Royal College**, which share a triangle of land with the city's almost forgotten racecourse, the **Turf Club** on Reid Avenue. The old grandstand is a sad reminder of the horse racing era of the 1940s and '50s, when the planters from the Hill Country would join Colombo's elite for the smartest occasion of the season. There are plans for a sports stadium to be built on this site, but don't hold your breath.

To the west is **Independence Square ⑤**, the setting for the great ceremonies of state and the New Year's Day fireworks. The Independence Commemoration Hall, a *faux* Kandyan audience hall, was not built until long after independence. It is a curious toad-like colour, probably because it is made from concrete pretending to be something grander, but from afar it manages to look imposing.

If you haven't got the time to travel all the way to Sri Lanka's ancient cities, you can seek consolation in a 1970s replica of the 8th-century Aukana Buddha *(see page 242)*, which stands opposite the **Bandaranaike Memorial International Conference Hall ①** on Bauddhaloka Mawatha. If you think this building looks similar to Beijing's Peoples' Square, your suspicions are correct; it was a gift from the Republic of China in 1971 at a cost of US$1.5 million.

Viharamahadevi Park

You will have by now earned a rest in **Viharamahadevi Park**, at the heart of Cinnamon Gardens. Originally known as Victoria Park, it was renamed in 1958 – presumably because the former was far too easy to pronounce. Do not let this put you off, though (the park is known by both names), and you can also ignore the signs outside claiming that the park closes at 6 o'clock.

Map on pages 154–5

The Sinhalese Queen after whom Victoria Park was renamed had a very colourful life. Viharamahadevi, poor girl, was cast adrift off the Colombo coast as a sacrifice to unfavourable gods. She fetched up on the shore at Kirinda, near Yala, and King Kavantissa, who knew a good thing when he saw one, grabbed her for his own queen. The royal couple's only claim to fame was their son Dutugemunu, who wrested Anuradhapura from Chola conquerors and united Sri Lanka for the first time.

Official gardeners will give an interesting tour of the park's trees and flora, including the last surviving cinnamon trees from what was once the largest plantation in the region and the easy-to-miss "Touch-me-not" – a remarkably animate plant that shrinks away if probed with a finger. Ebony, mahogany, lemon, fig and eucalyptus trees grow here amongst lotus ponds, and there is even an orchid house.

Elephants from the temple near Beira Lake are often kept in the park, but a more intriguing sight are the hordes of fruit bats and flying foxes waking and stretching their wings before dusk. As the gardeners relentlessly reassure you, these creatures eat only fruit and are not remotely interested in entangling their wings in your hair – or their teeth in your neck. For families, there is also a children's park on the southeastern side, with a mini zoo and a small train.

Overlooking the park, on the northeastern side, is the **Town Hall ⓤ**. Built in 1927, it is a neoclassical wedding cake, topped with a glimmering white dome apparently carved from royal icing. The clerks and bureaucrats toiling within must feel like glacé cherries. Appropriately enough it can be viewed whilst sitting at a clerk's marble table and spooning the froth off a *cappuccino* from the first-floor coffee shop of the **Paradise Road Store**. This emporium occupies a 19th-century mansion and sells locally made collectables, antiques and ceramics which are aimed at Western tastes.

Just across the street from the New Town Hall you will find the **Devatagaha Mosque**, the oldest building in Colombo 7, built at a time when the cinnamon estates were on the turn to scrubland and before the development which followed in the late 19th century. It is dedicated to the Muslim Saint Datar, who is also here. The tale runs thus: a poor widow could only make a living from pressing olives to make oil. It took her all day to make enough to fill her only pot, which she then took into town to sell. One day she was walking along the footpath from Borella to Galle Face, when she accidentally broke her precious pot, losing not only its valuable contents but all hope of earning tomorrow's meagre wage. The poor woman burst into tears and her sobs were heard by a wealthy family of Muslims who lived nearby. Having heard her story they gave her a new vessel from which flowed an abundance of olive oil, courtesy of Saint Datar. On the spot where the oil was first spilt, the Muslim family built a mosque in his memory.

A shopping spree in Kollupitiya

Those who find artefacts in a museum too well preserved and parks too gentle, should head down to Kollupitiya district, between Viharamahadevi Park

Between March and May is the best time to savour the aroma of flowering trees in Viharamahadevi Park, including the different perfumes of the seven varieties of frangipani, also known as temple blossom.

BELOW: strolling through a city garden

One of the elephants of Dehiwala Zoo putting on the afternoon show.

and the sea, and visit **Kollupitiya Market** before the vegetables wilt and the soft fruits rot. One of Colombo's many markets, it is worth a visit to try some local fare – even if your hotel offers full board. The neighbouring **Liberty Plaza** shopping centre cannot compete with it for smells and sounds.

Café Society

Colombo 7 is the place to find local yuppies flashing their new business wealth, as well as members of older families, who, like much-reduced gentryfolk everywhere, feel themselves far superior to their more affluent neighbours. Both groups like to hang out at **Le Palace**, a restaurant in a colonial villa on Gregory's Road. Among the attractions here are the best cakes in Colombo, whipped up by French *patissier* Jean Pierre. On verandahs overlooking the palms of the shady garden the *nouveaux pauvres* ruminate on their ancestry while pecking at swan éclairs floating on a pond of chocolate sauce artistically disposed over a ten-inch dinner-plate. The pastry is all they can afford here. Meanwhile, the *nouveaux riches*, who have had to leave their Ferraris at home due to the bumps on the roads, tuck into the *à la carte* and talk about their servant problems and their newest ruse to make another grand – or rather a *lakh,* the Sri Lankan equivalent, meaning 100,000 rupees.

A few outdoor cafés have sprung up between Colombo 3 and Colombo 7, and hopefully their popularity will lead to the opening of more. **The Commons**, at 74A Dharmapala Mawatha, is one of the newest, while the young set congregate at the **Rock Café** on Green Path, which is trendy, fast and very, very loud. The **Cricket Club Café** at 34 Queen's Road, is in a quiet garden sandwiched between Duplication and Galle roads, just around the corner from the British Council in Alfred House Gardens. Behind the **Barefoot** shop at 704 Galle Road (which sells good-quality crafts) is one of the coolest gardens in the dirty old heart of the city, where the sun refuses to shine. When you have been tussling with traffic on the city streets, the serenity of the old trees overhead is a perfect foil to the car horns and exhaust fumes. Artists and intellectuals meet here to put the world to rights, while two girls weave mats in colours of a Trincomalee sky. The menu might be limited but you may loiter here as long as you please over your carrot cake and lime juice.

Outdoor dining is only just catching on in Colombo. **Beach Wadiya** in Bambalapitiya allows you to wiggle your toes in the sand while a banquet fresh from the ocean is spread at your table. The **Curry Leaf Restaurant** at the Hilton offers the full ethnic experience under the stars and a complete introduction to every type of Sri Lankan food served from picturesque circular huts.

Dehiwala

The **Zoo** (open daily; entrance fee) at Dehiwala, about 10 km (6 miles) south of Fort, is one of the largest zoological gardens in Southeast Asia and has an impressive collection of birds, reptiles and other animals. It pioneered the policy of putting animals in an artificial habitat, rather than simply displaying

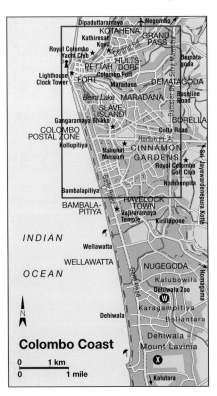

Colombo Coast

them in cages. However the whole concept of a zoo is now old-fashioned and, to many, distasteful. The performing elephants prancing around and sitting on stools are to many people more depressing than entertaining. You will see happier elephants elsewhere in this country which loves elephants and is accustomed to living and working with them.

Mount Lavinia

As a result of inept planning, most tourists seeking a bed in a guest house or small hotel are forced to venture to the far end of Colombo – namely 11 km (7 miles) or 30 minutes by taxi south to **Mount Lavinia ✗**, a beach resort which is just waking up to its potential in this respect. The lack of any middle or economy hotels is one very practical reason why, if you have a couple of days left to kill, the centre of Colombo is not to be recommended.

The beach at Mount Lavinia is pleasant enough, considering its proximity to the city, and the quiet, villagey pace of life is amplified even by a five-minute stroll up to the screeching madness of the Galle Road. The sea is usually safe for swimming, but can be rough and you should be wary of the strong undertow which crops up all along the Colombo coast. Use of the **Mount Lavinia Hotel's** pool will set you back a small fee unless you are a guest, but is worth it for a laze in the refreshing sea breeze and for a wander around the anachronistic splendour of this building, which was originally the residence of a British governor.

There are a couple of medium priced hotels on the toes of this grand old-fashioned dowager, and mushrooming behind her are some family-run guest houses which are good value. There are many beachfront restaurants which serve both cosmopolitan and local dishes. ❑

**Maps
City 154
Area 170**

TIP

After dark the beach at Mount Lavinia takes on a seedier side. Beware of pickpockets and pimps on the lookout for guileless travellers walking out alone.

BELOW: greens and grins at Kollupitiya market.

THE WEST COAST

Map on page 176

There is always something happening on the beach, besides sunbathing, whether it's fishermen pulling in their nets, or baby turtles making their first splash

The aeroplanes landing at Colombo International Airport are swallowed up into a forest of palm groves. They descend from the sky into an emerald bay of coconut trees, with not a building in sight. The tourists on board might share the sense of wonder (and trepidation) felt by visitors of the past, but concealed within the palm fronds are luxurious hotels ready to receive them. Liveried waiters, sleepy elephants, huge swimming pools and unspoilt beaches await them all along the island's beautiful West Coast.

Arthur C. Clarke, one of Sri Lanka's most celebrated residents, described it thus: "And always it is the same; the slender palm trees leaning over the white sand, the warm sun sparkling on the waves as they break on the inshore reef, the outrigger fishing boats drawn up high on the beach. This alone is real; the rest is but a dream from which I shall presently awake."

The Negombo Coast

There is no need to venture far from the airport to satisfy the average sunseeker, since there are expansive beaches within minutes, with hotels providing every comfort and fishing villages providing local colour. There are many interesting remnants of Portuguese and Dutch visitors who ousted the Moors and took possession of the Negombo coast. They came primarily for its cinnamon, "the bride around whom they danced" – and no wonder. Cinnamon gathered in the jungles owned by the ruling princes was in such demand for its choice quality that it was exported around the world, where it was sought after for its efficacy in the relief of air trapped in the bowel.

The warm, therapeutic aroma of cinnamon has a bitter history. The Dutch enslaved the *chaliyas* (cinnamon peelers) and punished with death anyone caught stealing this precious commodity. The sweetest, most prized variety grows along the silver-sand coastal belt near Negombo.

Just behind the coast, stretching north to Puttalam, the Dutch built a network of canals covering a distance of around 130 km (80 miles). Today, you can hire a bicycle and ride these canal paths. Common or garden bikes can usually be hired anywhere in or around Negombo. On an island where up to five people will share the same bike at the same time, it is a little harder to find well-serviced mountain bikes and helmets.

If you have been fortunate enough to experience the brilliant unchartered beaches of the Trincomalee coast and the miles of unspoilt beaches down south, the coast around **Negombo ❶** may be a bit of a disappointment. Its proximity to Colombo International Airport at Katunayake brings people here as their first

PRECEDING PAGES: fishing fleet at sea off Negombo.
LEFT: a fisherman unravels his nets.
BELOW: Catholicism on the march.

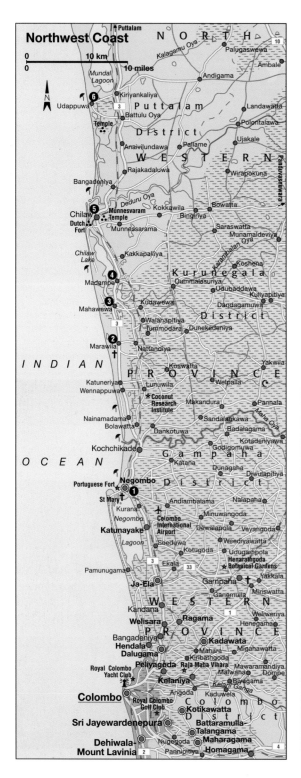

Northwest Coast

or last stop in Sri Lanka. A taxi to the airport costs just Rs500 if you're spending your last night at one of Negombo's many hotels and guest houses.

As in the other coastal areas, the early settlers who arrived on the coast were intent on bringing the Bible to the locals. Churches are dotted all along here, proving that the unsuspecting fisherfolk were successfully converted to Catholicism.

When the Dutch arrived, they took over the small **Fort** raised by the Portuguese and claimed it as their stronghold. The British put it to use as a jail which it still is today. Dutch relics do exist; a rest house faces the lagoon and there is a Dutch cemetery near the fort gate.

Fisherfolk

The Negombo lagoon is where you will see local fishermen at work with dugout canoes or *oruvas*. The prehistoric evolution of these ancient outriggers can be traced all the way back to the Roman historian Pliny. He mentioned the vessels

in the 1st century, but the *oruva* canoe had already existed in Sri Lanka for a long time by then – having first arrived here from the Comoro Islands off Mozambique and the South Seas.

The robust *Karava* fisherfolk bring their daily catch of crabs, prawns and seerfish to the markets. Try to catch a glimpse of a **fish auction**, if you rise early enough, to witness this unbelievable operation. These noisy outdoor sales (or *lellamas*) are usually held under the shade of a banyan tree.

Many of the *Karava* live on a tiny island called simply **Duwa** (the Sinhala word for island), where these dignified, lithe-bodied men and women get together annually to celebrate a highly emotional Passion Play in which the entire village is involved. There are many toddy and arrack taverns in town and community life is expressed in the enjoyment of them.

Travelling north

Heading north in the direction of Chilaw you will pass **Marawila ❷**, which has one or two small guest houses, and its close neighbour **Mahawewa ❸**, which is known for batiks and has many small and friendly batik factories where you can purchase fabrics for a slightly lower price than in town.

At the entrance to the town of **Madampe ❹** you will encounter the Riderless Horse. Legend has it that a careless Madampe citizen, who rode past the **Tanniyan-valla Bahu Devala** temple without paying due respect in the customary manner, was taught a lesson to remind him that a ride often goes before a fall. When his horse bolted and threw him to the ground, the now horseless rider vowed that if he survived the tragic cuts and bruises he would build an effigy of his horse to decorate the temple courtyard. The pacified gods were mer-

Map on page 176

No need to shop for sun hats, they will eventually come to you.

LEFT: Negombo Fort. **BELOW:** Karava cemetery on the coast south of Negombo.

ciful and received in due time a crude statue of a rearing horse which passers-by keep happy with morsels of broken coconut or a few coins.

The road runs inland from here, skirting Chilaw Lake before it reaches the fishing town of **Chilaw** ❺, which perches on the northern shore. It is a picturesque place, with a bustling fish market providing the main focus of activity in the otherwise sleepy town. The rest house provides sumptuous portions of baked crab and other seafood.

A few miles inland from Chilaw are the well-preserved ruins of the short-lived but ancient Sinhalese capital of **Panduvasnuwara**, where the temple of **Munnesvaram** is to be found on a *wewa* (reservoir) of the same name. Legend has it that the god Vishnu worshipped at this site in person. It was later destroyed by the boisterous Portuguese and subsequently re-erected by the British. For two weeks in early September a festival is celebrated here, with fire-walking the main attraction.

From wet zone to dry zone

In **Udappuwa** ❻, between the Mundal lagoon and the sea, the terrain changes dramatically; you are entering the Dry Zone. The fishing villagers are descendants of a North Indian warrior caste who migrated and settled on this coast over a thousand years ago. They were the first converts to Catholicism when the Portuguese arrived and mass baptisms were held where unsuspecting *Karava* folk were palmed off with surnames like Mendis, de Silva and Fernando. Their boats are given names like *Jude Putha* ("son of Jude"), *Santa Maria* or *Gothic*.

This section of coast is, quite astonishingly, untainted by hotels and guest houses. But an entrepreneurial Colombo slicker has purchased a large slice of

The best oruva *boats are made from* jak, *a hard wood that lasts up to 20 years, with the help of regular applications of coconut or shark oil to keep it water-proof.*

BELOW: faces of the West Coast.

Map
on page
176

land in the hope of getting the fisherfolk to build long-houses in the Indonesian tradition for their first taste of foreign tourism. These lovely unspoilt people wear Sinhalese clothes, speak in Tamil, and pray to the Virgin Mary; they live in huts close to the wide beach and at four in the morning you can see them unravelling their nets to cast off for their day's fishing, chanting the age-old *kavi* *"hodi helai helai laam!"* (a Sinhala *kavi*, as it so happens). They will probably take to Indonesian architecture, and welcome the tourists in some Polynesian tongue.

The A3 coast road continues to the town of **Puttalam**, an arid fishing settlement with no facilities for tourists. Here the A12 turns inland to Anuradhapura, making this an alternative route to the ancitut cities of the Cultural Triangle. It also leads to the **Wilpattu National Park** (*see page 125*).

Southwest beaches

The section of Sri Lanka's west coast south of Colombo has a great deal more to it than stunning beaches. You'll find hatching turtles (seen along much of the west coast between November and April), the longest reclining Buddha in Asia, and fascinating wreck dives, with rubber and cinnamon plantations and stretches of golden, deserted beach in between. Heaven, it seems can wait.

The main train line from Colombo to Matara runs down the coast but buses tend to be more convenient for shorter journeys. Three express trains run every day, but the timetables are so erratic on this stretch of line that they do not bother with them, and the trains stop only at main stations that tend not to coincide with the resorts. Air-conditioned intercity buses run about every 15 minutes and are speedy, if a little hair-raising.

The easiest way to travel around Sri Lanka is to hire a car with a driver. Make sure the vehicle has double air-conditioning, or else the driver and front seat passenger will arrive as cool as dudes while those behind will be desiccated and of ill humour.

BELOW: pulling in the nets is done with a *kavi*, or work-song.

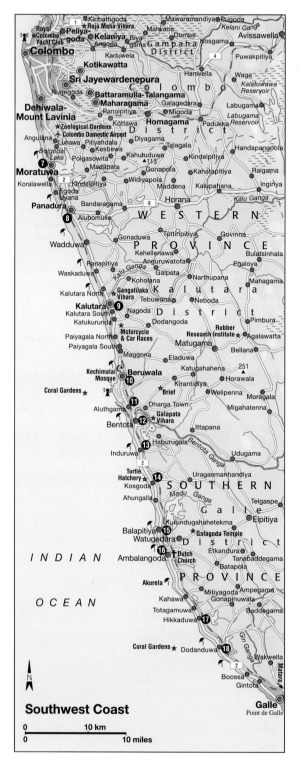

Southwest Coast

You will pass through the town of **Moratuwa** ❼ before you are aware that you have actually left Colombo. Next to it, **Panadura** ❽ is known for fresh fish, prawns and delicious toddy, which is tapped from the palm trees that stretch for miles southwards from here. Just 6 km (4 miles) out of Panadura, a 19th-century Veeragaha temple greets you on the road to Horana. The **Panadura Wildlife Resource Centre** runs canoe safaris, providing a tantalising glimpse of the mangrove swamps and many exotic species of bird, mammal and fish that live there.

Kalutara

The appearance of roadside stalls selling coir rugs, basketware and reed mats means that you are about to enter **Kalutara** ❾. The town is also known for its mangosteens – those dark purple shiny fruits containing luscious, translucent segments. Queen Victoria longed to taste one of these delectable fruits, but they did not travel well and she had to make do with mere description. If you try them yourself, be careful not to let the reddish-brown juice of the mangosteen's outer shell soak into your clothes since the stain is indelible.

Kalutara got its name from the Kalu Ganga or "Black River". As you cross the double-span bridge over the river, you will see a shrine and a Bo tree, with a till into which most drivers stop and make an offering; this is to ensure a safe journey.

If you choose to arrive by rail, the express train will let you off at Kalutara. Although a mere 43 km (25 miles) south of Colombo, it was once a bustling spice port in its own right – until the British replaced the inland estates with rubber plantations. There is still a definite buzz to the place.

As you pull into Kalutara South, you can't miss the gleaming *dagoba* of the **Gangatilaka Vihara** (open daily, 6am–7pm; entrance fee) rising above the town just south of Kalu Ganga Bridge. *Dagobas* usually contain relics of the Buddha and are traditionally sealed.

This one, built in the 1960s, is the only *dagoba* in the world which is hollow. Inside, the cool, echoing walls are lined with a continuous comic strip of 74 murals telling the story of Buddha. Many of these *Jataka* tales are, strangely, closely paralleled in the Bible. Guides give interesting tours of the entire temple (voluntary donation to enter), but often omit to explain that the main road runs through the temple to allow drivers to stop and make offerings for a safe journey before they hare off again like madmen.

To see how the locals can take anything as unyielding and stubborn as the stiff, thorny *watakeiya* palm leaf and lovingly transform it into patterned mats, purses, lampshades and linen baskets, visit the **Kalutara Basket Society** (open Mon–Sat), which is a five-minute walk from the big *dagoba*, behind the Town Hall. Rest assured, you will never use the term "basket-case" in such a pugnacious tone again.

Most people head further south before they unpack their bags, but there are a few moderate and expensive hotels. The **Sinbad Hotel**, near the Kalu Ganga, is one of the early pioneers of hotel life on this strip. It still has a pretty garden and provides watersports facilities on the lagoon.

When the Dutch deserted the bustling spice port at Kalutara, they left behind canals linking the spice plantations to the coast. The estates now produce rubber, but you can see traces of the old spice route by paddling through the tranquil waters of the old canals en route to the little known and intriguing **Richmond Castle**, a few kilometres inland. This magnificent hybrid of Indian and British architecture was originally a spice plantation mansion, built for the Padikara Mudaliyar, a wealthy regional governor, who copied the plans of an Indian Maharaja's palace that was designed by a London architect. After his death the house was left to a local school, but they were unable to meet the huge running costs. The house and 16-hectare (40-acre) grounds are open to the public. It makes a good canoeing or bike trek with riverside picnic.

If this is all too laid-back and you want to keep up with the Indiana Joneses, try a jungle adventure into the primaeval **Sinharaja Rainforest**, Sri Lanka's oldest rainforest. This should supply enough encounters with water monitors and torque macaques to make you glad of your twin double with attached shower, long after you have peeled the leeches out of your boots. Note that you require a permit to visit the park (*see page 195*).

Beruwala: mosques and beaches

North of **Beruwala ⑩**, located about 60 km (36 miles) from Colombo, some very pretty, secluded beaches mark the start of a sandy strip that extends all the way to Hikkaduwa and beyond, punctuated by hotels and small resorts. Beruwala itself has a fine beach of its own and is used by tour operators for package holidays, but it is otherwise a small and rather unremarkable town.

Beruwala has a large population of Muslims, and the town's most significant landmark, out on a rocky headland on the northern edge of the town, are the white minarets of the **Kachimalai Mosque**, believed to be the oldest on the island. Although you will be lucky to be allowed inside, this is an exquisite location from which to watch the sunset, with views over the bay and light-

Map on page 180

The doorway of a shop entices with shade, rather than displays of goods.

BELOW: a roadside fish stall.

house. As the oldest recorded Moorish settlement in Sri Lanka, Beruwala draws around 50,000 pilgrims from all over the island to its festival held at the end of Ramadan.

The **Barberyn Reef Hotel** (pronounced innocently by most drivers and guides as "barbarian") is a well-established hotel, which had an Ayurvedic health centre which its northern European clientele swore by long before indigenous cures became fashionable. The nostrums and potations are doled out by a highly qualified Ayurvedic doctor (who also happens to be a dead ringer for a Bombay movie star).

A Brief respite

Heading south towards Bentota, you will soon pass through **Aluthgama** ⓫, which means literally "new town". The express train from Colombo stops here and it is a gateway to the smaller resorts as well as being known for its raucous fish market. But if fish markets are not what you came all this way to see, and you need to satisfy a more cultural hunger and leave the mainstream tourists behind, just head inland for a complete change of scenery.

Sixteen km (10 miles) inland, beyond the village of Kalawila, you will find the paradise garden of **Brief**. There was nothing remotely brief about Brief. Indeed, the garden was a lifetime's work for its creator, the celebrated landscape artist, sculptor and bon-vivant Bevis Bawa – the elder brother of Geoffrey Bawa, award-winning architect whose work includes the new Houses of Parliament in Colombo. Bevis Bawa started clearing the surrounding rubber plantation in 1920, and he went on to create a verdant, romantic folly of inviting alcoves, nooks and bowers and garden sculpture that turned him into the

The Sri Lankan law which forbids any coastal hotel to tower higher than a coconut palm has meant that architecture is kept at a point where, given enough shrubs and trees, it can at least be disguised.

BELOW: the gardens at Brief.

Capability Bawa of Sri Lanka. Entering through a thick bamboo hedge via a statue-capped gate, you discover the Japanese garden, wide lawns, a pond and a hilltop lookout, several walled gardens and many other hidden surprises. Most visitors find themselves staying here much longer than they intended.

Map on page 180

Bevis Bawa died in 1992 and left no heir, but the 10-hectare (25-acre) estate was distributed amongst his faithful workers, each according to his years of service. "Brief", which got its name because Bawa's barrister father bought the land with money from a successful legal brief, has been left to his manager and fellow landscape gardener, Dooland de Silva. He is also happy to show visitors round the living art gallery house (a large mural by Australian artist Donald Friend dominates the hall), provided you make an appointment. The journey from Colombo will take two hours so telephone 071-28458 to contact Dooland.

You may need some help to find Brief: after Aluthgama junction, turn left through Dharga Town, then at Mango Tree junction turn right at the mosque; follow the hand written signs "To Brief", and finally turn right when you see the sign "Short cut to Brief".

Gaudy Sri Lankan souvenirs.

Bentota

Five km (3 miles) south of Aluthgama, you can find refuge in **Bentota** ⑫, a gentle, leafy sprawl of hotels and guest houses along the coast, which the English discovered as an unopened petal of perfection and quickly shortened to Ben Tot – making it sound like a relative of Ben Nevis.

The sea is calm here, as are the waters of the Bentota Ganga, which is ideal for watersports and boat rides as far as 35 km (23 miles) upstream. Travel just 5 km (3 miles) up the lazy river in the noonday sun (or take the Elpitiya road, south of the bridge) and explore the few remains of the **Galapata Vihara**, dating back to the 12th century. This is no ordinary temple; legend claims it was built by a minister of Parakramabahu the Great (AD 1153–86), who was responsible for most of the wonders at the medieval city of Polonnaruwa (*see page 261*). Galapata temple is linked by a maze of subterranean tunnels with all the other temples in the area.

BELOW: a turtle's brief career in modelling.

When the British discovered Bentota, and built a rest house for their officers en route from Colombo to Galle, it was a peaceful place to escape to. That tranquillity, however, was somewhat shattered after a modern complex with the equally ghastly name of the **National Holiday Resort** was built, comprising a shopping centre, post office, several hotels and a marketplace where you can practice your bargaining skills to buy tortoiseshell ware, drums, masks and handmade lace.

For those who want to sink into unadulterated luxury for a few days, **The Villa** is a hotel like no other. Designed by Geoffrey Bawa (*see above*), it is the last word in elegance, simplicity and style. Every one of the 15 rooms is unique, and the bathrooms are the largest to be found anywhere on the island. The unhurried but efficient staff will make you feel as though you are a house guest rather than a customer just passing through. As if in an effort to tip their hat at The Villa, you will notice as you drive through Bentota that "villa" has been added to the name of almost every two-star hotel and

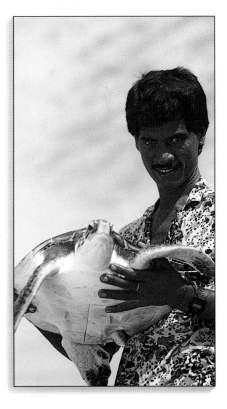

Ambalangoda is famous for its masks. The more garish the colours (particularly reds and yellows) the less traditional the masks are likely to be.

LEFT: all beaches come with free sunshine.

one-bedroom guesthouse – creating an entire town full of hotels called "Something or Other Villa".

The calm seas here make it the ideal sea for snorkelling, sailing, wind surfing, water-skiing, and deep-sea fishing from an outrigger canoe. The waters and beach of Bentota also attract a great number of turtles. The **Sea Turtles Project** (open daily, 6am–6pm; entrance fee), at the southern tip of town, is one of the many turtle hatcheries that have been set up along the southwest coast to protect turtle eggs until they hatch. Small tanks contain hundreds of one- to three-day-old turtles, as well as some larger ones, including an albino, kept for show. For Rs200, you can release a three-day-old turtle into the ocean to fend for itself. There is no doubt that the hatcheries that have sprung up are raking in the profits, and hopefully it is not at the turtles' expense. The implications of keeping them tank bound, when in the wild they swim frantically for the first days of their lives, is not known.

Having waved your little orphan into the sea, you can walk around the rocks under the hotel on the point to the quiet stretch of beach at **Induruwa** ⓭. The secret of this small and peaceful village will surely not last long. Flat basketware is the village speciality and the market on Tuesdays attracts buyers from Colombo, so stop and buy before it all gets whisked away. In the **Sri Lankan Handicraft Centre** (open daily), on the left of the Galle road as you leave Induruwa heading south, you can see basket weavers at work and visit *papier mâché* workshops.

Sri Lanka's first and original turtle hatchery is 5 km (3 miles) south of Induruwa in **Kosgoda** ⓮, reputedly the best beach for turtle-watching and signposted off the Galle Road. If you have not had your fill of baby turtles already, the **Victor Hasselblad Turtle Hatchery** stays open daily from 6am–6pm.

Southwards, visible on the inland side of the Galle Road, just north of **Balapitiya** ⓯, is what looks like a Dutch church and a Buddhist temple stuck to each other. The **Ambagahapityia Welitara** is, in fact, a Buddhist temple, but it was built in the time of the Dutch and so was influenced by their style of architecture. However, as many of the island's inhabitants will bear out, this cultural confusion does not make it any less Buddhist. The **Sri Pushparama Vihara** beside it houses some interesting murals. In Balapitiya itself, you will cross the Madu Ganga, along which you can take boat rides past a host of tiny islands.

Ambalangoda

A lovely drive south along the coast deposits you in **Ambalangoda** ⓰, 86 km (54 miles) from Colombo. The town has a gorgeous beach but is most famous as the home of mask carvers and puppets – a fact that you can hardly ignore as every small souvenir shop claims to be the main purveyor of so-called devil masks. The **Mask Museum** (open daily, 8am–5pm) is on the main road near the northern end of town, and should not to be confused with the Ariyapala shop across the road, which falsely claims to be a museum. Nonetheless, **Ariyapala**, a famous mask carver, has interesting displays and explains the meanings and

Map on page 180

traditions behind the devil masks used in the Low Country exorcism dances that originated here. The shop above has a huge selection of masks and wood carvings, although better prices and more traditional workmanship can be found at **Southland**, 353 Main Road.

Bandu Wijesuria's **Dance School**, next door to and under the same ownership as the Mask Museum, gives occasional performances of traditional Kandyan and Low Country dances. You should make every effort to catch a performance if you possibly can – this is the real McCoy or indeed the real McBandu. If you aren't that lucky, you are still likely to see some of his 250 pupils being drilled.

To see batik paintings of a particularly high standard, visit **Dudley Silva**, who has exhibited his remarkable Picasso-inspired work as far afield as Europe. He lives and works in his little Portuguese house at 53 Elpitiya Road (left after the museum as you head towards town), so he's open all hours. You'll have to pass his door in order to reach the **Galagoda Temple**, near Karandeniya, 5 km (3 miles) inland. There is an ongoing restoration programme, which is in itself interesting to see. Ask to be taken to the new entrance, unless you don't mind climbing the original 200 steps. In a long, unpretentious building hides a 50-metre (160-ft) reclining Buddha, the longest in Sri Lanka.

The astonishing view up-country includes Adam's Peak (*see pages 232–3*), seen most clearly in the morning, before 10am, and the area around is lush with cinnamon groves. If you visit at the right time, you may see members of the *Salagama* caste (a distinct caste to the cinnamon growers) harvest this prized bark off the laurel just after the rainy season has soaked it to the skin, making it easier to strip. Like Sri Lanka's other ancient art of mining gems, cinnamon-peeling is a highly skilled technique almost unchanged over the centuries. In

TIP

There are no life-saving facilities on most beaches in Sri Lanka, so watch out for the very strong currents. Drownings along the coast are not unheard of.

BELOW: *Oruva* boats on the beach at full sail; they go faster in the water.

Map
on page
180

One of the swankiest nightspots in Hikkaduwa – the most popular resort along the west coast of Sri Lanka.

BELOW:
cabbage coral.
RIGHT:
toddy tapper
performs without
a safety net.

1518, when the Portuguese returned to get their teeth into the island, the annual tribute they extracted from King Sitwaka for "protecting" him from his middle-eastern nuisance was a hefty 110 tonnes of cinnamon bark.

As you leave Ambalangoda, after the bus station and large shopping centre, the left turn towards the train station takes you to the stunning bell-topped archway of the **Sunandaramaya Mahavihara**. This is one of the earliest Buddhist temples on the south coast, which might account for its *thorana* (gateway), the largest on the island, being Hindu-inspired. On the outer wall of the shrine room are some rare murals depicting *Jataka* stories.

South to Hikkaduwa

The main road proceeds south past beautiful **Akurela** beach, with a fabulous reef, and then screeches right through **Hikkaduwa** ⓱, 100 km (62 miles) from Colombo – making it difficult to understand why the beach resort is currently so popular.

International surfers are attracted to this buzzy bit of coast, and divers come to explore the nearby coral reefs, but the beach is narrow, the currents are strong and the rash of hastily-built hotels and guest houses have just about erased this once beautiful bit of coast of its carefree character. Still, backpackers, independent travellers and package tourists alike seem to favour the Goa-meets-Bali beach atmosphere created by the diving and surfing scene, the beach restaurants and bars, shops and snake charmers. Furthermore, Hikkaduwa's broad range of accommodation caters to all pockets.

"Coral" is the key word in Hikkaduwa, and just as in Bentota, where every hotel calls itself a "Villa", here you will be hard pressed to find a hotel without "Coral" in its name. Numerous diving and snorkelling outfits cater to those interested in exploring Hikkaduwa's "Coral Sanctuary". Sadly, the coral reefs themselves are slowly dying, but they are still well populated by a variety of fish and turtles which can be easily seen even when snorkelling not far from shore.

For divers there are also fascinating, well-populated wrecks and dives to lower-level reefs which are still living. At the southern end of town, **Wewela** has the best surfing waves, and you can also body surf at **Narigama** where the beach widens for a change, allowing sunbathers to chill out in the swelter – but watch out for the strong undertow and currents.

As a much calmer alternative to the teeming thrust of energetic beach life, you should visit the lake at **Dodunduwa** ⓲. There is rich birdlife and an island with a serene Buddhist hermitage, which can be visited by prior arrangement.

Another place providing rural light relief is the **Sri Janandarama Mahavihara** just 4 km (2½ miles) down Baddegama Road, north of Hikkaduwa bus station. The one foot-long key that the monk uses to open the main temple is one of the sights, as is the list of foreign benefactors. This unremarkable temple has benefited from sitting next to a major resort and is well manicured and powdered, but it's a shame to think that it might be the only Buddhist temple many beach holidaymakers will see. ❑

COCONUT: SRI LANKA'S FLEXIBLE FRIEND

The life-sustaining coconut tree has often been called the Tree of Life because it can provide people with shelter, food, fuel and medicine

Sri Lankans use almost every part of the coconut tree within their daily lives – indeed, it has been described as being a Fairy Godmother to whoever grows it.

Although the coconut tree is one of the most distinctive features of Sri Lanka's landscape, it was initially a native of tropical America and had a long journey, via New Guinea, Malaya and Polynesia, before it touched down on the west coast of Sri Lanka, where it now flourishes. In the 19th century, the coconut tree formed the basis of the island's economy.

LEGENDS OF THE KING COCONUT

King Kusta Raja (the "leper king"), whose figure is carved on a rock at Weligama, where the nut was first established, discovered the medicinal value of the oil of the *thambili* (the golden king coconut), when it cured his mysterious skin disease. When Kandyan ceremonies to evoke protection were performed for King Panuwas in the 5th century BC, he demanded yellow coconuts to be placed at his feet. Even today the pale green leaves (*gokkala*) of the *thambili* are woven into fine traditional forms to provide decoration at weddings and other festivities. According to another legend, this tree of life grows best when planted near human habitations and within reach of the human voice.

◁ **SHELL ACCESSORIES**
Coconut shells are polished and often painted or lacquered, then turned into drinking cups, ladles, beads cutlery handles and a host of other utensils.

A FRUIT FOR ALL SEASONS

△ BRANCHING OUT

Coconut wood is used to make rafts and furniture. The thicker and tougher portion of the coconut branch is used for outrigger canoes and fishing boats.

▽ CELESTIAL FRUIT

The popular Portuguese Catholic saint, St Anthony, is here honoured by a typically Sri Lankan decoration: a pedestal of silver-painted coconuts.

The coconut is a major feature of Sri Lankan cuisine and is used in a variety of ways.

The bud at the top of the stem (*badas*) is eaten as a gourmet pickle, and the soft white kernel inside the nuts and the tender shoots which grow around the coconut palm are also considered delicacies.

Coconut milk is used daily in both savoury and sweet Sri Lankan dishes, while coconut oil provides a distinctive flavour to many dishes – as well as an unmistakable smell.

The sap, known as toddy, is bled slowly from the flower (*spathe*) into a clay pot. Fresh toddy is full of yeast and in its unfermented form is a health drink (*thelijja*). Once distilled, it becomes the national spirit, *arrack*, a hard liquor. The *spathe* is then boiled down and the resulting treacle is set into an unrefined candy (*jaggery*), which is often used to sweeten tea or as topping for curd.

What remains of the coconut is finally turned into *poonac*, a nutritious feed for cattle and pigs.

▷ SPINNING COCONUTS

The fibrous outer husk of the coconut is soaked in pits, vigorously beaten to extract the fibre, then spun into coir ropes, doormats, brushes, canvas, an organic filling for mattresses and strong fishing nets.

△ A STEADY TRADE

The continual harvesting, tapping and distribution of Sri Lanka's coconuts provides welcome, year-round employment for young male islanders.

THE SOUTH COAST

*This last outpost of the northern hemisphere has unexpected
inhabitants, including stilt fishermen and Hindu swamis,
plus long expanses of tantalising, unspoilt beaches*

Map
on pages
194–5

The south coast of Sri Lanka tends to be forgotten at the expense of the
more accessible and popular coastline nearer Colombo. But the road to
the deep south plunges you into a region rich in history and cultural interest,
and there are several vast and impressive nature reserves, including Yala, Bundala
and Uda Walawe.

It all begins at **Galle ❶**, which is believed to be the possible location of the
city of Tarshish, of Biblical fame, the source of a thriving trade in "gold, silver,
ivory, apes and peacocks".

Galle

In 1505 a Portuguese fleet set sail to intercept Moorish vessels carrying cargoes
of spice, but it was driven off course and landed at what was to become the
gateway to the south. The newcomers named the harbour Galle, after the crow-
ing cockerels that they heard at the end of the day – the Latin for chanticleer is
"gallus". Hence the name Punto de Gale, which the British later corrupted to
Point de Galle.

Today, the old town of Galle jostles with the new. The bus and train stations
are just north of the **Fort**, within walking distance of its imposing walls. Outside the walls Galle seems hurried, worried and not a
little scruffy, but once within the Fort the pace slinks
back through the centuries, and the surprising calm-
ness is delectable. The Fort is small enough to be
enjoyed in an afternoon's stroll, ending up on the
western walls to watch the sunset.

The only punctuation to this oasis for the senses is
that of unusually relentless hawkers who follow you
with handmade lace and other wares. The lace can be
very fine even though its vendors' timing isn't, but if
you pause for even a cursory glance your assailants
will not leave you for the rest of the afternoon. Exaggerated gesticulations of repulsion – imagine they are
offering you a rat kebab – should do the trick.

The **Cultural Museum** (open Tues–Sun; entrance
fee) is housed in a Dutch colonial warehouse on
Church Street as you enter the Fort. Just beyond this
is the **New Oriental Hotel**, which is neither new nor
oriental but the oldest hotel on the island – built by the
Dutch in 1684 as their governor's headquarters. The
lobby, with old maps on the walls and rattan *chaises
longues* on the verandah, is a time machine trans-
porting you back to the 1860s when it first opened.
Staff will proudly show you around the spacious, if
tired, surroundings, including the dusty, musty old
billiard room and the beautiful leafy garden surrounding the small swimming pool; a small fee is
charged to non-guests who want to swim.

PRECEDING PAGES:
palm-fringed river
scene near Bentota.
LEFT:
almost deserted
Bentota beach.
BELOW:
Galle lighthouse.

A shop of intricate intrigue in Galle.

Next door, the small **Groote Kerk** (Great Church) is the oldest Protestant church in Sri Lanka – dating from 1755, although the original structure was built 100 years earlier. It holds services in English twice monthly. The **National Maritime Museum** (open daily, 9am–5pm; entrance fee) covers all aspects of life in and around the sea, including scale models of whales and an extraordinary "walk into the sea" diorama showing the construction of coral reefs.

An evening stroll around the **fort walls** and bastions in time for the sunset is something of a tradition, even among the locals. You can walk along the top of the walls, which are partly built of fossilised coral, nearly all the way round. Starting at the modern lighthouse at the bottom of Church Street (uninteresting in itself but offering a stupendous view if you can locate the keeper), work your way round so that you are on one of the western bastions when the sun goes down. As you near the western side of the fort, watch your step over the large arrow slits in the walls for you might trample on several romantically entwined young couples. Sheltering under gaudy umbrellas for privacy, they arrive early to nestle down in the best seats for the nightly performance of the dying sun.

On the promontory on the east side of the harbour is the **Closenberg Hotel**, with rattan easy chairs on its verandahs and white-clad waiters ever ready with a tray of drinks; another fine place from which to watch the sunset. This was once the residence of a Captain Bailey, who bought it from the British Crown in 1857 and named it "Villa Marina" after his wife. The old-fashioned rooms in the main part of the house have massive teak furniture and mosquito nets. But the newer rooms with balconies facing the sea provide more privacy.

There are some interesting drives out of Galle, offering a wild, luscious, jungly contrast to the stark fort-town. About 3 km (2 miles) before arriving in

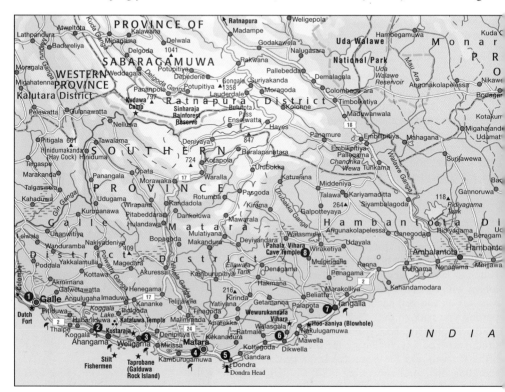

Galle you will have passed a new five-star hotel designed by Geoffrey Bawa, **The Lighthouse**, which has a panoramic view of the coast. Heading north on the Udugama Road, about 20 km (12 miles) from the town past lowland tea estates, is one of Sri Lanka's few remaining pockets of primaeval rainforest – the **Kottuwa Rainforest**. Despite its abundance of orchids, hanging creepers, sheets of moss and exotic birds, it is less well-known than the much larger **Sinharaja Rainforest Reserve**, another 20 km (12 miles) further north. This reserve contains spectacular rainforest scenery and wildlife – indeed, the highest concentration of animals unique to Sri Lanka are found here. There are guides to show you around, but you need a permit from the Forest Department in Colombo if you want to stay overnight in the reserve's camp.

Unawatuna Bay

The small resort overlooking **Unawatuna Bay**, a few kilometres out of Galle, was once a suburb where Dutch commanders and merchants built their quiet, country residences. Even in the late 1980s Unawatuna was a calm and peaceful haven. Recently, its golden beach, clear waters and offshore reef have been discovered by younger tourists and, now peppered with a rash of guest houses and beachfront cafés, Unawatuna is possibly well on its way to ruin. But if you can stand the harassing fishermen-turned-beach-bums, who are a pest to women travellers, you may enjoy the low-key, Caribbean feel.

The reef off the far end of the beach can be reached from the shore, or you can sail out further in a traditional catamaran, which skims across the waves like some kind of prehistoric pond skater. There is talk of setting up a coral sanctuary here (following in the footsteps of Hikkaduwa, yet again) to prevent exploitation

Map on pages 194–5

BELOW: a floral display at Kottuwa rainforest.

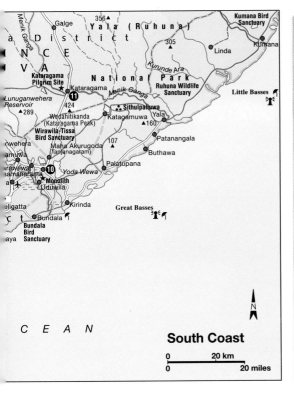

of a reef that shelters more species of fish than the Great Barrier Reef. Snorkelling equipment and scuba diving gear can be hired.

Koggala

During World War II **Koggala** ❷, just beyond Unawatuna, was forcibly evacuated and turned into an air force base – the old airstrip is on the right as you enter on the main road. The town doesn't seem to have ever quite regained its former life and consists of little more than a main road forging through a "Free Trade Zone". But it is well worth visiting the **Martin Wickramasinghe Folk Art Museum** (open Tues–Sun; entrance fee). Set in the beautiful gardens of this well-known local author, the museum has an interesting selection of exhibits, though a lack of background information leaves them rather out of context. Further inland, **Koggala Lake**, with its islands teeming with birds and numerous temples on the far side, is ideal for an afternoon's exploration.

On the way out of Koggala, about 4 km (2½ miles) along the inland road, is the **Kataluwa Temple**. Several different styles of fresco are featured here, including some from the Kandyan period and some remarkable paintings of *kaffringha* dancers with a troop of western musicians.

Weligama

As you enter the charming small town of **Weligama** ❸, 23 km (14 miles) from Unawatuna, the road splits. The coast road, which skirts close to the sea, will bring you to the Rest House on your left and, almost opposite, to **Count de Maunay's Island**, which floats mysteriously on the gentle waters of the bay, looking as though it could up its anchor and skim off over the horizon if it felt

BELOW: Count de Maunay's Island.

so inclined. Known also as "Taprobane Island" and locally as *Yakinige-duwa* or "She-devil's Island", this tiny enchanted paradise was created by a French count in the 1930s as his vision of Eden. You can easily wade out to it at low tide but will find security forbidding as it is still privately owned. As enticing as the bay at Weligama may seem, the water is not clean enough to swim in.

If you take the inland road, just west of the centre of Weligama, you come to the **Kustaraja** ("leper king") in a small park – a legendary character 3 metres (12 ft) high carved into a rockface. He is supposed to have arrived in Sri Lanka afflicted with leprosy but was cured by drinking only *thambili* (the juice of the king coconut) for three months. If you've already tried one of these ambrosial drinks, you'll know that there's no need for encouragement from mythical kings to drink away.

Matara

Matara ❹, 160 km (100 miles) from Colombo, has a population of around 40,000 and is the eighth biggest town on the island. It is also the terminus on the southern railway line where time stands still. An ancient settlement, Matara has been occupied by the Portuguese, Dutch and English, and reflects the different influences of these various visitors. Most of the old town lies within **Matara Fort**, which was erected by the Dutch. As in Galle, the fort is a quiet refuge from the busy commercial town, and the best small guest houses are found in its Mediterranean-style, peaceful back streets. The much smaller **Star Fort**, built in 1763, houses the **Museum of Ancient Paintings**, and in a factory nearby, on Dharmapala Mawatha, you can see traditional drums being made, and you can also buy authentic instruments.

Map on pages 194–5

Weligama is well known in Sri Lanka for its lace. Visitors should be prepared for the direct selling techniques of some of the locals.

BELOW: human herons.

TIP

The lighthouse garden at Dondra Head is a good picnic spot, especially if you have managed to buy some fresh hoppers (*see page 104*), which are particularly good in this town.

BELOW: the beach near Tangalla.

Dondra ⑤, 5 km (3 miles) southeast of Matara, means "the city of the gods" and is the southernmost point of Sri Lanka, marked by an octagonal lighthouse which is the tallest on the island, standing at 54 metres (176 ft). From here, beyond the view of local fishing boats riding the indigo waves under faultless skies, there is nothing but horizon and more horizon until Antarctica. The Portuguese ravaged the **Maha Vishnu Devala**, a 7th-century shrine with a roof of gilt copper that once shone like a beacon out to sea. The tawdry modern buildings still host a ten-day fair and *perahera*, venerating the Hindu god Vishnu (as opposed to Buddha) coinciding with the Kandyan *perahera* in July/August.

Just before the next main coastal town of **Dikwella ⑥** (meaning "long bridge"), 22km (13½miles) from Matara, you'll pass **Polhena** beach, which has an inshore reef and good waves for surfing. Two kilometres (1 mile) along the road out of Dikwella towards Beliatte is the **Wewurukannala Vihara**, with the tallest Buddha in Sri Lanka, 50 metres (164 ft) high, which was built in the1960s. As though to prove the size of this huge seated Buddha, there is an eight-storey building behind it, but this is not just for show – it contains a staircase lined with brightly-coloured comic strip style paintings of the Buddha's life. The oldest part of the temple complex is 250 years old but holds little of real interest. However, the rest holds an unusual and gory display of figures and paintings depicting the punishments meted out in hell and warnings of how to avoid being sent there. Not for the faint-hearted! (Be warned that in every part of the temple will be people asking for donations.)

Six km (3½ miles) past Dikwella, by the 188 km marker, a right-hand turn leads to the spectacular **Hoo-aaniya Blowhole** at Mawella. High seas, especially during the southwest monsoon in June, force water 23 metres (75 ft) vertically

Map on pages 194–5

through a natural rock chimney to the surface and then 20 metres (65 ft) into the air. Breathtaking in season, but otherwise pathetic, though you should be careful not to make disparaging remarks. Villagers say that when the sea is really rough the spout reaches the height of "three coconut trees".

The pink beaches west of the bluest blue of **Tangalla Bay ❼**, 195 km (121 miles) from Colombo, look inviting but you should be wary of the steep drop-offs and strong waves. You may prefer to head instead for the beautiful white sandy beaches to the east of town – one of the most appealing spots along Sri Lanka's southern coast. The offshore reef breaks the surf and provides good diving and calm water. There are many small guest houses at both ends, with larger modern hotels along the better beaches. For its size, the town has a relaxed atmosphere with a busy market and many reminders of its Dutch heritage.

Mulgirigalla

Just 16 km (10 miles) north of Tangalla, past Beliatte, is the Pahala Vihara Cave Temple of **Mulgirigalla ❽**. Allow at least an hour for a leisurely ascent and try to arrive early to beat the heat – not least because you will have to do the entire climb barefoot and bareheaded. Halfway up is a unique Victorian monks' graveyard, beside the entrance to a small school for trainee Buddhist *bhikkus* (monks).

Heading east from Tangalla, a road heads north from Nonagama to **Uda Walawe National Park**, where some 600 elephants roam freely around the park's 308 sq km (119 sq miles) of land. There are many places to stay overnight on the edge of the main park, and jeep safaris with a guide are available to view many species of deer, wild boar and jackals.

One of the small dagobas on the higher levels of Mulgirigalla.

BELOW: the sacred rocks of Mulgirigalla.

MULGIRIGALLA – ROCK TEMPLE

Mulgirigalla, "the summit of the rock", was confusingly known as Adam's Berg or Adam's Peak until the 18th century. The Portuguese, infamous for their destruction of Buddhist sites, misunderstood the monks who explained that the frescoes were of the "first man". Rather than Buddha, they decided that these were images of Adam and left the cave temples untouched. In the 17th century, a Dutch general misled some visiting Persians who had landed in Matara asking to be taken to Adam's Peak. Having no intention of marching 160 km (100 miles) through difficult territory, he led them on a roundabout route from Matara to Mulgirigalla dragging the journey out for six days.

Probably founded in the 1st century BC, this 105-metre (350-ft) rock temple is smaller than Sigiriya but also rises almost vertically out of the surrounding forest. With well-preserved and beautifully painted cave temples carved into five levels, the rock was also the site of an important discovery; the ola-leaf scripts discovered here in the 19th century were the key to the translation of Sri Lanka's most informative ancient text, the Mahavamsa. It is also the site of a Buddhist graveyard, a rarity enforced on the monks by the British who disapproved of cremation.

Map
on pages
194–5

*One of the more
peaceful denizens of
Yala National Park.*

BELOW: offerings at
Kataragama.
RIGHT: a child
receives the
blessings of a
Hindu swami.

Back on the coast, **Hambantota** ➒ is the largest town on the southeastern coast and has Sri Lanka's largest population of Malay Muslims. Its name is said to derive from *sampans*, the boats which the Malays arrived in, and *tota* or harbour. From Sampantota it is but a short step to Hambantota, although the story smacks of wishful amateur etymology.

Hambantota is famous for its buffalo curd which it claims to be the best in the country. There are many stalls selling it – easily recognisable with their strings of clay pots swinging from the awnings. Hambantota's other big industry is the ancient method of salt-making, and you will see many evaporating salt pans on the roads in and out of town. The main tourist attraction is the **Bundala Bird Sanctuary**, which stretches along the coast east of Hambantota and is one of the best parks for instant gratification: in a four- or five-hour jeep ride, you may see elephants, 2½-metre (8-ft) crocodiles, and flamingos – which are among the 150 species of bird found in the area. Afternoon safaris in the dry season (December–May) provide visitors with the best chance of seeing the wildlife.

Tissamaharama

The main reason for visiting **Tissamaharama** ➓, usually just called Tissa, is as the gateway to **Yala National Park** (*see page 126*) – one of the island's best-known reserves, and one of its biggest, encompassing an area of 1,300 sq km (500 sq miles). The best way to visit the park is to hire a jeep and driver in Tissa, but sometimes the park is out of bounds (due to the activity of the Tamil tigers), so check as soon as you arrive in town. Tissa's active army of "Safari Touts" is hard to avoid, but most hotels can also organize trips.

Tissa's other attractions are a number of ancient *dagobas*, and the local tanks (artificial lakes), including the Tissawewa, by the pleasantly situated Rest House in Tissa itself, and the Wirawila, on the Hambantota-Wellawaya road. These lakes form a busy bird sanctuary and you may also see crocodiles, monkeys or elephants.

Kataragama pilgrimage site

The visually bland town of **Kataragama** ⓫, 16 km (10 miles) north of Tissa, has been described as "the holiest place in Sri Lanka". Devotees from the Hindu, Buddhist and Muslim religions flock here all year round, although the biggest numbers come for the Kataragama Festival in July and August, when conch shells blow, trumpets blare and drums beat out as voices rise in unison to a chorus of *Haro Hara*! Weird self-imposed tortures are endured by devotees with tongues transfixed by spikes, or butchers' hooks penetrating their skin.

The town is split by the Menik River, with a small residential area on one side and the extensive religious complex, containing shrines and temples to all three religions, on the other side. The main deity, Kataragama Deviyo, is synonymous here with the 12-armed Hindu war god Skanda, whose lance, or *vel*, is held within the Maha Devala, the most important shrine in the complex. All three religions worship at this simple white shrine, with three daily services or *pujas* (at 4.30am, 10.30am and 6.30pm). ❑

THE ROAD TO KANDY

*A journey through spectacular scenery to the famous city
of Sinhalese history, culture, religion and pageantry
reaches the heart and soul of the country*

Map
City 210
Area 224

When the Portuguese first came ashore near Colombo in the early 16th century, they were escorted to Kotte, the capital city of one of Sri Lanka's three major Sinhalese kingdoms of the time. The Portuguese admired the fine city, and then razed it to the ground. They proceeded to take over the whole of the island, but never managed to conquer the remote highlands around Kandy.

Successive capital cities dotted the escarpments on the ascent to Kandy – an anglicised Sinhala word, *kande,* meaning hill – which was finally established as an impregnable natural fortress in the 17th century. It proved so safe that those wily Sinhalese monarchs were able to maintain autonomous rule despite the pressure of foreigners filching their spice trade down on the coast. Impenetrable jungle, sheer rockfaces and torrential rivers proved to be natural protection against foreign forces who were used to engaging the enemy at sea. The independent kingdom deep within the jungle that persisted in glorious isolation, long after the colonial powers had subjugated the rest of the island, contributed to a legendary status that the word Kandy still retains.

Despite modern road and rail links, the sense of rarefied isolation clings to the beautiful city of Kandy and surrounding countryside. You can catch glimpses of the wild terrain and lush vegetation as you travel along the road through manicured rice paddies, coconut, rubber and tea plantations. The number of hair-pin bends are too numerous to count, and give credence to the secure nature of the former capital.

PRECEDING PAGES:
Kandy city and lake.
LEFT: modern
Kandyan chief
in Perahara
procession.
BELOW: outside
the Kelaniya Raja
Maha Vihara.

From Colombo to Kandy

The Kandy road traditionally begins at Queen's House in Fort (Colombo), and there are numerous pleasant and surprising experiences in store for those who have the time to dally.

The journey has hardly begun when the first stop is called for at **Kelaniya**, on the outskirts of Colombo. The temple and environs of Kelaniya trace its history back to the time of the Buddha who, it is believed, came here on his third and last visit to the island. A temple was built around the area where the Buddha trod, followed later by an entire city. Not surprisingly, the location is of significant spiritual value to Buddhists. The architecture of the temple and paintings inside reflect Sinhalese art forms derived from many South Asian civilisations but with a leaning towards Buddhist culture. A variety of recumbent carved statues of the Buddha are of special interest.

A quaint legend is associated with Kelaniya. As a consequence of tipping a Buddhist monk into a vat of boiling oil, the reigning local prince found that the deities retaliated by overflowing the sea in many parts

of his kingdom. To placate the offended deity, he deftly arranged to sacrifice his favourite daughter Vihara Mahadevi (later to have a Colombo park named after her) and cast her adrift in a gold-encrusted boat on the ocean. Eventually, the tide dragged her in on the southern shores near a minor kingdom ruled by a handsome prince called Kavan Tissa, whose court soothsayer had given him strict instructions that he should marry a girl only if she were to arrive by sea in a golden boat. Needless to say, the prince could not believe his good luck and married Vihara Mahadevi immediately. The first male child born to them, called Dutugemunu, became a legendary hero who defeated the Tamil King Elara in an epic battle and united the country under one king for the first time. A traditional *Perahera* is held in January at Kelaniya Temple.

On a well-travelled side road 11 km (7 miles) out of Colombo is the village of **Sapugaskande**, built on a hillock. The Buddhist temple is the main attraction here, primarily for the unusual murals found inside the shrine room. These are the work of artists taught by a Burmese sage, who had been summoned to Sapugaskande to settle a dispute among the senior monks on the rights of persons of all castes to higher ordination, and who stayed to pass on his painting skills. The unconventional frescoes are just one example of the cross-cultural influences shared by the Buddhist countries of South Asia. The view in all directions from the temple is stunning.

Continuing inland, just north of Miriswatta, 27 km (17 miles) from Colombo, you can visit the **Henarathgoda Botanical Gardens**, which contain a whole array of plants indigenous to a wide range of tropical countries. The most historic species is the original rubber plant propagated from seeds taken from its native Brazil, and smuggled down the Amazon in bales of cotton.

Three award-winning movies – The Outcast of the Islands, Purple Plain and, most famously, The Bridge over the River Kwai – were filmed among the lush hills and waterways of Sri Lanka's central highlands.

BELOW: paddy fields en route to Kandy.

Another worthwhile detour from Miriswatta is to **Uruwala Temple**, on the south side of the Kandy road. The care with which the temple's buildings and artifacts are maintained is touching evidence of the piety and devotion of Sri Lanka's Buddhists. The monks can provide enchanting details associated with the temple complex, some of whose structures are hewn from the rock.

There is another temple worth visiting in the village of **Waruna**, 36 km (22 miles) out of Colombo. Carved out of solid rock on three levels, the temple features buttressed walls, high overhangs and drip ledges that protect a series of ancient frescoes, now reduced to mere outlines. The strenuous climb to the roof of the temple is worth it just for the view of rich tropical vegetation that you'll have from the top.

A few miles further inland towards Kandy you'll pass **Cadjugama ❶**, where young women beckon travellers to stop and buy the freshly roasted cashew nuts (*cadjunuts*) that gave the village its name. Cashews are a luxury ingredient used in many traditional Sri Lankan dishes; raw cashews, for example, can be cooked in coconut cream with spices, or "devilled" – roasted with chilli.

With food still on the mind, continue on to **Nelundeniya** (just east of the turning to Kandy at Ambepussa), a traditional village that provides visitors with a fascinating sociological and culinary experience. The village is organised and run with government patronage in order to preserve and demonstrate Sinhalese crafts, village society and culinary arts.

From Nelundeniya, a minor road leads south to the hamlet of **Dedigama ❷**, the mid-12th century capital of one of the three principalities into which Sri Lanka was divided in the pre-colonial era. The village has many remains and artifacts from that time, some housed in the local museum, and most bear the

Map on page 224

Views in front are rather more limited if you manage to get stuck behind a rice wagon.

BELOW: cashew nut seller, Cadjugama.

stamp of Dedigama's most illustrious son, King Parakramabahu I – the famous Sinhalese King who was rewarded with the title "The Great" for managing to unite the island under his rule and for building many artificial lakes for irrigation purposes.

Just north of Nelundeniya, on the other side of the Kandy road, is the great king's second capital city, **Beligala ❸**, which once housed the sacred Relic of the Tooth, now in Kandy (*see page 212*). The stonework of the ruined city juxtaposes natural rock and hewn columns to form a series of unusual and beautiful structures.

Elephants young and old are given sanctuary in a natural habitat at the government-run **Pinnawella Elephant Orphanage ❹**, just north of Kegalle, 80 km (50 miles) from Colombo. Abandoned or injured baby elephants are reared here and are trained to eventually become working animals. Feeding and bathing time in the river provide the best opportunities to admire the animals close-up. The orphanage opens daily (entrance fee; extra for video cameras).

The ascent to Kandy

The view in all directions is spectacular on the approach to Kandy. The city nestles in a wide plain surrounded by a ring of guardian mountains, with quaint names – Bible Rock, Lion Rock, Ship Rock, Camel Hill, Tuber Rock and Balloon Rock. The new entrance to the city is **Kadugannawa Pass**, a sheer ascent of 250 metres (820 ft) in a matter of 5 km (3 miles), complete with hairpin bends. There are breathtaking views southeast towards the ocean.

At the end of the final hairpin bend, the road passes through a mini-tunnel carved out of a solid rock promontory. A local legend speaks of the tenacity of

TIP

The Pinnawella Elephant Orphanage provides most visitors with the best chance of seeing a large number of elephants at close quarters. The animals are free to roam around the sanctuary but come together at specific bath and feeding times.

BELOW: fledgling elephants at Pinawella

the Kandyan Kingdom, which could never fall until an invading force pierced the solid rock encircling the city. Ironically, after the Kandyan Kingdom was annexed in 1815, the British fulfilled the terms of the legend.

Immediately on your left after the bridge over the Mahaweli River, still about 6 km (4 miles) from the heart of Kandy, the **Peradeniya Botanical Gardens ❺** provide a warm welcome to the city. The 60-hectare (147-acre) garden (open daily; entrance fee) is the largest in Sri Lanka and is a walkers' paradise – although you can also bike or drive through the Avenue of Royal Palms, the bamboo-fringed riverside drive, and the bat drive, where flying foxes hang around upside down. Allow plenty of time to enjoy the great variety of flowers, plants and mature trees, and don't miss the giant Javan fig tree, which covers an impressive 1,600 sq metres. The gardens were the setting for the South East Asia Command Headquarters during World War II, when Lord Mountbatten was in charge of operations.

Kandy – the Sinhalese capital

The Kandyan kingdom, the last independent state in Sri Lanka, withstood the onslaught of three invading European nations for over two centuries. The islanders looked upon the ruler of Kandy as their king, but political and economic boundaries gave way to emotional and religious ties. The Buddhist Chapter headquarters, Malwatte and Asgiriya, were venerated from a distance by lay persons and monks alike, but Kandy was considered the last bastion of independent Buddhist thought, which gave spiritual strength and virtue to the Kandyan people. An example of their strength and determination was the ferocious and tactical war waged three years after the annexation. The Kandyan

Map on page 224

The bridge over the Mahaweli River marks the western edge of Kandy. Where the river bends, fringed by rainforest, you can cross the Halloluwa Suspension bridge, built in 1939. Miss your footing through the worn plankway and you'll dive hundreds of feet into the fast-running waters.

LEFT: Peradeniya Botanical Gardens.
BELOW: airhead.

rebellion was almost successful in driving the British out of the country. Timely reinforcements from an Indian garrison turned the Sinhalese victory into defeat.

Kandy  is the perfect size to be explored on foot, the higher altitude making the climate conducive to long and leisurely strolls. The city is visually rich, with its narrow streets lined with characterful old buildings and crowded with people. The **Municipal Market** has superb displays of fruit and vegetables, textiles and clothing, and the lake provides an attractive focal point.

And when you have walked your feet off, you can repair to the old-fashioned **Queen's Hotel**, bang in the middle of town, to enjoy the well-maintained ozone-filtered swimming pool and the excellent club sandwiches, or the buffet lunch in the dining room if you prefer. Even if it wasn't a pilgrimage site, people would keep on coming to Kandy.

Carved figure in the National Museum, Kandy.

Kandy Perahera

The number of visitors to the city reaches a spectacular peak in July. A courtyard on the south side of the **Temple of the Tooth Ⓐ** becomes the hub of ornate and frenzied activity during the two-week **Perahera**. Many dozens of caparisoned elephants, dancers, drummers and other performers come together to parade the sacred Tooth Relic (*see page 212*) through the streets. The rituals and ceremonies associated with Perahera have persisted for many centuries and have changed remarkably little over this time.

The belief among the people is that the country will not suffer from famine, revolution or calamity as long as these rituals are perfectly practised. Whatever the quality of the ritual, calamity is likely to come your way if you arrive in Kandy during *Perahera* without planning ahead. The whole town goes into

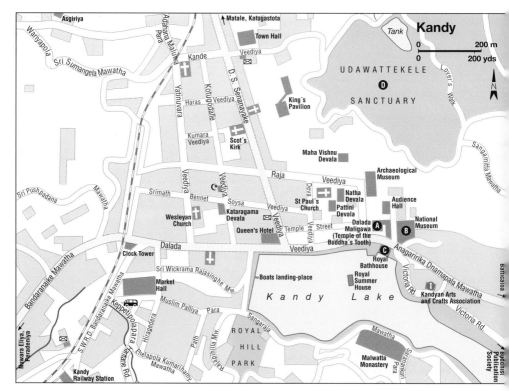

carnival mode for a fortnight and every hotel room is booked up. Due to this annual overflow, local people have been pressed into opening up their homes as seasonal guest houses – with the result that Kandy has become the bed and breakfast capital of the island. Outside *Perahera* time, you can find some remarkable bargains in simple homes around the lake or dotted round town, and can end up staying in charming establishments with names such as Lake Cottage, Scenic Summit, Blue Haven and Elephant Bath.

Royal Palace Complex

The buildings of the **Royal Palace Complex**, consisting of the King's Palace, the Queen's Palace, the Audience Hall, the Royal Bathhouse and Royal Summer House, represent the final flowering of Sinhalese architecture and craftmanship.

The airy rooms of the Queen's Palace, complete with cloisters and a central courtyard, have been converted into the **National Museum** ❸ (open 9am–5pm except Fridays; entrance fee), where royal regalia and pre-colonial artefacts are displayed in the rooms where once the courtly concubines lounged. There are also sad mementoes of the capitulation to the British in 1815, which was officially agreed by the Kandyan chiefs who met in the **Audience Hall**. Carved teak columns support the roof and cooling air circulates in its shade.

You should consider buying the so-called Cultural Triangle Ticket, which will get you into a range of sights, including the **Archaeological Museum**, housed in the surviving portion of the King's Palace, and the four **Hindu Devales** (shrines), which are perhaps as old as the city itself and are well worth exploring. While Sinhalese Buddhists were in the majority in Kandy, the ancient rulers of the kingdom gave equal prominence to every racial and religious

Maps:
City 210
Area 224

TIP

Don't trust the hotel recommendation of a trishaw driver – he is trying to earn himself a pay-off. Good guest houses refuse to deal with touts. If you ring them from the station they will come and collect you.

BELOW:
the Queen's Hotel.

Tales of the Tooth

Many Buddhists believe it is the most precious thing in the world. Indeed, wars have been fought over it. Yet it is never put on public display: it is kept in a golden lotus beneath six caskets of diminishing scale. The outer one, about 1.2 metres (5 ft) in height, is of silver gilt, but all the others are of beaten gold. It is the Tooth.

On attaining Nirvana, the Buddha was cremated, but mourners managed to rescue parts of his mortal remains. Some important relics were passed on to Sri Lanka, including a cutting from the sacred Bo-tree, his begging bowl, his collarbone and strands of hair. Others have since turned up on the island – nail clippings, for example.

The collarbone demonstrated its sanctity when it arrived in Anuradhapura, rocketing to an altitude of 1,500 metres (5,000 ft) and belching flames and streams of water. The Bo-tree cutting also shot into the sky on arrival, emitting a beautiful halo of six colours.

Buddha's left eye-tooth, however, remained in the Kalinga kingdom in India, until seven centuries after his death, when its future was thrown into doubt by a militant resurgence of Hinduism. It is said that it fell into Hindu hands, but attempts to destroy it with a sledge-hammer succeeded only in breaking the hammer. The Hindus gave it back.

When King Guhasiva of Kalinga faced defeat, the Tooth was hidden in his daughter Hemamala's hair and she was then spirited away to Sri Lanka. Its arrival caused a sensation, and a suitable temple was built as its new home. The *Perahera* procession was initiated soon afterwards, with the Tooth paraded through the streets of the ancient capital on the back of a white elephant.

With the growing tradition that whoever possessed the Tooth had the right to rule Sri Lanka, the relic was moved around according to the vicissitudes of troubled times. When Marco Polo arrived at the behest of Kublai Khan in the late 13th century, invaders from south India had carried off the Tooth and no Sinhalese king could control the situation. King Parakrama of Polonnaruwa fought a war to get the Tooth back from the Tamils, and from then on a special bodyguard was assigned to look after it.

In the 16th century, the Portuguese captured the Tooth and shipped it to Goa where, before the assembled eyes of the Portuguese viceroy, a bishop and numerous dignitaries, it was pounded to dust, the dust burnt, and the ashes thrown into the sea. That should have put paid to the Tooth, but apparently not so. The remnants re-assembled themselves on the seabed, enabling the Tooth to fly back to the island of its own accord.

It was while the Tooth was briefly in unbelieving British hands after the fall of Kandy in 1815 that the caskets were opened up. They decided that the discoloured object encircled by a gold thread was definitely a tooth, but that at 5 cm (2 inches) in length it was more likely to have come from a crocodile than a human being. But then they forgot that the footprint on Adam's Peak (*see page 232–3*), which some believe to be the Buddha's, is 1 metre (3 ft) long.   ❑

LEFT: worshippers lighting coconut oil lamps at the Temple of the Tooth in Kandy.

group. Robert Knox noted "Not only was there complete freedom of worship, but Kandyan Kings granted lands to Buddhists, Hindus, Muslims and Christians. The Christian religion, he [the king] does not in the least persecute, indeed he honours and esteems it".

The *devala* devoted to Lord Vishnu is revered by Buddhists, for the role played by that god in the preservation of Buddhism. The *devala* dedicated to Goddess Pattini, a popular deity who favours chastity and good health, is worshipped by people of all faiths. God Natha is the third deity revered in Sri Lanka. He has a special place in the hearts of believers as the preserver and nourisher of faith and love. The god of Kataragama, Skanda, is the fourth deity worshipped for his forthright manner in which he solves problems and gives solace to those who are grieving.

The **Royal Bathhouse ⊙**, on the edge of the lake, is a beautiful pavilion with the traditional Kandyan roof, supported on white columns. Inside is the ticket office, but you won't see any bathing beauties here any more.

The Temple of the Tooth

The **Temple of the Tooth** (or **Dalada Maligawa**) contains the most sacred relic of Buddhism and the most precious symbol of Sinhalese pride. Carried around by the ancient kings, the tooth in question has witnessed all manner of calamities. Most recently, the Temple of the Tooth was devastated by Tamil Tiger bombs in 1997, prior to the proposed Independence anniversary celebrations in Kandy. Since then, it has not been easy to gain access, and, indeed, it remains practically impossible even to poke your nose through the door.

Once the Temple is restored and normality returns, bemused tourists will no

Map
on page
210

BELOW: the Temple of the Tooth.

doubt be allowed back in to point their cameras at closed doors, from behind which the sound of drumming promises a dramatic entrance that never happens. The sense of anticipation and mystery is intentional. The tooth itself is never seen, kept locked up in a diminishing series of caskets which are closely guarded. After all, the Chinese went to war to wrest this prize from its guardians. The *puja* ceremonies of veneration are held at dawn and dusk every day; when the temple reopens, the dawn version will remain an intimate affair, without the coachloads who arrive at dusk to testify to the fame of this dental relic and to add the strobic flashes of photography to the mysterious twilight ritual.

Around the Lake

For a morning constitutional or an afternoon stroll, it is traditional to stretch one's legs with a circuit of **Kandy Lake**. The shady path provides magnificent views of the hills and of the town, which shimmers in the slanting sunlight, its blemishes airbrushed out by the moist atmosphere.

The lake was created in 1807 by the last Sinhalese King, using reluctant feudal labour. It stands as an indictment of the late Kandyan monarchy that they frittered away national energy on the making of an ornamental lake at a time when their kingdom was under serious threat; their efforts benefitted only their conquerors, who later turned the lake into a popular boating pond.

The island in the lake was the **Royal Summer House**, which the salacious and unhistorical refer to as the harem – as if the king would put his courtesans so far out of reach.

BELOW: a relic of British rule beside the lake.

Passing the Royal Bathhouse, the promenade transforms imperceptibly from city street to parkland walk. This leads you to the **Kandyan Arts and Crafts**

Association and Tourist Information Centre, where you can buy beautiful crafts, most of which are made on the premises. A lunch of rice and curry at the adjoining restaurant is a mouthwatering experience, too. Even if you eat or buy nothing, the buildings themselves give you a taste of Kandyan architectural style. The roofs are constructed in a series of overlapping folds of red tiles that resemble an origami Sydney Opera House, or a squashed pagoda. The walls are a lattice of spindles that make the most of the breeze coming off the lake.

Another detour from the shore of the lake allows you to explore Buddhist culture and history by visiting the **Buddhist Publication Society**, at 54 Sangaraja Mawatha. Alternatively, there is the **Samadhi Cultural Centre**, at 171 Wattarantenne Place.

A suburban jungle

A pause between sightseeing trips is an engaging moment to experience the natural beauty of the 5-km (3-mile) walk through **Udawattekele Sanctuary ⓓ**, a natural reserve situated to the north of the city.

The Workshop of the Tooth.

You can wander into this suburban jungle almost without realising it. It is difficult to say whether the last villas of town are encroaching on the wild forest or whether they are being slowly engulfed by the latter's dense foliage. An experienced guide is formally required, but there are good paths and tracks, and if you have a sense of direction you can experience the elation of creeping up on a troupe of monkeys eating, grooming and socialising. As they scatter at your approach, you will probably find yourself tiptoeing so as not to disturb this dark and chattery place. The sunlight is filtered through a canopy of leaves, alive with the song and flash of exotic birds. Among the wide range of exotic

LEFT: a denizen of the neighbourhood. **RIGHT:** the Temple of the Tooth seen from Udawattekele.

flora and fauna, you may also stumble upon a Buddhist hermit sitting outside his home beneath an overhanging rock, or you might find yourself looking down on the roofs of the Temple of the Tooth, unbelievably close to town, and yet a world away.

Excursions to the east

Kandy makes an excellent base for excursions into the surrounding area. An additional attraction of exploring these stunning landscapes, especially in the late afternoon, is seeing working elephants being bathed in the rivers after a hard day's toil. They snort out water in glee as their handlers scrub them vigorously with elephantine loofahs.

The vista from the road that runs east of Kandy is dominated by a range of mountains, the **Knuckles Range**, whose name vividly describes its outline. They are only the beginning of a spectacularly scenic route.

On the many occasions that the Kandyan monarchs were threatened by invaders, the city would empty and everyone would trek to the natural citadel of **Hunnasgiriya** ❼ and remain there until the danger had passed; the royal treasures, including the Tooth Relic, always accompanied them. The view from Hunnasgiriya, about 35 km (22 miles) east of Kandy, is breathtaking, and a walk around the ruins of **Medamahanuwara**, the city of refuge built on the summit, is a powerful and sobering reminder of a culture under seige.

The switchback road over the Knuckles Range leads to the Mahaweli River, with views of the land once inhabited by the aboriginal tribes of Sri Lanka. This area of jungle bound by the river and the plains beyond is the sacred land of the Veddhas (*see pages 70–71*), known as **Bintenna**. Unless you know that

TIP

The roads around Kandy can be hazardous. One 8-km (5-mile) stretch has 18 switchbacks. You should also watch out for monkeys in the middle of the road.

BELOW:
Lankatilaku Vihara.

Map on page 224

it is safe to proceed to the east coast, there is not much point in going much further. One place of at least historical interest, though, is **Mahiyangana** ❽, at the end of a hair-raising journey down to the plains. This was one of the locations visited by the Buddha 26 centuries ago – at least according to the *Mahavamsa* chronicles, which honour many spots on the island with such an assertion. The aboriginal people were the immediate beneficiaries of that visit, since they converted to the practice of Buddhism after watching him levitate. A temple in Mahiyangana marks the spot where the Buddha is said to have preached.

Returning to Kandy, you can glimpse 18th-century social life in the Kandyan Kingdom, as reproduced in a series of wall paintings in the **Degaldoruwa Cave Temple**. Alongside are paintings from the lives of the Buddha, which have all the personal trappings of the time. Note how the dress and decorations in the paintings are a mixture of Western and Eastern cultures.

Fine craftsmanship is demonstrated in the weaving of vegetable fibre mats, which are dyed in striking colours, in the village of Henawala, about 13 km (8 miles) east of Kandy.

Excursions to the southwest

Easily accessible from either the road to Colombo or the road to Nuwara Eliya are several places of historic and cultural interest, which should not be missed. Three temples of architectural significance lie in close proximity, and can be visited by following an easy circular route.

The first, approximately 14 km (7 miles) southwest of the centre of Kandy, is the **Gadaladeniya Vihara** ❾, which was built on a hilltop in around the 14th century. Faded paintings from that time provide many clues as to the manner in which the temple was built, and an indication as to who laboured in building such a magnificient stone temple in the middle of nowhere. The art is South Indian, so the general assumption is that the workers were imported labour.

BELOW: wrestlers carved on a column of the Kataragama Devala, Embekke.

Another temple of the same period but more in the traditional Sinhalese style is **Lankatilaku Vihara** ❿, a short drive to the south of Gadaladeniya and reached after a long climb up steps cut into the rock. The elaborate stone- and woodwork in the shrine room and the *devales* for the four guardian deities attest to the toil of the many craftsmen.

The **Kataragama Devale** ⓫ at Embekke, an easy one-mile stroll from Lankatilaku, was also built in the 14th century to house an image of the god Skanda, the Kataragama deity. The entire wooden structure is intricately carved with mythical and other figures.

All three places of worship were built at the time when the king of Kandy ruled from **Gampola**, a town 10 km (6 miles) south of Kandy.

Also in the area are two craft villages of special interest: **Kiriwavula** has a traditional brass foundry, where intricately designed items are made for export and local sale, while **Manikdiwela** has a sophisticated hand-loom fabric industry.

Excursions to the north

The road north of Kandy leads to **Matale**, 25 km (15 miles) away, where a British garrison was stationed in the early 1800s. Fort MacDowall has since disappeared, but the small busy town, encircled by hills, has a definite place in history for its contributions to the "Year of Revolutions". The Matale Rebellion of 1848

Map on page 224

Anyone for hoppers?

BELOW:
Kandyan dancers rehearse their traditional steps.
RIGHT:
Kandyan drummer displays intensity.

is commemorated by a monument in the town park.

One of the unfortunate repercussions of that unsuccessful uprising is still being felt to this day. One of the rebel leaders sought refuge in the caves of the nearby monastery of **Aluvihara**. The British pursued him and destroyed much of the old temple, including a library of priceless *ola* (palm-leaf) manuscripts. These comprised the earliest written version of the Buddhist scriptures (the *Tipitaka*), the teachings of which had previously been passed down by word of mouth. They were the lifetime's labour of 500 monks working in the 2nd century BC. The laborious task of replacing the library has been painstakingly carried out ever since; the first of the "three baskets" of the *Tipitaka* was completed in 1982.

You can watch handiccrafts being made in a number of villages between Kandy and Matale. **Palle Hapuvida**, for example, has a cottage industry treasured for many centuries, in which workers embellish wood products with colourful, warm lacquer using their nails. A community of craftsmen display a variety of metalwork and wood carving skills in the earnestly named **Kalapuraya Craftpersons' Village**.

In the neighbouring villages of **Gunepana** and **Amunugama**, two schools have been set up to train Sri Lankans in the art of traditional dance and drumming. The public is welcome to watch the students as they go though their paces. Nearby, just a few miles along a side road northeast of Kandy, the fine art of *repoussé* is practised by metal craftsmen in the village of **Madawala**, and a bonus awaits those who also explore the ancient temple in this village. A three-storey image house, built on short stone pillars, contains a beautiful selection of religious paintings and artefacts. ❑

KOHOMBA – KANDYAN DANCE

A nightlong ceremony in honour of the god Kohomba became the focus of a style of dance perfected in Kandy under royal patronage. The religious performances require about 50 male dancers, dressed in silver belts and beaded breastplates and with anklets and headdresses jangling as they swirl and skip to the rhythm of 10 drums. The dancers express their devotion to the god in movements culminating in worshipful obeisance.

Out of the Kohomba Kankariya ceremonies a secular entertainment evolved, called *Vannama*, in which the dancers portray the movements of a specific animal. However, the mimicry is strictly stylised, and the dance remains abstract rather than representational. These are often interspersed in performances of the Kohomba Kankariya, with a competitive display of virtuosity from different dancers.

Today, Kandyan dance is often performed by women, especially in shows put on for tourists, and tends to emphasise the graceful rather than the acrobatic elements of the dance. Nevertheless, it is a thriving tradition of movement that traces its origins to the famous sanskrit treatise on music and dance written by the sage Bharata about two thousand years ago.

UP COUNTRY, LOW COUNTRY

*A tour of the highlands holds the promise of encounters with
pilgrims, waterfalls, tea pluckers and assorted wildlife
and ends in lowland landscapes studded with gems*

Map
on page
224

Hermann Hesse beautifully described this area in 1911: "The wind had just swept clean the whole valley of Nuwara Eliya, I saw deep blue and immense, the entire high mountain system of Ceylon piled up in mighty walls, and in its midst the beautiful, ancient and holy pyramid of Adam's Peak. Beside it at an infinite depth and distance lay the flat blue sea, in between a thousand mountains, broad valleys, narrow ravines, rivers and waterfalls, in countless folds, the whole mountainous island on which the ancient legend placed paradise."

The mountainous region of Sri Lanka, which is usually referred to as Up Country, is most famous for its tea plantations, but it was coffee that impelled the first planters to clear the forests. Back in the 1860s, the scourge of the virulent *Hermelia vastarix* blighted the coffee plantations and, financially ruined, the planters turned their aspirations to tea with even more determination. The abundant rainfall combined with sunshine, cold nights and mists offered the perfect climate for producing high grown, aromatic teas; so the world-famous industry of Ceylon Tea was born.

But there is far more to these uplands than endless valleys of close-cropped tea bushes, processing factories belching out fragrant aromas and the bright flash of South Indian Tamil workers in their pimento, fuchsia and cerise sarees picking their way through millions of "two-leaf-and-a-bud" so that the very best will end up in your tea cup.

Everywhere you turn, a waterfall more impressive than the last tumbles white water down spectacular mountains, blowing air scented with wild mint and eucalyptus. There are quaint, sleepy hill towns; botanical wonders and the Peak Wilderness; trout fishing; world class golf courses; the ancient gem city of Ratnapura; the holy mountain of Adam's Peak; fascinating wildlife; caves and caverns associated with mythology; and then sitting right at the top of all this is Nuwara Eliya.

Nestled gently into the foothill of Lanka's highest peak, Mount Pidurutalagala (2,524 metres/8,281 ft), this erstwhile haunt of the British colonials has probably had more hype and tripe written about it over the years than almost any other tourist spot on earth. Suffice to say that to travel there is probably better than to arrive.

PREVIOUS PAGES: Hill Country at dawn.
LEFT: a landscape of hand-plucked bushes.
BELOW: ploughing a paddy field.

From Kandy to Nuwara Eliya

Leaving **Kandy**, the town that served as the nerve centre of Lanka for two centuries, an ascent of 1,400 metres (4,700 ft) takes you through stunning vistas, deep valleys and dramatic chasms, all neatly cloaked in the glistening green leaves of *Camelia sinensis*. As

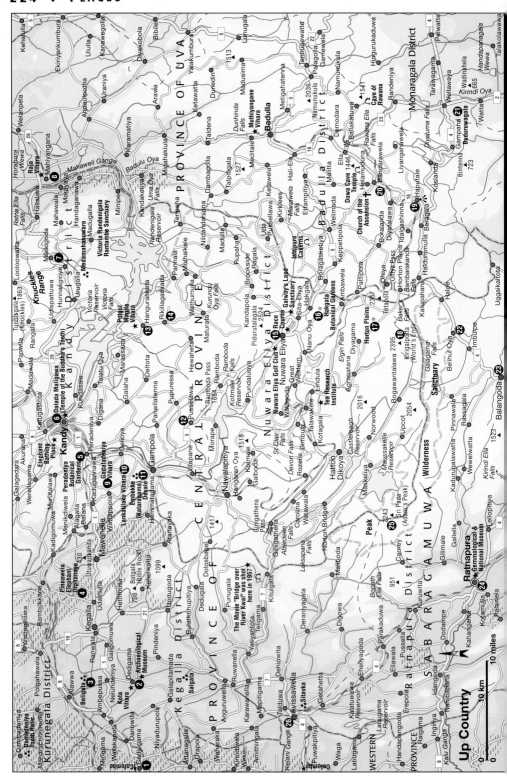

the road ascends, the herb-scented air grows cooler and the clouds crowning the peaks get closer.

Map on page 224

The Kandy to Nuwara Eliya road is 80 km (50 miles) long and a well-sited rest house at **Pusselawa ⑫**, half way, is a good stop for lunch. An alternative route, and a very pretty one, is on the B39 through **Hanguranketa ⑬**, which in the 17th century was a sacred refuge for the Kandyan King Raja Sinha II. The **Potgul Magila Vihara** is of some importance as it contains an ancient collection of *ola* manuscripts between covers of handcrafted silver and chased brass. The outer walls of this "inside out" *dagoba* display murals more normally found locked within a temple's relic chamber. Also worth inspecting is the beautiful moonstone.

Just a few kilometres south at **Rikillagaskada ⑭**, where route B39 meets B40, an innovative Scotsman, James Taylor, gave tea cultivation its first shot. Taylor arrived in Ceylon a strongly built 16-year-old on assignment to a coffee plantation in Deltota where the ill-humour of the proprietor drove him on to better things. Today you can visit Loolecondera Estate where Taylor's first tea flourished 120 years ago and buy boxes of it to take home.

The views across the Great Valley toward Hunnasgiriya are spectacular. Look for the Sleeping Warrior on the Knuckles range; or the North Wiltshire also known as Brandy-Gala; to the east is Friar's Hood (Toppigala). There are more tea estates cosily cladding the undulating hills and dales on the winding route through Ragala. The **Kurundu Oya Falls** drop 189 metres (630 ft) above the Mulhalkele Bridge. Picturesque waterfalls cluster round the town of Nuwara Eliya. The **Lover's Leap** falls 30 metres (100 ft) behind the brewery; **Glassaugh** with a fall of 60 metres (200 ft) is north of Nan Oya. The most beautiful are the twin falls at Ramboda where the 109-metre (357-ft) **Panna Oya** meets the **Ramboda Falls**.

BELOW: Rawana Ella Falls.

Nuwara Eliya

Such an inspiring journey might build up your expectations of **Nuwara Eliya ⑮** (pronounced New-*rel*-ya). It is easy to see why the early British settlers fell for it. After the heat and dust of Colombo, the salubrious climate and the breathtaking landscape are a soothing balm, as Sir Edward Barnes discovered when he was governing the island in 1828 and used it as his up-country retreat.

A little later the British explorer Samuel Baker, famous for discovering the source of the Nile, spent some time convalescing here and determined "to make it a regular settlement… a little English village round my residence." Without further ado he imported Hereford cows and planted strawberries, carrots and leeks which thrived in the eternal spring climate. He planned to build a brewery and sent for all he would need including an arsenal of sporting firearms, farm hands, artisans, a bailiff, a blacksmith with forge, farming machinery and a horse-drawn carriage. The only means of transport then was through the Ramboda Pass using bullock wagons and elephant carts. Yet it all arrived safely, except the carriage. Baker's coachman explained it to his master the best way he

knew how – by letter: "Honord Zur, I'm sorry to hinform you that the carriage and osses has met with a haccidint and is tumbled down a preccipice and its a mussy as I didn't go too."

Years later the beets, cabbage, leeks, potatoes and strawberries are still going strong. And with them the on-going myth, kept alive by practically every guide book and travel brochure on the Hill Country, proclaiming that Nuwara Eliya is "little England in the hills".

Sadly, this once lovely little town, whose name is supposed to mean City of Light, would be more appropriately called City of Blight. For a sprawling mess of hurriedly put up shelters and cheap, flimsy housing has taken over from the mock-Tudor villas and English gardens. The pristine Englishness of the 1940s and '50s, when horse races and flower shows attracted the cream of Colombo society to stay at the smart hotels, has disappeared. A shanty town mars one end of town, while lorries snarl up the other as they wait to load vegetable produce to transport to Colombo.

Victoria Park, once a beautiful town park near the lake, is strewn with litter, its park benches making beds for beggars. The racecourse which hosted the most glamorous event of the year, the Nuwara Eliya Races, is left to the weeds and a few stray ponies that small boys work like donkeys in the hope of scraping together a few rupees. During the over-excitement of the 50th independence celebrations, some of the very best French horses were exported to Sri Lanka for a grand parade. Only after this very expensive cargo arrived at the port was it realised that these aristocratic animals could not be left out in the extreme heat of Colombo, let alone be expected to parade. They were brought to Nuwara Eliya, and now live in the stables at the disused racecourse, but out of fear for

BELOW: terraced vegetable plots.

Map on page 224

their safety or perhaps out of embarrassment, they are kept locked away and no-one is allowed to see them or use them.

There are numerous attractions to tempt you away from Nuwara Eliya, but if you need to fill a couple of hours here, explore north of the higgeldy-piggeldy main street and out of town for a collection of remarkable art by a celebrated artist, David Paynter, a member of the British Royal Academy. A number of Paynter's Gaugainesque portraits hang on the walls of a children's home started by the artist's father, Reverend Arnold Paynter, in the 1940s. A dairy farm and vegetable garden just about keep the orphans – casualties of the war – afloat financially. Though shrunk in size due to lack of support, the home still stands in some of the prettiest woodland foothills, just beside the barred entrance to **Mt Pidurutalagala**. You can no longer climb this peak since the island's main television transmitter tops the summit (the prescribed alternative is **Single Tree Mountain** on the Badulla Road). There are wonderful treks in the forests behind it which will give you a glimpse of what Hermann Hesse was talking about.

If you are looking for a place to rest tired feet after an afternoon's walking, or would like to fit in a round of golf while in Nuwara Eliya, the Hill Club is the place to head. Not much has happened over the past 40 years to change the club's dignified atmosphere or the well-kept garden, which now overlooks an 18-hole golf course. Its neighbour, the Grand Hotel, no longer deserves its name. The Victorian Governor of Ceylon, Sir Edward Barnes, would probably turn in his grave if he knew what had become of his former mansion. Whistle-stop tourists from Colombo are trundled in here for a single night and whisked out the next morning before they have time to take in the dishabille of this once well-kept hotel. The only in town hotel that has not gone to seed is St Andrews.

Billiard room service at the Hill Club.

BELOW LEFT:
Nuwara Eliya's disorganised sprawl and buzz.
BELOW RIGHT: the Grand Hotel.

A comfortable establishment set in beautiful surroundings, it is a good choice for an overnight stay if you plan to linger a little longer in the lush countryside of the Hill Country. But if you want to be one up on the rest of the troop, then The Tea Factory, a luxury hotel in the converted shell of an old tea factory surrounded by its own tea plantation in Kundapola, commands a unique position with stunning views.

The Hakgala Gardens

South of Nuwara Eliya is another prominent peak, **Hakgala**, and at its feet the delightful **Hakgala Botanical Gardens** ⑯ established in 1860 (second after the Perideniya Gardens near Kandy). The gardens started as an experimental cinchona plantation from which the anti-malarial drug quinine is derived but is now known for its roses, ferns, an orchid house and a summer house with one of the loveliest views in Lanka.

The rock of Hakgala (Jaw Rock) rises 450 metres (1,500 ft) above the gardens and is said to be the place where Prince Rama hid Sita. According to legend, there is a spot by the Sita Amman Kovil where the soil is darker than elsewhere, because when Rama sent a troop of apes in search of his beloved Sita it so enraged King Ravana that he set fire to the tail of Lord Hanuman, angering the monkey god and causing him such discomfort of the rear end that he tore round in a fierce rage setting fire to the trees of the forest; the darkened soil bearing proof to this.

At the edge of the gardens is the **Hakgala Natural Reserve**, home to a host of wildlife including the bear monkey and sambhur (*see pages 125–130*) and a unique array of birdlife.

BELOW: landscape near Nuwara Eliya

The Wilderness

Beyond Hakgala lies **Horton Plains** , a windswept plateau over 2,000 metres (6,500 ft) high, forbidding and awesome, interspersed with forest and Lanka's second and third highest mountains, Pattipola and Totapola (2,357 metres/7,740 ft). These misty, silent grasslands streaked with icy rivulets, offer some excellent walks, the most famous being to **World's End** , a 4-km (2½-mile) hike from Farr Inn, a former rest house but now a central landmark on the plains and a comfortable enough guest house. In the early morning, a crescent of silver glimmers in the far distance pinpointing the Indian Ocean. The escarpment drops dramatically for 230 metres (750 ft) and falls away steeply for another thousand or so.

The **Peak Wilderness Sanctuary** stretches through alpine ruggedness for 40 km (24 miles) west of Adam's Peak. Elephants have been known to live at these heights, although now you are more likely to see deer, jackal and occasional leopard in these dense forests.

Eastern exploration

Travelling eastwards through a landscape of thrilling waterfalls, the road dives dizzily to **Haputale** , which was one of tea millionaire Thomas Lipton's favourite haunts. Here, in the Benedictine monastery of Addisham, you'll find a natural bird sanctuary with blue magpies, paradise flycatchers, green barbets, brilliant orange plumaged mini-verts hornbills, golden orioles and a host of other bird life.

The house resembles Leeds Castle in Kent, England, and was in fact built by a Kentish gentleman, who filled it with imported carpets, porcelain, furniture and glassware. He even had an English chauffeur for his Daimler. Today it is run as a monastery, which produces homemade jams and jellies from wild guavas and fruit cordials for sale (open 9am–12 noon and 3–5pm). Though in no way a full commercial guest house, Addisham can accommodate up to 12 people by prior arrangement.

The picturesque town of **Bandarawela** was once hailed as possessing one of the healthiest climates in the world, and nothing much has happened here to change that. The Bandarawela Hotel is a former tea planters club with comfortable period furniture and enormous bathtubs. This is still the best area for what in tea planter's jargon is termed "flavoury tea", and where some of Lanka's best is produced. Pears and strawberries also reach their prime here as the climate is drier and milder than at Nuwara Eliya. Between here and Welimada in the hamlet of **Mirahawatte** lies the **Uva Herbarium**, a garden dedicated to growing herbs and re-establishing forests. Many species of birds of the Uva are easily photographed here, and picnicking is a delight.

Low Country

The road from Haputale to Ratnapura descends through abundantly beautiful scenery. From Ratnapura it is easy to return to Colombo or the West Coast. Alternatively there is a road heading east from Bera-

Map on page 224

BELOW: bridge over the Kelani river.

Tea & serendipity

The Chinese Emperor Shen-Nung is generally credited with inventing tea 5,000 years ago, a feat he accomplished by chance when a few leaves dropped off a wild tea bush and drifted into the pot of water he was boiling. Rather than waste the contaminated water, he drank it, and so became the first human being to experience the "cup that cheers".

Sri Lanka has an association with happy accidents that is borne out by events. By chance, tea became Sri Lanka's chief export in the 19th century after the island's coffee plantations were devastated by coffee rust in the 1860s. A few tea plants brought from China found a very welcome home in the crisp, high sierra which had the ideal climate. Large tracts of the hill country, and what could be called the foot-hill country, were hurriedly deforested and closely planted with tea bushes, interspersed with an occasional gum tree to act as windbreak and for shade.

Tea begins its journey from hillside to cup with a gentle tug between the thumb and forefinger of a plucker, invariably female and of Tamil descent, who can be found in swarms on the picturesque landscapes, with baskets strapped to their backs.

The process of converting a green leaf into black tea is a tricky and precise art of transformation that takes place in tea factories. These were often constructed in England and shipped out piece by piece. With louvered windows to assist in the drying process, these white aerated barns stand out against the glossy green hillsides, and look rather like Mississippi riverboats after a spectacularly high tide.

Withering, grinding and fermenting are the successive steps of conversion, followed by a blast in a stove to dry out all but two percent of the moisture contained in the leaf, and the end result is a quarter of the original bulk. It is then given elegant names based on the the size of the flake, such as pekoe, orange pekoe, broken orange pekoe, broken orange pekoe fannings, and even dust, a low quality and inexpensive tea.

The language of tea can get flowery in describing the subtle variants of flavour. There are even "flowery" teas, which have a "show" of silver or gold "tips" and fetch high prices. The strong flavours of the best Ceylon teas are popular in the Middle East

Flavour experts will then classify the tea as "malty, pointy, bakey, thick, coppery, dull or bright" according to strength, flavour and colour. The graded teas are then auctioned and exported with the buyers relying on the expertise of tasters to guide them.

In 1975 the Land Reform Bill put the tea industry in government control leading to a decline of the estates and several smaller tea factories closing down. One of these victims of nationalisation, the Hethersett Tea Factory, has, in a final stroke of serendipity, been reborn as a luxury hotel. The polished wood and brass have been restored, the working equipment, including overhead line shaft and pulleys using camel-hair belts, have been maintained in their original condition, whilst 60 luxurious rooms have been carved out of the lofts for tourists to stay in. ❑

LEFT: tea merchant samples a range of teas.

gala which crosses the A2 road that leads to the South Coast. This route also has the advantage that it passes one of the most evocative ancient sites on the island. **Buduruwagala** ㉑ can be reached by following a small road through a hamlet, and on up a steep slope. In a clearing of the forest a huge rock is adorned with seven colossal figures carved in the 9th or 10th centuries.

The journey west passes some waterfalls, which when swollen by monsoon rains are spectacular. The **Diyaluma Falls** drops 171 metres (560 ft) in a single leap, and the **Bambarakanda Falls** does a triple jump that totals 241 metres (790 ft). At **Belihul Oya** ㉒ there is a Rest House which makes a good break in the journey. It is situated beside a stream, which fills deep pools with crystal clear mountain water.

The **Hituwalena Cave** at Kurugala is a holy place, this time for Muslims. The cavern is said to be the mouth of an underground passage that reaches all the way to Mecca. It can be reached by turning off the road at **Balangoda** ㉓. This town has been the centre of archaeological investigations into "Balangoda Man", a hunter whose home this was from about 5,000 BC. Apart from skeletons, buried in pairs facing east, other finds include simple decorated pottery, bone implements and stone tools.

The Ratnapura forests abound in the *vesak* orchid, so called because it flowers in May, the month of the Buddha's birth, celebrated during the festival of Vesak. Just 3 km (2 miles) out of town is the ancient **Saman Devala** built by Parakramabahu in the 13th century and destroyed during Portuguese rule. When the Dutch restored it, they managed to incorporate a Portuguese church into the *devala*. But this hasn't prevented it from hosting an annual *perahera* during July and August. If you have timed your holiday to reach Sri Lanka for the

Map on page 224

Hindu temple decoration.

BELOW: misty Bandarawela.

TIP

It is bad form to ask how far it is to the top of Adam's Peak as you climb. Just exchange the greeting "karu-vanai!" (Peace!).

more famous Kandy *perahera* and find that overcrowded hotels prevent you from staying in town, you may be consoled by the Saman Devala version with its giant two-faced effigy.

City of Gems

Ratnapura ㉔, the ancient "city of gems", is 101 km (63 miles) from Colombo, right in the heart of the low country, where rubber grows and gems are sometimes found in paddy fields in the middle of nowhere. If you come to Ratnapura with the express notion of buying a gem at a bargain price you might be disappointed. If there are bargains to be had in the gem trade you can bet your last rupee that a European tourist is on the receiving end (*see pages 118–120*). But as in places like Galle, you will encounter the odd hustler trying it on.

The small but instructive museum called the **Gem Bureau**, a mile or so out of town, is also a training centre for young artisans and has a handicrafts gallery. The tranquil **Hotel Kalawathi**, with a rare herb and vegetable garden where you can try herb baths made from indigenous species, lies about 6 km (4 miles) from its main rival, the Ratnapura Rest House. The **National Museum** (open Monday to Thursday 9am–5pm) has a fossil display of elephants, rhinoceroses and hippopotamuses found in gem pits from the Balangoda area. The **Gemmological Museum** (open daily 8.30am–5.30pm, no entrance fee), as its name suggests, displays precious stones and has a cafeteria.

Adam's Peak

Ratnapura is the starting point for the classical route to **Adam's Peak ㉕** via Gilimale and Carney Estates, although there are much less arduous ways of

BELOW: the great sculptures of Buduruwagala.

getting there these days. "When Adam was expelled an angel took him by the arm and set him down here," wrote the Papal Legate Marignolli over 500 years ago when he descended from the most famous of Lanka's mountains.

The Peak has been the object of worship and pilgrimage by kings and commoners alike over the centuries. The "season" for pilgrims is during the calm bright months from January to April when the incredible sunrise produces the famous spectacle known as the "Shadow of the Peak", which leaves all who have seen it spellbound.

"The scene is most extraordinary," a European observer wrote in 1896, "men, women, old and young, some almost decrepit, some who actually die on the way, many who have to be pulled or carried up, people from India, from China, from Japan, from Burma, from Spain, from Siam, from Ceylon, from Africa, priests and laymen, princes and paupers, may be seen striving, toiling, perspiring upwards."

Herman Hesse had a transcendental experience on Adam's Peak. He later tried to duplicate the moment in India, but it eluded him. He then returned to Sri Lanka, climbed the Peak, and it happened again.

Where the Ratnapura road joins the one from Colombo to Nuwara Eliya is **Avissawella ㉖**. Near this bustling town lies a buried city of immense repute, Sitavka, named after Sita, the wife of Rama in the *Ramayana*. In this epic tale, Sita was abducted from India and brought to Sri Lanka by Ravana, the demon king, in a "peacock plane". Ravana imprisoned Sita in the vicinity of Sitavka, where he is reputed to have had his capital nearly 3,000 years ago.

On a more mundane level, the **Avissawella Rest House** provides a good rice and curry lunch. ❑

Map on page 224

Gems of Ratnapura.

BELOW: Ratnapura, the city of gems.

THE CULTURAL TRIANGLE

*This popular tour takes you deep into the past of
ancient Lanka to find sacred caves,
ruined temples and entire lost cities*

Map
on page
238

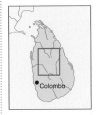

Colombo

Sri Lanka's so-called Cultural Triangle stands on its point on **Kandy**, the last Sinhalese capital. Within this area are the great sites of ancient Lanka: at top left is **Anuradhapura ❶**, the first capital, where centuries of kings built ever larger domed monuments to Buddha. Nearby is **Mihintale ❷**, a monastic city which grew up around the cave that sheltered the first disciple of Buddhism, Mahinda. The medieval capital, **Polonnaruwa ❸**, is further south. It contains complete buildings and colossal rock sculptures. In the middle is **Sigiriya ❹**, where a usurper built his royal palace on top of a loaf-shaped rock. Any one of these four sites is enough to impress even the most worldly traveller, taken together they are overwhelming. Each is covered in detail in the chapters that follow.

A central point from which to take excursions is **Habarana ❺**, a village with hotels built for just this purpose. Alternatively, there are hotels and rest houses at each of the sites, so it's possible to spend a night or more in each. The best way to see the area is by hire car, complete with driver who will also act as a guide. You can pick and choose what to see according to taste and the amount of time you have, but remember the Triangle also includes numerous lesser sites, most of which can be visited en route. Others are less accessible unless you have a lot of time. When planning your itinerary study the map and the places described in this chapter for a number of tempting detours.

Finally, this chapter highlights examples of ancient Sinhalese art outside the Triangle but close to the holiday centres for those people who are unable to complete a full tour.

Buddhist shrines and monasteries

Dambulla ❻, at the crossroads in the centre of the region, is the most visited monastery. It is the most impressive cave temple in Sri Lanka, with five caves under a vast overhanging rock, carved with a drip line to keep the interiors dry. This rudimentary architecture was embellished in 1938 with a loggia of arched colonnades and gabled entrances which oozes out of the rock.

On entering these elegantly portalled caves you may think you have stepped into an ornate tent, hung with bright carpets. The ceilings are painted with intricate patterns of religious images following the contours of the rock. There are images of the Buddha, the *bodhisattvas* and gods and goddesses. There are innumerable painted sculptures, including a life-size effigy of the last Kandyan king and much older statues of Hindu gods.

Only a 10-minute detour from the main road on your way back to Kandy from Dambulla is the 8th-century **Nalanda Gedige ❼**, a curious hybrid of

PRECEDING PAGES:
an Anuradhapura
panorama.
LEFT: the rock temples of Dambulla.
BELOW: the colourfully painted caves
of Dambulla.

Buddhist and Hindu architecture set in very peaceful surroundings which are particularly enchanting, especially after rain when there seems to be water everywhere. The temple is noted for its stone carvings of sexual subjects, which are very similar to the famous *Kadjuraho* carvings in India.

Further south on the same road, is the monastery of **Aluvihara** ❽, occupying a number of caves in a picturesque valley about 8 km (5 miles) north of Matale. It was in these caves that the Buddhist doctrines were first committed to paper – or rather *ola* leaf – in the 1st century BC. The *Tripitakaya* was written in an ancient script called Pali on long leaves of the *ola* palm which were then loosely bound to make books. Much of the library was destroyed by the British in 1848, after a rebel leader took refuge in the caves. The work of replacing the lost manuscripts continues today, and you can see monks painstakingly filling *ola* books in a scriptorium.

The various caves have different functions and contrasting moods. Several are beautifully painted with frescoes, one contains a large reclining Buddha, also

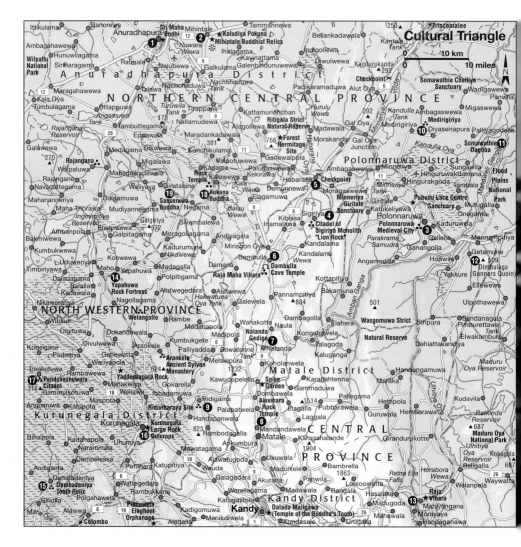

brightly painted, and one is dedicated to the Indian scholar Buddhagosa. The strangest of all contains a salutary depiction of the afterlife awaiting miscreants. As your eyes adjust to the gloom you will see colourful statues of sinners being punished by demons, an unfaithful woman being chopped into pieces, and a male sex-pest having the top of his skull removed so that the demons can reach in with spoons and ladle out his brain.

Some 17 km (11 miles) west of Aluvihara is **Ridigama ❾**, close to the Colombo road. Here you will find a cave temple with a gilded Buddha and various other works of art.

Beyond Polonnaruwa

Map on page 238

Exploring beyond Polonnaruwa will be rewarded by several interesting sites. Thirty-eight km (24 miles) north of Polonnaruwa via the Habarana road, through Hingurakgoda you reach **Medirigiriya ❿**. Built on top of a bare rock, this beautiful *vatadage* contained brahmi letters in the centre. There are three concentric rows of pillars surrounding four seated Buddhas facing the cardinal points. It is a most enchanting place as it is set in a natural reserve. You will pass two beautiful ancient tanks, Giritale and Minneriya, on the way to Habarana.

About 40 km (25 miles) northeast of Polonnaruwa, is the **Somawathie Dagoba ⓫**. A rock inscription states that the income from the ford of the nearby Mahaveli River was to be used for the upkeep of the *vihara*. There is a large stone elephant carved on a rock near the river bank. It is surrounded by a wildlife sanctuary where you might catch a glimpse some of the biggest elephants on the island. You might have to wait until happy hour – they show up only after 6pm.

Southeast of Polonnaruwa is the rock spire of **Dimbulaga ⓬**. Meditating

Stone Buddha in the Samadhi position of deep meditation.

BELOW: Buddhist teachings in the cave temple of Aluvihara.

monks from earliest Buddhist times up to the present day have used this hermitage of 500 rock caves. New monks are ordained in the Mahaveli River, and it was here that a saintly monk called Kassapa came to reform and unite the Buddhist order. Even now their presence in the smallest village has a moralising influence on the life of the village community.

There are three beautiful temples easily accessible from Kandy, the **Lankatilaku** and **Gadaladeniya** (*see page 217*), which date from the 14th century, when Gampola was the capital. A little further is **Mahiyangana** ⓫, one of the locations visited by the Buddha 26 centuries ago, according to the Mahavamsa chronicles (which honour many spots on the island by such claims). Successive monarchs, the monkhood and devotees worked towards developing a religious centre. The well maintained and ornate *dagoba*, with an impressive pinnacle, is the result of successive monarchs adding to the structure; it is supposed to contain a lock of the Buddha's hair.

Regardless of whether you believe that Buddha really stood on this spot or accept that his hair is indeed within the *stupa*, there is a sacred sense of place here that has been revered by a hundred generations.

Ephemeral capitals

After the fall of Polonnaruwa in 1236, the harassed kings moved their royal residences to a series of inaccessible crags, always carrying the Sacred Tooth and Bodhi tree with them. Close to the road that links Anuradhapura with Colombo is **Yapahuwa** ⓮, which ranks as one of the great architectural wonders of the island. It is easily found, since the rock rises to a height of 91 metres (33 ft).

The town was built sheltering on the south side of the crag, protected by two

semi-circular ramparts and a moat. The palace is reached by climbing a very impressive staircase, decorated with friezes of musicians and dancers and guarded by lions. The three flights lead you to the porch which has richly decorated pillars and balustrades. After the chasteness of classical Anuradhapura you will notice a marked change in style, reflecting the influence of the Pandyans. The royal court moved here from **Dambadeniya ⑮**, a beautiful spot, a short detour from the road to Colombo; sadly almost nothing of the old court buildings survives.

Despite its massive fortifications, Yapahuwa served as the capital for only a dozen years, and after a brief return to Polonnaruwa, the kings settled in **Kurunegala ⑯**, where they remained for 48 years. There is nothing left to see here, apart from some carved steps leading to a building of unknown function, but the town has two rest houses and could be used as a base for excursions.

Another 12th-century royal palace was built at **Panduvasnuwara ⑰**, where you will find a small museum by the side of the road. It is a lovely area to walk around and speculate on what things might have been like in the past. The citadel contained the one-pillar palace in which Princess Citra, the daughter of King Panduvasudeva, was kept prisoner. The story goes that she was imprisoned in order to prevent the realisation of a prophecy that a son born of her would kill all her brothers. The locals who hang around the area enjoy offering their versions of the tale.

With Tamil kingdoms becoming a permanent feature in the north, the Sinhalese capital was subsequently transferred to Gampola, Rayigama, and finally Kotte. The latter was much admired by the Portuguese, who then destroyed it. During the colonial period the small independent kingdom of Kandy preserved

Map on page 238

BELOW: elephant wall protects the *dagoba* at Mahiyangana.

Map
on page
238

Sinhalese culture, until the last king was deposed by the British in 1815. Today the Sri Lankan parliament has moved out of the colonial buildings of Colombo to a new complex at Kotte, built in a modern version of the Kandyan style, so keeping alive the artistic traditions that began in Anuradhapura more than 2,000 years ago.

Rock cut sculptures

Worthy of a detour is the **Aukana Buddha** ⑱, 50 km (30 miles) south of Mihintale. This isolated colossus is the most perfectly preserved ancient statue in Sri Lanka, though it is often wrongly dated. For many years it was attributed to the reign of the 5th-century King Dhatusena, but the style of carving points to a later date. Whatever the date, it is a magnificent image, carved out of the living rock with supreme assurance. Although it stands erect, firmly planted on both feet, the body is graceful. This effect is helped by the beautifully flowing drapery which appears almost diaphanous.

The Buddha's heavy right hand is raised in the posture of blessing, his other hand delicately touches his shoulder, as if holding his pleated robes in place. His expression is serene, and from his curled hair there sprouts the flame signifying super-enlightenment. It is only when you lower your gaze to the massive feet resting on the lotus-decorated plinth that dizziness and a crick in the neck remind you of the vastness of this statue. It rises to 13 metres (42 ft), canopied by a reconstruction of the brick image house said to have contained it when it was first built. Unfortunately, to modern eyes this gives it the appearance of someone sheltering under a railway bridge.

Best seen at dawn, Aukana (which means "sun eating") is an astonishingly accomplished piece of work, and the unknown sculptor must have been a great master, but did his inspiration match his technical brilliance? It is a matter of taste. It seems clear that the artist was aiming for a sublime style in which expressiveness would be out of place, but if the blank expression fails to interest you, then the monumental Buddha at Sasseruwa will be more to your liking. A good copy of the Aukana Buddha was erected in Colombo in the 1970s. It stands opposite the Bandaranaike Conference Hall on Bauddhaloka Mawatha.

A journey of around 10 km (6 miles) brings you to **Sasseruwa** ⑲, and another image at the site of an ancient cave monastery which provides a fascinating contrast with the Aukana Buddha. The standing image is nearly as large (12 metres/39 ft), but if anything it has even greater impact. It makes up for in vivacity what it lacks in sophistication and refinement. The statue stands in a niche created by the removal of stone around it, as though he was always there, standing within the stone, waiting for the sculptor to uncover him.

There are some mysterious examples of rock-cut art in the Up Country at **Buduruvalagala**. Two *bodhisattvas*, each attended by two figures of uncertain identity, stand on either side of a larger central Buddha figure. This courtly group stand in a romantically overgrown glade. ❑

BELOW: Bodhisattva Avalokitesvara at Buduruvalagala.
RIGHT: the Aukana Buddha.

ANURADHAPURA

A long succession of Sinhalese kings adorned their ancient capital with royal palaces, pleasure gardens, artificial lakes monasteries and monuments to the Buddhist faith

Map on page 247

Anuradhapura was the greatest monastic city of the ancient world. At its height it was home to thousands of monks at dozens of monasteries, served by a large lay population. It was the royal capital of a succession of 113 kings who oversaw a flowering of the arts that produced magnificent palaces, intricate and exquisite sculptures, ornate pleasure gardens and of course the huge *dagobas*, the domed buildings that protected the most sacred relics of Buddhism. The gentle sway of the Buddhist faith inspired the kings of Ancient Lanka to allow freedom of worship and to build the world's first hospitals. There were even animal hospitals provided for their non-human subjects. Perhaps the most impressive achievement was in irrigation, with reservoirs constructed to preserve the monsoon rains, and a system of sluices put in place to keep the rice paddies productive.

The fame of the city spread; the Greek ambassador to India, Megasthenes, admired the limousines of the ancient royalty, the state elephants, which were an important export, along with gems and spices. The mass of Roman coins which have been found show that Lanka was not short of trade and possibly even enjoyed some early tourism. In the early 5th century, the Chinese Buddhist pilgrim Fa Hien came in search of the Buddhist texts in Anuradhapura as Buddhism was then already waning in India.

LEFT: a Thuparama guardstone.
BELOW: leaves of the sacred Bo tree.

Originally founded by a minister called Anuradha, the city developed around 500 BC under King Pandukabhaya. In 161 BC King Dutugemunu united the island with Anuradhapura as the capital. It was fought over and finally abandoned in 1073 when the capital was transferred to Polonnaruwa. By that time the city had served as the capital for about 1,400 years. From then on the jungle enveloped the palaces and temples, which slowly began to crumble. The British explorers who first surveyed the ruins in the 19th century justifiably felt they were rediscovering a "lost" city. Subsequent archaeologists of Anuradhapura have had an invaluable aid in the form of the *Mahavamsa,* the great chronicle which records the founding of the city's monuments in *Pali* verse. Restoration continues, sometimes amounting to rebuilding, since this is not a dead city but a living pilgrimage site. Tourists, pilgrims and even monkeys flock here for their own reasons.

The most crowded part is around the sacred **Bo Tree Ⓐ** (*Sri Maha Bodhi*), especially on the full moon, *poson* in June, when the area is packed with worshippers. People come because this is a sapling of the original tree under which the Buddha attained enlightenment in Bodhi Gaya in India.

It is the oldest tree in the world and has been tended devotedly for 23 centuries, even when the city was

conquered by Tamils. Seedlings from it have stocked temples throughout the island and around the globe. Today it is propped up on a frame of iron crutches and protected by a golden railing, swathed in colourful prayer flags offered by the pilgrims. The tree retains its beauty, turning a soft pink when it sprouts new leaves, but otherwise it seems to shrink away from the celebrations, preferring to keep a dignified distance from the crowds.

Near the sacred Bo Tree is the **Brazen Palace** Ⓑ (*Loha Pasada*), a grand name for what is now an unimpressive forest of short stone pillars, most of them rough-hewn, and all tilting at varying angles. These paltry remains convey nothing of the splendours described in the *Mahavamsa*. These chronicles tell of a palace nine storey high, each floor with 100 rooms, and a throne of ivory with a seat of mountain crystal. Despite its name it was not a royal palace, but a residence for monks (the name brazen refers not to the inhabitants, but to the copper roof). Otherwise this magnificent palace was made entirely of wood, which unfortunately meant that it burned down more than once. The 1,600 pillars you see today are all that remains of the work completed by King Parakramabahu in the 12th century.

Dagobas

The quintessential form of Buddhist architecture began as a mound of earth and developed into the *stupas* of India, the *chedis* of Thailand, and the *pagodas* of China and Japan. In Sri Lanka they grew to unprecedented size under the patronage of Anuradhapura's fervent kings. The basic *dagoba* consists of a dome standing on a square base, topped with a pinnacle.

The gigantic white dome looming to the east of the Basawakkulama tank is

BELOW: the ruins of the Brazen Palace.

the **Ruwanweliseya** ⊙, also known as Maha Thupa or Great Stupa. It was built by Dutugemunu, the hero king of the *Mahavamsa,* who was supposedly inspired by seeing a bubble floating on water. To attempt to recreate the weightless quality of a bubble on such a vast scale might seem futile, but somehow it works. You don't see the thousands of tons of masonry that were required to raise this dome to its full height of over 55 metres (180 ft); all you see is the skin of white paint that seems to envelop a pocket of air.

The stupa is surrounded by an army of full size sculpted elephants (nearly all of them modern replacements) standing ear to ear along the whitewashed perimeter wall. This elephant wall has an imposing effect, but its function is also symbolic: the elephants seem to support the platform of the *dagoba*, just as in Buddhist mythology they hold up the earth. This symbolism is continued in every detail of the *dagoba*. The dome represents heaven or, alternatively, you could see it as representing the head of Buddha. The conical spire is an elaborate accumulation of *chatras,* parasols that indicate kingship. They may also remind one of the protuberance that appears from the Buddha's head to signify super-enlightenment.

Within the dome is a chamber containing sacred relics of the Buddha. The gatehouses at the four cardinal points of the *dagoba* mark the outer wall. Inside this is a "sand courtyard", from which rises the so-called elephant wall. Above it, to the southeast, is a model *dagoba* featuring four large limestone Buddha statues; to the left is a statue of the Buddha of the Future, known as Bodhisattva Maitriya. A statue believed to be of Dutugemunu stands under an awning looking towards his masterpiece.

North of the Ruwanweliseya is the **Thuparamaya** ⓓ, built by King

Map on page 247

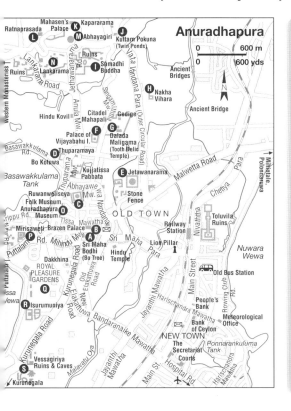

A protective gana or dwarf, an attendant of Kutera, the god of wealth.

Devanampiyatissa before massive buildings became fashionable. It may be small, but it is very sacred to Buddhists, since it is believed to enshrine the right collarbone of the Buddha. What you see today is not ancient at all, but a reconstruction of the mid-19th century. It is not even the right shape since the original resembled a heap of rice, rather than the present bell-like form. The crowd of listing stone pillars that surround it like windblown palms are the remains of a *Vatadage,* a type of building unique to Sri Lanka. Their capitals decorated with carvings of *hamsas* (geese, a protective bird), these monolithic columns are arranged in four concentric circles of decreasing height and would have protected the old *dagoba* under a conical roof.

East of the Ruwaneliseya lies the vast **Jetawanarama** **E**, the largest *stupa* in Anuradhapura with a 113-metre (367-ft) diameter base standing on massive brick foundations set into a huge bed of concrete. It rises 122 metres (400 ft) in height, and its perimeter walls enclose 8 acres (3 hectares) of land. The complex is the vision of King Mahasena, who was also responsible for the biggest tank of them all (the Minneriya), but the Jetawanarama was his pet project. It compares with the biggest of the pyramids. Another elaboration on the basic *dagoba* was the *vahalkada* or frontispiece, one of which was built at each of the four cardinal points. The Jetawanarama's eastern *vahalkada* was decorated with beautiful figures of alluring women posed so elegantly they appear to be moving, even dancing, wearing elaborate but scanty attire.

Palaces and temples

BELOW: the small Thuparamaya *dagoba.*

Continue north of Thuparama to the **Palace of Vijayabahu I** **F**, built for the king who liberated Sri Lanka from the Chola empire. This was his provincial

royal residence. About 100 metres (109 yards) north are the ruins of the **Maha-pali Refectory**, with an immense trough that would have been filled with donated rice, and the **Dalada Maligama** (Tooth Relic Temple). This housed the first home of the Tooth Relic brought to Sri Lanka in the 4th century AD. The Chinese traveller Fa Hien who visited the site when the relic was still here gives a vivid description of its exhibition. Beyond this is the enigmatic **Nakha Vihara**, a square *dagoba*, decorated with stucco figures, which is now a misshapen assemblage of bricks with empty niches where statues once stood.

The Abhayagiri complex

North of the city lies an area which almost became a rival capital. This was the Abhayagiri Vihara, whose monks followed a lax form of Buddhism, which incorporated Hindu influences and presented a challenge to the orthodox Theravada school. During the reign of King Mahasena (AD 276–303), the monks achieved a short-lived victory, and their precincts sprouted palaces, bathing pools and sculpture of the highest artistic standards. The first relic you arrive at gives only a hint of what is to come. The weathered limestone image of the **Samadhi Buddha** is depicted in the serene state of *Samadhi*, or deep meditation. The surrounding area is so peaceful that just walking through it has a calming effect on the weary traveller.

A little further north is a sight that one might expect to see in Tivoli or Versailles. The **Twin Ponds** *(Kuttam Pokuna)* could only have been produced for a highly sophisticated client who had the confidence to keep them simple. There is no ostentation in the design of these two stepped pools and yet the effect is impressive. They are not identical twins, however; one pond is longer

Map on page 247

LEFT: the Samadhi Buddha.
RIGHT: the Twin Ponds.

by 12 metres (40 ft), a ratio that is carefully calculated, for this is the grand classical style in which perfect proportions and restraint make up for the comparative lack of ornament. And for whom were these regal facilities created? The monks, of course, who bathed in the water that gushed out of a carved lion's head, after it had been put through a system of filtration. They performed their lavage under the protective gaze of a five-headed cobra believed to bring good fortune.

Beyond this is an outstanding moonstone (*see the information box, below*) at the threshold of the Queen's Pavilion of **King Mahasen's Palace** . As with the Brazen Palace, one would get a better idea of how this palace must have looked from reading the *Mahavamsa* than by gazing at the remnants in the grass, but at least there is its wonderful semi-circular doorstep, elaborately and vibrantly adorned with symbolic carvings.

To the north are the great columns of the **Ratnaprasada** (Gem Palace), the chapter house of the monastery. To protect their wealth, the monks placed a guardstone at the entrance which is the finest in Sri Lanka. The bejewelled figure is a *nagaraja* or Cobra King, with a seven-headed cobra forming a hood over his elaborate crown. Every detail of his dress is beautifully depicted; every belt and tassel is clearly defined and miraculously well preserved. His body is caught in an exaggerated, elegant posture and the feet touch the ground lightly; he is proffering the symbols of prosperity; a *purna ghara* or "pot of plenty", the Sri Lankan equivalent of a cornucopia and a flowering branch. Above his head is an arch depicting *makaras,* dragon-like creatures with the feet of a lion and the ears of a pig that represent time, either consuming or regurgitating a ribbon of history. In this instance good fortune is represented by a writhing mêlée of

BELOW: the famous moonstone of the Abhayagiri monastery.

HOW TO READ A MOONSTONE

The stone doormats at the thresholds of Sri Lankan temples have a lot more to say than "welcome", but you have to know how to interpret them. Though not rigidly prescribed, they always reflect cosmic symbolism. The outside ring depicts a flame, symbolising desire, the rapaciousness that Buddha taught should be conquered to avoid suffering. In the next ring a stately frieze of animals symbolising vitality walk from left to right, the direction of good omen. In Anuradhapura moonstones these included a bull, horse, elephant and lion, but the Polonnaruwa specimens omit the bull out of respect for Hindus.

Next, you come to the circle with the twisting creeper symbolising the life-force. According to Buddhism, when you surpass this craving, you are able to choose good over evil and go in search of the truth. This stage is represented by the goose or *Hamsa*. The next ring, an exquisite scroll with an ornamental lotus flower in its centre, is symbolic of purity and the approach to Nirvana, or enlightenment.

The moonstone continued to evolve; a 14th-century example in the National Museum, Colombo, is horseshoe-shaped, the centre a full circle, and a 16th-century example in the National Museum, Kandy, is broken into writhing forms.

naked dwarves and fruit. At the foot of the *nagaraja* is an attendant dwarf, or *gana,* who seems to be chortling at the jolly scene.

The ruins of the **Abhayagiri**  monastery itself are fascinating to historians. This once housed 5,000 monks and was the most powerful institution after the king. To the south is another monastery, the **Abhayagiri Vihara**, founded by King Vattagamini in 88 BC, who donated it to the abbot of the Vessagiri Monastery. Mahayanism and Tantrism were taught by this Abhayagiri sect. The Mahayana doctrine introduced Bodhisattva worship, in which men give up the chance of entering Nirvana in order to help humanity, while Tantrism involved the worship of the mother goddess. Despite their laxity in doctrinal matters, the monks of the Abhayagiri sect reorganised the monastery complex. Instead of the jumbled collection of buildings huddling round the stupa, they arranged everything in concentric squares. An outer enclosure contained the monks' living quarters, refectory, bath-house and latrines, and an inner precinct, on a raised platform, contained the religious buildings including the Bo Tree and the *stupa.* However when the power of this sect declined the monasteries went back to the comfortable informality of their old ways. Just south is the **Abhayagiri Museum**, funded by the Chinese in honour of the 5th-century Buddhist academic Fa Hien, and the **Lankarama** , built in the 1st century BC, which is circled by a crowd of pillars three deep, the remains of another *vatadage.*

Multi-hooded cobra, or Naga.

If you have time, you can explore the forest hermitages known as **Western Monasteries** to experience serene meditation and the simple ascetic life. The Pansa Kullika monks take an extra vow to emulate the Buddha's practice of gathering rags from corpses, which he then washed and wore. The monks are easily recognised today by their dull brown robes.

BELOW:
children at play.

Southern sites

Back in the middle of town, the **Anuradhapura Museum**  occupies a British colonial building, and has a variety of unique and interesting finds from Anuradhapura and nearby. The most useful for archaeologists is a reliquary found at Mihintale in the form of a model *dagoba*, giving vital clues as to how they originally looked. You can get an idea of how the Thuparama Vatadage would have looked with its roof intact from a scale model.

Among the other curiosities are a stone urinal carved with a relief depicting the god of wealth throwing money down the hole, and a whole collection of stone toilets embellished by their makers with the representation of a rival monastery, so that by using it the monks could express their lofty contempt for their brothers. Next door is the **Folk Museum**, with a collection depicting rural life in the north central province.

Heading away from the museum along the Tissa Wewa road, you find the **Mirisaweti**  *dagoba* built by Dutugemunu who later built the Ruwaneliseya. This area is pleasant to walk through. To the north is a refectory where you will find a food trough which held enough for 1,000 individual servings. The monks had to eat all their daily rations before 12 noon and were not allowed to eat anything else between meals.

Map on page 247

Tanks

Anuradhapura gets its annual quantity of rain in one go thanks to the northeast monsoons and, over its long history, three reservoirs were built so that every possible drop of rainwater was retained to irrigate the paddy fields. They were so successful that Sri Lanka became known as "the granary of the east". Most of these ancient irrigation channels still provide water for the farmers of the dry zone paddy fields.

West of the Brazen Palace is the **Basawakkulama**, a tank or *wewa* identified with King Pandukabhaya. Called the Abhaya Wewa in ancient times, it was built around the 4th century BC and enlarged and improved on several occasions. To its south is the beautiful **Tissa Wewa**, built by King Devanampiyatissa, overlooked by the rest house. The tank covers 65 hectares (160 acres) and water travels 85 km (54 miles) from the Kala Wewa, feeding 70 tanks on its way. The shore of the tank is always cool and is a lovely place to watch the sunset.

The **Nuwara Wewa** is the largest tank in Anuradhapura created in the 2nd century AD, and was constructed by gradual enlargement. It is 7 km (4½ miles) across and 12 metres (40 ft) deep. In the annals of ancient civilisations these irrigation works have had no parallel.

The area to the east of Tissa Wewa was given over to the **Royal Pleasure Gardens ●**, also known as the "Park of the Goldfish", covering approximately 160 hectares (400 acres). A network of pipes channelled water all over the garden. Along the shore you will see two pools set into the boulders. The **Northern Bath** is cut into rocks which seem almost to have come to life. Using both flat relief and fully moulded carving the rocks have taken on elephant forms and appear to be bounding into the cool water, waving their trunks and

BELOW: Tissa Wewa.

trumpeting with joy. The water that fed this pond was made available only by the efforts of those reliable bulldozers, the elephants, so it is fitting that they should share the fruits of their labour.

Map on page 247

The rock temple of Isurumuniya

At the southern end of the grounds is the **Isurumuniya** ⓡ, dating from the reign of King Devanampiyatissa in the 3rd century BC, which brings a tour of the ruins to a splendid climax. The rocky outcrop has over the years accumulated a roofed porch, a bell-domed *dagoba*, and other architectural additions connected by stone steps and paths. All of these man-made additions cling to the surface of the rock like barnacles and anemones on the hull of an upturned shipwreck. It has the quality of the mighty Sigiriya Rock without the vertigo. At its foot is a museum where you will find a collection of fine stone carvings.

The Isurumuniya Lovers.

The most famous sculpture is of the **Isurumuniya Lovers**, carved in the 6th century AD in the Indian Gupta style. Folklore identifies the young couple with Saliya, King Dutugemunu's son, and the low-caste maiden for whom he gave up the throne. According to the legend, Saliya first fell in love with the beautiful commoner while strolling through the Royal Pleasure Gardens. However, a far less romantic interpretation of the figures is that they are representations of a Hindu god and his consort.

Returning to the centre of town through the Royal Pleasure Gardens may give you a chance of finding romance, as the lovers did. The indefatigable will have the energy to explore the **Vessagiriya Ruins and Caves** ⓢ further south. These three large outcrops of rock once housed 500 *vessas* or members of the *vaisya* caste, a group ordained by Mahinda. ❏

BELOW: the rock temple of Isurumuniya.

MIHINTALE

Map on page 238

This is a monastic city of caves, temples and ruins, where Buddhism first took hold on the island and left behind an assortment of relics and monuments on the rocky hillside

The history of Mihintale is the history of Sri Lankan Buddhism, which begins with the story of an Indian missionary called Mahinda, since this is, literally, Mahinda's Mountain. This was where King Devampiyatissa met with a strange hunting accident that led to his conversion. He was on a deer hunt one day in the year 247 BC when his quarry gave him an unexpected jolt. Instead of the deer he expected to uncover, he found a man in monk's robes. It was the Indian prince Mahinda, sent on a mission by his father, King Tissa, who with the zeal of a recent convert had imprinted his new-found religion on his own country and was looking to spread the word. Buddhism soon overwhelmed the island, embraced with fervour by the Sinhalese people, whilst in India it declined. Always happy to backdate for spiritual purposes, the legend claims that the Buddha himself sanctified this mountain three centuries before the advent of Mahinda. Regardless of your beliefs, the beautiful shrines, *stupas*, caves, and above all the wondrous setting, make Mihintale unforgettable.

All over the world, high places are given religious significance, with the result that devotees are always climbing steps – sometimes on their knees. The three flights of steps at Mihintale, totalling 1,840, take the pilgrim through the shadows of the spreading temple trees to the summit. They were built in the reign of Bhathika Abhaya (22 BC to AD 7), but a later paved road provides a short cut. The first flight of steps is wide and shallow. The climb is sufficient to require regular deep breaths and a meditative pace.

LEFT: the Ambasthala Dagoba.
BELOW: a guardian stone.

At the end of the first flight to your right is the 2nd-century BC **Kantaka Cetiya**, one of the earliest religious monuments on the island, excavated in 1934. The 130-metre (425-ft) base consists of three giant steps of dressed stone, a characteristic of Sinhalese *stupas*. Above them the dome has worn down to resemble a heap of masonry, reaching 12 metres (40 ft) in height. It would originally have been much more impressive at over 30 metres (100 ft) high.

The highlights of the building are the four ornamental facades called *vahalkadas* facing the cardinal points. The eastern facade is the best preserved, with horizontal rows of carvings separated by strips of plain stone. There are beautiful friezes of dwarfs and elephants among the symbolic patterns, and on either side the wall is finished off with a tall carved pillar holding rather weathered lions aloft. The south facade also has some very ornate pillars carved with symbolic animals and plants. There is also a small relief figure of a *naga*, which is one of the earliest figure sculptures on the island. Despite its worn appearance, you can see that it is gracefully posed, with the weight on one leg, so even in these archaic times the Sinhalese sculptors were very sophisticated.

TIP

Do not take a photograph of a Buddhist monk unless you have his permission. It is considered disrespectful.

South of this ancient *stupa* is something even older: an inscription on a rock in large *Brahmi* characters – the forerunner to the *Pali* script. It is found on a rock shelter that would have been inhabited by Buddhist monks in the 3rd century BC. These rock shelters constitute the bare minimum in desirable residences. A channel was carved in the overhanging boulder to act as a dripstone moulding and help keep out the rain, but that was all. If you crawl through the cave you will find a sheer cliff face where the resident monks would sit on narrow ledges for a spot of meditation. Thousands of them perched on the precipice like sleeping cormorants; cross-legged and sublimely unaffected by vertigo.

The ascent

The second flight leads to the remains of some monastic edifices. At the entrance of the **Dhatu Ghara** relic house are the Mihintale Tablets – inscriptions on two stone slabs that formed the rules and regulations that governed the monks. They met to discuss matters of interest at the **Assembly Hall** (*Sannipata Sala*) and they ate communally at the **Monks Refectory**, which is the central courtyard.

Beyond it are two huge vats for food hollowed out of single blocks of stone, lying at right angles to one another among the few stones that once supported wooden buildings. They are referred to as rice canoes (*bat oru*) on account of their resemblance to dug-out boats, although they are definitely not very buoyant. They were filled with rice donated to the monks by devout locals.

To the summit

BELOW: stone stairway in Mihintale.

The third flight of steps, narrow and steep, takes you on a spiritual ascent to the highest plateau, where the lovely **Ambasthala Dagoba** marks the place where

Mahinda surprised King Devanampiyatissa in mid-hunt and quizzed him about mango trees to test his intelligence. The Mango Tree *stupa* is supposedly built over the exact spot where Mahinda stood, and a statue of the king is placed where he stood, a respectful distance away. The great sage Mahinda preached his first sermon from the **Rock of Convocation** (*Aradhana Gala*) near here.

From this plateau trails spread out in all directions. One leads to the 1st-century BC **Mahaseya Dagoba** the largest *stupa* in Mihintale which enshrines a single hair relic of the Buddha. Another path wends its way to **Mihindu Seya** where a small golden reliquary resembling the earliest Indian *stupas* surmounted by a *chattra* (umbrella) was discovered, along with a bronze statue.

Above them all towers the enormous boulder that covers **Mahinda's Bed** (*Mihindu Guha*). The bed itself is a smooth slab of stone, the covering rock was the roof. This is where the sage reposed, apparently oblivious to discomfort. Such spartan arrangements testify to the power of Buddhism that it could impel a prince to leave his palaces and live under a rock.

Another path leads past a long pool in the shadow of a large low rock which is carved in low relief with a mythical five-headed cobra. This is the **Naga Pokuna**, the Pond of the Serpent. *Naga* is supposed to be the guardian of treasure, protector of water and the maker of rain. The carving on this natural rock emphasises his association with water and it is said the *Naga*'s tail reaches right down to the bottom of the pool. The pond is part of an elaborate irrigation network that connects it with **Sinha Pokuna**, the Pond of the Lion, by means of stone channels, which never runs dry even at the height of a tropical drought. The outstanding lion gargoyle spurts water into a handsome square bath surrounded by a wide step carved with a frieze.

Map on page 238

Part of the carvings that decorate the Kantaka Cetiya.

BELOW: monks posing by the Kantaka Cetiya.

Map on page 238

RIGHT: Buddhism at home in the hills.
BELOW: by contrast, a Hindu shrine near Mihintale.

Off the beaten track

On a high peak are the ruins of **Et Vihara** ("the *stupa* of the elephant"). It has a panoramic view of the sacred valley on one side and of **Kaludiya Pokuna** ("the pond of black water") on the other. This artificial pond at the foot of the western slope of Mihintale served a monastery of the 10th or 11th centuries. It is a very peaceful and beautiful spot. The monastic college consists of a facade and roof built onto a natural rock overhang to create something half-way between a cave and a building. The monastery also has the simplest form of guardstone, where no sculptures appear on its face. The minimalist decoration is misleading, however, since these monks were definitely not roughing it like the troglodytic pioneers of Buddhism. They were happy to forego a sculpture here and there, so long as they enjoyed the comforts of indoor toilets and bath houses. These luxuries were served by an advanced hydraulic system of artificial moats and ducts running through the buildings. Half a kilometre (547 yards) from the pond is the **Ragagiri Kanda** ("the Mountain of Kings") where a whole series of hermit caves is set into the hillside.

Near the base of the westernmost hill is **Indikatuseya Dagoba** ("the *stupa* of the Needle"). The base of the *stupa* survives, unadorned with carving, but with broad bands of dressed stone like the base of a colossal doric column. The dome that once surmounted it has shrunk to a small mound of brick awaiting restoration. The guardstones at the foot of the steps are missing, but as you wander around the other ruins you will find a flight of steps complete with moonstone and a pair of guardstones depicting *Naga* in human form, but the building they embellished is reduced to a collection of stone pillars. This site caused great excitement among Buddhist scholars when Sanskrit texts belonging to the Mahayana school were found here. They had been transcribed into Sinhala characters and inscribed on copper plaques in the 8th or 9th century.

Ancient medicine

At the foot of the mountain are spread the ruins of a **Hospital** (*Vejja Sala*) which dates back to the 3rd century AD, some 400 years before the earliest hospital in Europe. Among the remnants of walls and pillars are monolithic basins for bathing the sick known as *bet oruva* or "medicinal boats". Like the rice boats, these are hewn from a single rock, but they have a particularly gripping sculptural quality.

The internal cavity is shaped to immerse a recumbent body without wasting precious herbal oils. The result is a simplified human shape that tempts you to lie down and try it for size. Stones used for grinding medicinal herbs unearthed here can be seen at the museum, along with medicine jars whose blue glaze indicates that a link must have existed between Persia and the island.

When you leave Mihintale you may not be converted, as King Devampiyatissa was, but you cannot fail to be impressed by the ascetic courage that led the earliest monks to live under bare rocks, whilst admiring the sophistication of the later monasteries which provided their inhabitants with ample stores of free food and an efficient plumbing system. ❑

POLONNARUWA

*Taking inspiration from their Hindu conquerors,
the resurgent Sinhalese kings moved to this city,
triggering an amazing artistic renaissance*

Map on page 262

Polonnaruwa was the medieval capital of Sri Lanka. In its prime, the city was protected by 6 km (3½ miles) of strong encircling walls. Strategically, it commanded all the crossings over the Mahaweli River, guarding the increasingly powerful Southern Province, Ruhuna. In AD 993 the Cholas looted and burnt Anuradhapura and used Polonnaruwa as their military base for 77 years, resulting in an interesting blend of South Indian Hindu culture and Sinhalese Buddhist art and architecture.

The valiant Vijayabahu I, who defeated the Cholas in 1073, devoted his long reign to the development of irrigation and Buddhism. Civil war followed his death and in 1161 Parakramabahu, the hero of the *Culavamsa,* the lesser chronicle in which the history of Lanka was recorded, captured Polonnaruwa and assumed control of the whole island. Regarded as being the last great king of Sri Lanka, Parakramabahu's greatest contribution was his protection of the Buddhist faith. Nissanka Malla, his nephew and successor, also embellished the city with many new buildings, but he was in the habit of simply sticking an extra brick or two onto a structure and claiming it as one of his. Around 1293, Polonnaruwa returned to the jungles after the capital city migrated southwards.

LEFT: the Lankatilaka image house.
BELOW: the statue known as the Sage may portray King Parakramabahu I.

Around the tank

"Not even a drop of water from the rain must flow into the ocean without being made useful to man," declared the Grand Monarch Parakramabahu when he constructed the **Parakrama Samudra** which covers an area of 2,430 hectares (6,000 acres). This monumental feat of engineering had 11 channels leading water off in different directions to feed a network of irrigation canals and minor tanks. The government-run **rest house** is right on the shoreline of the tank, the rooms open onto a verandah with beautiful views.

Close to the rest house is the **Archaeological Museum Ⓐ**. It may not look impressive but it is interesting for its superb Chola bronzes and other artefacts. On a promontory by the lake is the **Dipuyyana Ⓑ** (the Island Garden) which was Parakramabahu's royal retreat. The *Chronicle* compares its splendour to the Versailles palace of Louis XIV. The surrounding water must have kept the gardens wonderfully cool throughout the year.

Among the pleasures to be enjoyed in the gardens were the **Baths**, a collection of circular and square pools which were fed by underground pipes from the tank. Parakramabahu's intrusive successor built the windowless stone **Mausoleum** next door, now an uninspiring sight due to neglect, although some of its red, white and blue painted plaster is still intact. Even less remains of a wooden columned **Audience Hall**

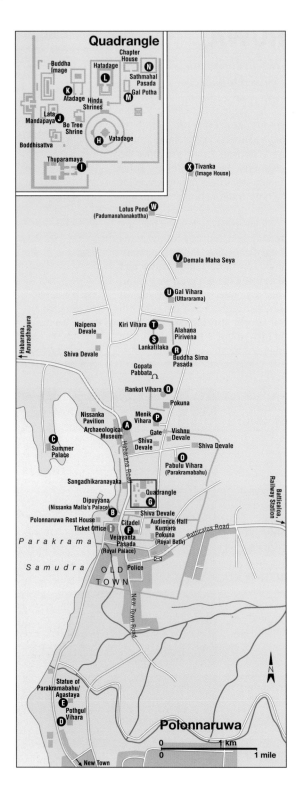

that was built beside it. However, one of Nissanka Malla's buildings is of great importance, though not for its architectural merit. The columns of his royal **Council Chamber** were inscribed with the positions to be occupied by the King's Council, following a strict protocol, giving us a picture of the political scene at the time.

There is an island pavilion in the lake where brick couches provide rest and views across the vast expanse of water. On a peninsular projecting from the northern shore is the **Summer Palace ☉** of Parakramabahu, which has become home to a variety of birds.

A detour south along the *bund* to see the **Pothgul Vihara ☉** (Southern Monastery) is worthwhile particularly if you like puzzles. Here you will find four small *dagobas* surrounding a circular brick building on the central platform. The acoustics of this enigmatic building are excellent, even without the corbelled roof that it would have had when it was built. This has lead to a suggestion that it was a lecture theatre where the tenets of Buddhism were read aloud. A little further north there is further evidence to back up this theory.

The **Statue of Parakramabahu/ Agastaya ☉** is a huge 12th-century rock sculpture of great quality. A barefoot figure, clad only in a sarong, steps forward out of the wall of rock from which he was carved. His broad face, with its beard and walrus moustache, has a look of seriousness softened by spirituality, as he holds a sacred manuscript from which he appears to be reading aloud. It seems certain that he is a religious teacher, which would coincide nicely with the theories about the function of the Pothgul Vihara.

The subject of the statue is a matter of debate: a Saivite *rishi* named Agastaya is the most probable candidate but it has also been suggested it is a representation of the city's great hero, Parakramabahu and is a memorial to him. Whoever it represents, this 3.5-metre (11½-ft) figure is a masterpiece.

The Inner Citadel

The administrative centre of Parakramabahu's capital was surrounded by walls that can still be clearly seen. Within them the **Vejayanta Pasada ⓕ**, the royal palace of Parakramabahu is still impressive, and the massive brick walls of the main hall stand amidst the ruins of about 40 intercommunicating rooms. The palace and its courtyard were surrounded by walls which were further protected by an outer wall. According to the *Culavamsa*, the palace rose to seven storeys, but since the upper floors were wooden no trace of them remains.

Further east is his **Audience Hall**, containing exquisite stone carvings. You can imagine the great king seated under these elegantly carved pillars holding formal council. The base of this building is supported by bas-relief elephants. The entrance has two flights of steps with moonstones flanked by *makaras* – mythical dragon-like animals. Outside the citadel's eastern walls is where the ladies of the court would have taken their evening dip in the **Kumara Pokuna** – or Royal Bath.

The Quadrangle

The centrepiece of the ancient city, the **Dalada Maluwa** (the Terrace of the Tooth Relic), was a sacred precinct containing 12 magnificent buildings. Today it is known as the **Quadrangle ⓖ**.

As you enter, the circular **Vatadage ⓗ** is to your left. This is one of the oldest monuments in Polonnaruwa, with additions (the very elaborate *makara* balustrade was Nissanka Malla's) and subtractions. It has lost the conical roof, and most of the *dagoba* that was the central core of the building and the reason for its existence. It has even lost one of its guardstones at the base of the steps.

The name of the Sathmahal Pasada means "Seven-storey edifice", which is all anyone knows about the building.

BELOW: the ancient Vatadage predates the city.

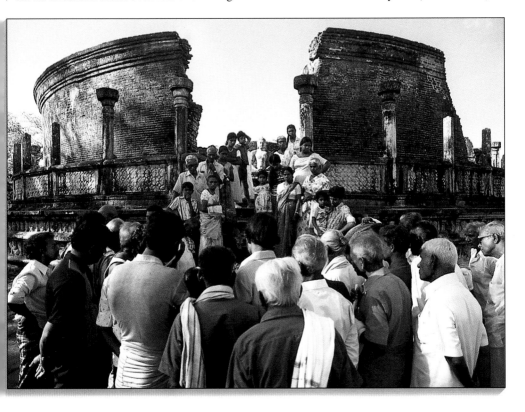

These stones depicting *naga* king figures with seven hooded cobra heads were believed to prevent evil from entering the premises. Along with the moonstones symbolising the stages on the Buddhist path towards Nirvana, they became ubiquitous features of Sinhalese buildings.

The well preserved **Thuparamaya** is an image house built for the worship of the Buddha. It is in a style of the stunningly original form of architecture that flowered at Polonnaruwa. These barrel-vaulted and domed buildings had brick walls of great thickness, stuccoed and painted with figures and architectural subjects. The roof of the Thuparamaya is intact and several images are still in place inside.

Passing a lone statue of **Boddhisattva** you will find the extraordinary wobbling columns of the **Lata Mandapaya** ❶ (flower-scroll hall), built by Nissanka Malla. The columns are representative of lotus stems and are part of a "baroque" period in Sinhalese art in which an austerity of style gave way to heavy ornamentation.

The **Atadage** ❷, or the House of Eight Relics, was the first Tooth Temple built by Vijayabahu in the 11th century. A neat plantation of 54 stone columns, some of them intricately carved, others embedded in brickwork, would have supported a timber upper floor in which the relic was kept. An image of the standing Buddha almost 3 metres (10 ft) high stands among the columns. As you stand in front of the statue, your imagination is free to rebuild the stairs, of which only the bottom ones made of stone survive, and then climb them to the upper floor. You can also imagine what carvings and paintings ornamented this most sacred temple, as they have all been replaced by air.

The **Hatadage** ❸ resembles the Atadage in plan as well as in name, and it

TIP

The ruins of Polonnaruwa are spread over a wide area. There are bicycles for hire at several places in the town to enable you to tour around and stay cool.

BELOW: the Thuparamaya image house.

was built for the same purpose, when the protection of the Tooth Relic became a symbol of royal power. Its thick stone walls that still contain three Buddha images are inscribed with Nissanka Malla's name, though this doesn't necessarily mean it was built in his reign.

The **Gal Potha** (Book of Stone), is an enormous stone slab which you can see beside the temple. It has glowing inscriptions praising the work of Nissanka Malla, leaving no doubt who the author might be. *Ola* leaf parchment was the usual medium for writing, but these rectangular leaves were small and easily overlooked, so the vainglorious king had this giant petrified version, 8 metres (26 ft) long, dragged all the way from Mihintale, 100 km (60 miles) away.

The **Sathmahal Pasada** **N** (Seven Storey Edifice) is of a simple stepped design, but is deeply perplexing to historians. The *Chronicles* make no mention of it, and archaeologists are stumped as to its origin. All they can say is that it is unlike anything else seen on the island, and then conjecture about Babylonian ziggurats. Each floor has a niche on each face to contain figures, remnants of which survive. It is very satisfying to look at this mysterious edifice and appreciate its inspiring shape and religious power, and for once know almost as much as the experts.

Beyond the city walls

Going north, a long trail will take you through the busy streets of the medieval city that has long since disappeared, its lesser buildings gone, its inhabitants replaced by tourists and monkeys. Turning right at the crossroads is the ancient street on which lies the **Pabulu Vihara** **O**, a brick *dagoba* supposedly built by

In order to list his great achievements and virtues, King Nissanka Malla required a slab of stone 8 metres (26 ft) long.

BELOW: the guardstones and moonstone of the Hatadage.

Rupavati, one of Parakramabahu's queens. It is surrounded by image houses – an innovation of the Polonnaruwa period, although the early style of the sculptures suggests that they may have been brought here from Anuradhapura. At the end of this road is a **Shiva Devale**, the only all-stone temple in perfect condition. This shrine was probably built by the Cholas in the 11th century – its alternative name, *Vanam Madevi Isvaram,* commemorates the queen of Rajaraja I, the Chola conqueror. It has a character that contrasts with the Sinhalese buildings, as despite its modest size it is ebullient rather than serene. Some superb bronzes were found here.

Return to the crossroads and travel north, passing more Hindu temples, then on through the northern gate entrance. Here a footpath on your left leads you to the **Menik Vihara ℗** with terracotta lions at its base. An image house with standing Buddha sculptures is nearby.

The first monastic complex to the north is **Alahana Pirivena**, the royal cremation grounds where Nissanka Malla's colossal (55 metres/180 ft) 12th-century **Rankot Vihara ℚ** (Golden Pinnacle) is modelled after the Ruwanweli. Two Brahmi inscriptions found above the ledge at **Gopata Pabbata** (Hill of the Cow Herds) – a picturesque crag of rock with a natural cave – are the earliest signs of human occupation at Polonnaruwa, dating back to the 2nd century BC. A spreading banyan tree crowns the rock with its far-reaching roots stretching down the rock face.

On the highest platform is the **Buddha Sima Pasada ℝ**, the chapter house whose sacred functions were to enforce the rules of the Sangha Buddhist sect. The impressive walls of **Lankatilaka ⓢ** image house soar to a height of 16 metres (55 ft), and the unique brickwork is of extraordinary variety. Inside

LEFT: traces of frescoes.
RIGHT: the serene head of the Gal Vihare's seated Buddha.

Map on page 262

the shrine stands the headless statue of a Buddha, and the interior walls are adorned with excellent murals. It is larger than the Thuparamaya, with a more elaborate plan. The outside walls are horizontally divided into five floors and adorned with reliefs of architectural subjects, which give an indication of the type of domed roof it would have had. Inside is a single tall space, which is still very impressive, though open to the sky.

To the north is the milk-white **Kiri Vihara** ❼, the best preserved *dagoba* with its original lime plaster stucco intact, and the remains of small structures clustered around it.

The Gal Vihara rock sculptures

Sri Lankans, whilst quick to boast of the age and size of their monuments, are strangely reticent about the artistic quality of the best. If you have come to Sri Lanka and you haven't heard of the **Gal Vihara** ⓤ you can be forgiven, although once seen it will certainly remain in your memory.

Out of a cliff-face of granite, unknown artists carved three figures of the Buddha and a chapel. The earliest figure shows the Buddha standing on a lotus plinth in the "blessing posture", his arms folded and his eyes half-closed. The sculptor was working in a material that to some extent dictated the output. Dark strata in the rock sweep contour lines across the delicately carved features of his face like the slipstream from a dream.

Later, in the reign of Parakramabahu, this image was joined by the other figures. The seated Buddha meditates cross-legged against an interesting relief of buildings, another hint of how Polonnaruwa's temples originally looked. The rock-cut chapel alongside contains a further seated Buddha surrounded by atten-

BELOW:
the Gal Vihara.

dants waving fly whisks and other decorations showing traces of paint. On the other side is the largest figure, a 14-metre (46-ft) reclining Buddha of such beauty that it inspired hundreds of years of Sinhalese art, but was never matched. Here the variations in the colour of the rock appear as a veil of ripples washing over the figure of the Buddha as he slips into Nirvana. The rock was not always kind to the sculptor; a pale line of rock has inflicted a scar on the chin of the Buddha. But the reverent tenderness with which every detail, including the bolster-like pillow, has been carved with such graceful skill that it is easy to forget how difficult the sculptor's task must have been.

Later works in this idealised style are cold and mechanical in comparison but the Gal Vihare figures manage to convey an emotional power while sustaining the most exquisite serenity. The liquid flow of the robes and the calm facial expressions are interpreted beautifully.

Northern sites

The **Demala Maha Seya** Ⓥ is a failed emulation of the giant *dagobas* of Anuradhapura, conceived by Parakramabahu I, who successfully imitated the ancient kings in most respects. If completed it would have been 191 metres (625 ft) high and would have rated as the largest of its kind in the world. The vast mound of bricks was made by Pandyan prisoners of war from Parakramabahu's Indian campaigns. The small *dagoba* on the top is the work of a later and lesser king, looking like a dwarf standing on the shoulders of a giant.

Continuing north, to the left is one of the few surviving relics of the Jetavana Monastery. The area once consisted of around 500 buildings, of which most remain unexcavated. The elegant **Lotus Pond** Ⓦ was built in tiers of eight-

BELOW: the 12th-century Lotus Pond.

petalled lotus flowers, a clever and original idea that didn't really catch on, perhaps because there were too many sharp corners for comfort. You would certainly have to watch your step climbing in, but once seated on a petal with all your fellow monks forming a circle, the whole experience must have been very refined.

The most important building in the Jetavana Monastery is the **Tivanka ⊗**, the image house which copies the style of the Thuparama and the Lankatilaka. Its walls are covered in stucco decoration depicting small temples and figures. The name derives from the image of the Buddha in the narrow antechamber which is seen in the *tivanka* or thrice bent posture. Bent at the knees, waist and shoulders to set the body in flowing diagonals, this pose denotes ease and grace, normally reserved for female statues.

The most important paintings of the Polonnaruwa period were found on the walls of the Tivanka, though since their excavation they have deteriorated for lack of proper protection. These frescoes are in a classical style unlike contemporary Indian paintings or later Sinhalese work. The colour scheme is confined to reddish brown, yellow ochre, green and white, a Pompeiian palette that gives precedence to the exquisite draughtsmanship. The *cella* is decorated with scenes from the life of the Buddha, the antechamber with incidents from the *Jataka*.

Outside there are stucco friezes of lions and a particularly delightful parade of *ganas* (dwarfs), grimacing and clowning in amusing poses, whilst apparently supporting the entire weight of the building. The majority of these frescoes date from the reign of Parakrambahu, who attempted to restore Polonnaruwa, but others are much older. ❑

Map on page 262

BELOW: cattle roam this ancient landscape.

Map on page 272

SIGIRIYA

Soaring above the surrounding plains to towering heights, the cloud-hugging rock of Sigiriya is regarded by many as one of the wonders of the world

The summit of this almost inaccessible rock was the unlikely setting for a courtly paradise of elegant pavilions, amid gardens and pools, all perched 180 metres (600 ft) above the surrounding jungle. The rock was transformed into an immense recumbent lion by the addition of a brick-built head and foreparts of which only the artfully sculptured paws remain. The impact of the Lion Rock, as it is called, must have been awesome, since even its remnants beggar belief. Executed daringly, on a stupendous scale, it prompts one to marvel at the creative vision that was behind this eighth wonder.

The creator of Sigiriya was perhaps the most interesting monarch Sri Lanka has produced – the brave, murderous and brilliant Kassapa who reigned between AD 477–495. The son of King Dhatusena, Kassapa was born to a non-royal consort. Knowing that his half-brother Moggallana, younger but of royal blood, would succeed him, he seized the throne, imprisoned Dhatusena, and later killed him for not disclosing the whereabouts of his treasures. (Patricide is considered to be one of the five great sins according to Buddhism.) Moggallana fled to India intending to return with an army.

Seven years after his ascent to the throne, Kassapa moved into his amazing palace at Sigiriya, built for defence in preparation for the revenge attack. The rock's natural defences were augmented by some ingenious strategies. Broad moats and stone perimeter walls were constructed on a scale not found elsewhere in Sri Lanka. In the event of an enemy approach, the outer moat was built so as to flood the entire area between the two moats. A boulder-catapult still stands on the summit waiting to be unleashed upon an intruder. To encourage the sentry guards to stay awake, the sentry points on the rock summit were strategically placed so that a momentary lapse of attention would send the drowsy guard plunging to his death.

One fateful day in AD 495, 18 years after seizing power, Kassapa descended to confront returning Moggallana and his army, quite a distance away from the citadel. At the height of battle, by a stroke of misfortune, Kassapa's elephant turned aside sensing a hidden swamp. Fearing that Kassapa was retreating, his army backed away, leaving him stranded. Courageous as he was, once Kassapa realised his situation he drew his sword and beheaded himself, leaving no room for capture by his enemies.

Sigiriya was not just the fortress of a paranoid tyrant, it was the palace of a ruler who wanted to assert his right to kingship with symbols, and to show through great works that he was the rightful monarch. He only had a short reign but his achievements have lasted 15 centuries.

LEFT: Sigiriya, the "Lion Rock".
BELOW: the gardens at the foot of the rock.

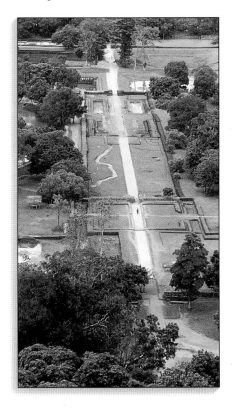

The Water Garden

The **Water Garden Ⓐ**, still well-preserved, is a combination of the hanging gardens of Babylon, the boulder gardens of China or Japan, and the water gardens of ancient Rome. The terraced gardens flow down to the boulder gardens and then to the geometrically laid out water gardens in the western precinct. With running water and fountains, pools and ponds, aquatic flowers and birds of gorgeous plumage, tropical trees in bright blossoms, these royal gardens must have been a place of serenity for mind and body.

The entire water garden is in a walled enclosure. Elaborate gatehouses made out of timber and brick masonry are marked by the cavities left by the massive timber doorposts, but nothing more survives. Almost adjacent to the western entrance is a miniaturised water garden of splendid beauty, discovered not long ago. With winding waterways, shallow reflecting pools, corbelled water courses and marbled floors, and an intricate layout of tiled roof buildings, this garden covers an area almost half the size of a football field. An ideal location to get a glimpse of the splendour of Sigiriya.

Adjacent is a central island, surrounded by four L-shaped water pools, originally almost entirely occupied by a large hall or a pavilion. These pools appear to have been used as bathing pools, with polished walls, flights of steps and surrounding terraces, similar to that of a modern day swimming pool. Reinforcing the symmetrical layout, towards the Lion Rock, are four large moated islands located on either side of the walkway. "Cool water palaces" once occupied the two inner islands.

Abutting these islands are fountains fed by waters from the artificial Sigiriya Lake under gravitational pressure. Using symmetrically perforated limestone

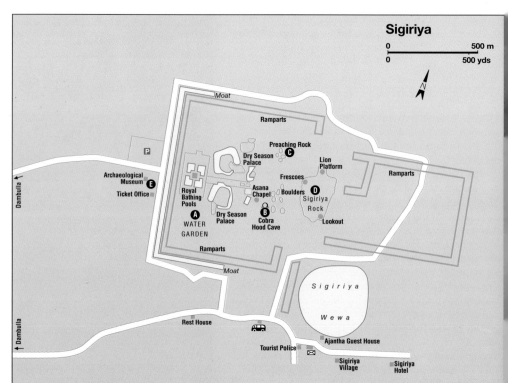

Map on page 272

plates to fashion their spouts, these fountains operate in rainy weather even today. Another remarkable pool, octagonal in shape, is hidden from the main western walkway, and adds further amazement. Surrounded by a wide terrace following its shape, the pool is sheltered by a gigantic boulder almost the height of a six storey building, a bold arrangement of water harmonising rock, with the pond located at the very point of transition from the water gardens to the boulder gardens.

The Boulder Garden

The boulder garden is in sharp contrast with the geometrical symmetry of the bordering water garden, yet the fusion of the two gardens is remarkable. With similarities to the boulder gardens of China and Japan, picturesque boulders of varying size grace this area. Linked together by winding pathways and paved passages, with boulder arches and limestone stairways, edifices of little known character stood on almost every boulder, whilst there were rock caves beneath them. The intriguing honeycombed holes on these boulders are nothing but footings for brick and timber edifices.

Equally fascinating are the rock carvings on these boulders, especially those on an enormous split boulder. On the fallen half, known as the **Audience Hall Rock**, is a 5-metre (16-ft) long carved throne facing a levelled square; and on the standing half is a water reservoir, dug into the rock, hence its name, the **Cistern Rock**. Another boulder of interest is the picturesque **Cobra Hood Cave B**, so named because of its shape. Buddhist monks from as early as the 3rd century BC used this cave, though its painted ceiling is dated to the period of Kassapa (5th century AD). The **Preaching Rock C**, located on the side of the

BELOW: the steps of the terrace garden.

SIGIRIYA – PALACE OF THE GODS?

In a brilliant exposition, Paranavitana, an eminent Sri Lankan scholar, claimed that Sigiriya was a deliberate attempt to emulate the mythical Alakamanda, the Himalayan mountain paradise of the God of Riches, Kuvera, for long associated with Anuradhapura kings. One reason for this was that Kuvera's attendant dwarves, or *ganas,* are seen on countless buildings.

According to this theory, Kassapa dwelt as Kuvera, and ruled as a god king, a concept that did not receive any religious favour, which perhaps explains why subsequent rulers never thought of making Sigiriya their abode.

Moggallana chose to rule from Anuradhapura after his victory over Kassapa, and he offered the rock, which is recorded as a Buddhist monastery in the 3rd century BC, back to the Buddhist clergy.

Thereafter, Sigiriya seems to have existed as a monastery up to the 14th century, and then disappears from history to reappear as a distant garrison of the Kandyan Kingdom in the 16th and 17th centuries.

Other questions remain unresolved, however. For example, had Sigiriya been put to any other use? Was there an observatory on the summit to gain an insight into meteorological phenomena?

Octagonal Pond, is also impressive. Its tiered platforms are believed to have been used by orating monks. Clearly, the boulder garden, with its many caves, had been used as a monastery long before Kassapa incorporated it into his royal pleasure garden.

An undated Buddhist monastery complex including a *stupa*, a *bodhigara* and an image house is located in the boulder garden area. Of particular interest is the basin at the entrance to the *bodhigara*, intended for the cleansing of feet before entering the monastery. Large trees adorn the site, especially *Halmilla* (*Berrya cordifolia*), a precious timber, characterised by its heart-shaped leaves and six winged propeller-like fruit. With terraced and turfed areas, the gardens are ideal for a short rest, either on the way to the summit or when returning, because of its central location and tranquil atmosphere.

The Terraced Gardens

Merging with the boulder garden are the terraced gardens, with each terrace rising above the other, similar to the hanging gardens of Babylon. Rubbled walls retain the mounting earth. Impressive brick-built staircases with limestone steps traverse the terraces, providing access to the uppermost terrace and onwards to the **Sigiriya Rock** itself. The once magnificent **Sigiriya Wewa** could also be reached from here. This lake is the main source of water for the water gardens. As seen today, it is only a fraction of its original size. Ancient visitors to Sigiriya had not only appreciated the frescoes but also the lake itself, as evidenced by inscriptions describing the lake as having clear water and colourful water lilies. Enjoy an evening walk on the trail along its *bund*.

It is difficult to imagine the maze of pipework buried under your feet as you

TIP

If the vertigo doesn't get you, the wasps might. The climb is made even more challenging by the Sigiriya wasps that sometimes make themselves a nuisance here.

BELOW: paws for a breath at the Lion's Platform.

stroll along. This intricate network covering the entire Sigiriya complex, with control valves, ring mains, manholes, silt traps, by-pass conduits and the like, is comparable to modern networks. Stone drains encased in clay carried water horizontally, and downpipes, made of two stone semi-circular sections held together by metal straps, carried water vertically. You will also see many open channels cut into the rock itself used for collecting water drained from the summit. Excess water overflowed to irrigate the lower areas of Sigiriya. Conservation was paramount in the minds of the Sigiriya designers.

The Gardens of Sigiriya are indeed a unique achievement, not only because of their complex hydraulics, but also because they are so well preserved, their antiquity preceded only by the ancient gardens of the Romans such as the gardens of Pompeii and Herculaneum, and the imperial gardens of Hadrian at Tivoli. The water garden, the boulder garden and the terrace garden make a harmonious picture on a grand scale.

Map on page 272

Lion's Platform

Sigiriya Rock has a half-way stage at its northern end, where a large plateau offers rest and stalls selling refreshments. The drink-seller who has climbed up the rock with his stock of bottles and cans, has earned his rupees, and you have earned a drink; but this is only the beginning.

The two enormous lion's paws are all that remains of the giant beast that gave the rock its name, for, incredible though it may seem, the entire rock was transformed into a mountainous lion by the addition of brick-built foreparts, stuccoed and presumably painted. There were originally steps leading up between the paws and into the lion's mouth. What an entrance! The sheer audac-

BELOW: fresco with a Sigiriya maiden.

BELOW: climbing onwards to the summit.

ity of the idea is breathtaking, and the surviving paws themselves are of a scale to make you shudder. They are expressively moulded, intimidating in themselves. By building this sculpture Kassapa was certainly trying to intimidate his enemies, but at the same time he was also claiming his kingship over the "lion race" – the Sinhalese.

Mirror Wall

Above the Lion's Platform and beneath the fresco pockets is the highly polished Mirror Wall. Coated with polished lime, this wall reflects like glass, even 1500 years after it was built.

Scribbled on the surface of the Mirror Wall are nearly 1,500 pieces of prose and poetry composed by the ancient visitors who flocked to Sigiriya from all over the island. These poems, which testify to the sightseers' appreciation of art and beauty, were written between the 7th and 13th centuries and are said to be Sri Lanka's oldest graffiti. Most of the graffiti is written in Sinhalese, but some of the poems are written in Sanskrit and Tamil. Apart from the very obvious beauty of the fresco pockets, the scribblers must have been inspired by the sight of the regal lion, the majestic castle, the exquisite ponds of the water gardens, the lovely Sigiriya lake, and also by the other visitors, especially the beautiful maidens who climbed Sigiriya to savour its splendour.

A vivid picture of Sigiriya and its grandeur during Kassapa's reign and thereafter is reflected in this graffiti. Sigiriya was not only a place of worship but also a haven of pleasure for many who visited after his death. It was a lovers' rendezvous and a place of merriment for early sightseers who thronged to Sigiriya. Indeed, this graffiti is a repository of evidence for the study of history, culture, and language.

Remarkable frescoes

Fascinating amongst the pictorial art of Sigiriya are the glamourously sensuous paintings of feminine beauty. This was a daring endeavour by Kassapa, since Sri Lankan art was inspired by Buddhism, a religion that preaches the cessation of lust to achieve ever-lasting happiness.

These figures of women, some of golden colour and others dark, pictured in isolation or in pairs, are depicted as rising from clouds and are known as "the cloud damsels". Somewhat less than life-size, they are depicted in three-quarter profile. One has to examine the paintings in detail to enjoy their loveliness; striking diversity in mood and personality, face and body, clothes and make-up can be seen. Indeed, these differences are truly remarkable. Flowers are used in profusion in their hair, in baskets, and in various forms. Whilst these flowers enhance their sensual charm, one wonders whether the painters of Sigiriya added these deliberately to compare the beauty of a woman's face, the softness of her skin and the beauty of her body, with that of a fresh flower.

Originally there were some 500-odd paintings drawn across the precipitous face of the Sigiriya rock, forming a gigantic gallery of paintings which covered an area almost twice as large as a football field.

Extending as a wide band from the western face of the rock to its northeast corner, these paintings may perhaps be the largest mural ever attempted by man. Painted mainly on the open face of the rock, with drip-ledges for protection, only a few survive; 23, to be exact.

Map on page 272

These remarkable remains, in an extremely good state of preservation, are located in a rock pocket above the Lion's Plateau, reached today by a spiral staircase. The remnants of the layered plaster coats on which these paintings have been drawn in tempera are still visible, some on the open western face of the rock. These frescoes were of such quality that visitors from all corners of Sri Lanka thronged to Sigiriya. Recent archaeological explorations have unearthed miniature terracotta figurines of these beautiful ladies. About 10 to 20 cm (4–8 inches) long, these must have been produced to be carried away as souvenirs by those who visited Sigiriya. The Sigiriya beauties have long waists, narrow hips, and thin faces – with expressions suggesting a seriousness of purpose.

What were the real reasons for these paintings at Sigiriya? There are many. Whilst some have portrayed these damsels as ladies of Kassapa's court in a devotional procession to the nearby shrine at Pidurangala, others have suggested that they are *apsaras* (celestial nymphs) in keeping with South Indian traditions. Another suggestion is that they represent clouds and lightning moving about the peak of Mount Kailasa. Archaeological explorations would provide greater evidence to resolve this mystery.

Surprisingly, these are not the only paintings at Sigiriya. Though less well preserved, later works were found in caves in the boulder garden. These paintings differ from those found on the upper rock surface. For example, the paintings on the high ceiling of the Cobra Hood cave combine geometrical shapes and motifs into a harmonious whole.

BELOW: the view of the gardens from the summit.

The palace on the summit

Would you dare climb a multi-storey building without a lift? Reaching the summit of Sigiriya is a similar feat! Emerging from the jaws of a regal lion, now destroyed by the torrential downpours and gusty winds it has suffered over 15 centuries, visitors set foot on forbidden territory, once reserved exclusively for royal use.

A unique palace, with layout and ground plan clearly visible, it is strikingly different to those found in Anuradharapura and Polonnaruwa. Whilst the inner palace occupies the high western sections, the outer palace occupies the lower eastern sections, and the palace gardens cover the south, they all converge on a large and lovely rock-cut pool, probably used for water storage. With thousands of marbled steps and walkways, this 1.2-hectare (3-acre) site is stupendous and the views breathtaking.

Rediscovered in the first decade of the 19th century, planned antiquarian research began only during the early years of the 20th century. Recent excavations and restoration work under the "Cultural Triangle Project" sponsored by UNESCO have aroused much interest. The **Archaeological Museum ❺**, just west of the water gardens outside the main complex, bears some of the fruits of this labour. ❏

FRESCOES: LANKA'S ANCIENT ART

An extensive collection of wall paintings offering insight into ancient lifestyles exists in the image houses and preaching halls of Buddhist temples

The survival of art from prehistoric times is a rare phenomenon since the materials used for pigment were perishable. But wall paintings by Sri Lanka's first inhabitants, the Veddhas, are found in 33 rockshelter sites, portraying stylised animal forms, hunting figures and symbolic motifs. They offer an insight into primitive imagination and lifestyles.

Lanka's tradition of wall painting dates from the 2nd century BC and continues up to the 20th century. Many of the later frescoes have the detail of Indian miniatures, with the complexity of a Russian icon. They provide a record of upperclass social life of the time, including architectural detail and social customs. All have been well preserved in image houses, relic chambers of *stupas* and monastic residences.

Sri Lanka's murals fall into three distinct categories. Firstly, there are the early fragmentary paintings, which include the female figures from the 5th-century palace of Sigiriya. Secondly, there are the murals of the Kandyan school, which arose from 1750–1815, before British colonisation, whose style has been preserved largely thanks to a renaissance in Buddhist art. Lastly, there is the Southern tradition, which used much decorative detail, with costumes reflecting significant changes occurring with Portuguese and Dutch invasion.

▷ **DOWN SOUTH**
Purvarama temple at Kataluva, whose murals may have taken four years to paint, has some of the finest examples from the Southern tradition.

△ **TALL TALES**
The shrine room at the Weherahena temple employs the technique of elongated strip narration depicting tales from the Buddha's life.

◁ **THE LAST KINGS**
The Kandyan tradition used heavy line work to create visual impact, using only red and yellow against monochromatic backgrounds.

△ **ROCK CAVERN**
The most magnificent cave temple is at Dambulla. Its gilded interior murals follow the natural rock so closely that they are often mistaken for cloth.

Art from the 5th century is extremely rare because organic pigments do not often survive thousands of years. In many temples, ancient art has been over-painted in more recent times in a style which makes the Buddhist texts easily intelligible to today's worshipper.

Since attaining World Heritage recognition as the Eighth Wonder of the World, the ancient rock palace of Sigiriya, with its bare-breasted queens and ladies-in-waiting, received priority restoration treatment on account of its great age, beauty and rarity. Of the original 550 figures, only 23 remain today due to vandalism through the centuries. These damsels, who are thought to represent clouds and thunder, are notable for being the only non-religious frescoes in Sri Lanka.

The Sigiriya artists used a mix of alluvial clay, paddy husks, sand, lime and vegetable fibres to paint onto three layers of plaster. For colour they used vegetable dyes, in a style similar to the Ajanta rock paintings of India. To view these legendary ladies at their glowing best, visit the temple in soft late afternoon light.

▷ **SUBHODRAMA**
A little-known temple in a Colombo suburb has naïve figures costumed in textiles and geometric motifs juxtaposed with Grecian cherubs.

▽ **LADIES-IN-WAITING**
These heavenly women of Sigiriya displaying ornate jewellery were painted 1,500 years ago to decorate King Kassapa's fortress.

THE EAST COAST

Sri Lanka's entrancing eastern seaboard stretches for more than 300 km (200 miles), providing solitude and superb scenery, but must be treated with caution

Map on page 150–1

Even the place-names of the East Coast sound different from the rest of the jaw-breaking names of the island; Passekudah, Sittandikundi, Valkarai, Kalmunai, Kokkilai – all seem like noises made by the wind. Trincomalee derives its name from the Tamil words *tiru-kona-malai*, meaning mountain sacred to Konesvara.

Trincomalee

This famous harbour, one of the largest and best sheltered in the world, has at various times been the envy of the Danes, Dutch, Portuguese, British, French and Japanese. During World War II it became a naval base to protect the fleet of the combined Allied Powers.

The British explorer Samuel Baker described it thus: "Few things surpass the tropical beauty of this harbour, lying completely land-locked, it forms a glassy lake surrounded by hills covered with the waving foliage of cocoa-nut trees and palms of great variety. The white bungalows with their red-tiled roofs, are dotted about along the shore, and two or three men of war are usually resting at their ease in this calm retreat…"

The men of war in the water these days are of the fishy variety. In July in particular large numbers of Portuguese man-of-war drift towards the shore, many becoming stranded on the beaches. Touch them at your peril for they are known to paralyse their victims with their sting.

The mention of Trincomalee to any Sri Lankan is likely to induce wistful sighs and longing looks as they picture the water, warm as tea and clear as gin, the skies as pink as paradise, and jungles where wild elephants roam. Sadly, it is these impenetrable jungles that have enabled the Tamil Tigers to infiltrate the area.

Safety first

The safest way to get here is either by a 30-minute flight on the Lionair route from Colombo or by chauffeur-driven car. The train from Fort Station takes seven hours but it is vulnerable to attacks by guerrillas hiding in the jungles and is not recommended for tourists. A couple of hotels now offer to transport their guests to and from Trincomalee by car.

Since the security situation changes constantly it is essential to get up-to-date information on travel to Trinco when you arrive in Colombo. Whatever you do, don't arrive by bus or train after dusk, as this is when the attacks on public transport usually occur.

A small clutch of guest houses is beginning to establish itself, and the town is waking up despite its war wounds. The Tamil locals who fled to India at

PRECEDING PAGES: the Tirukonesvaram Kovil in Trincomalee **LEFT:** fishing boats near Kuchchaveli. **BELOW:** fish drying in the sun.

Trinco provided safe harbour for Jane Austen's "problem" brother, Sir Charles, who is buried at the St Stevens cemetery alongside a certain PB Molesworth, the first manager of Ceylon Rail, who dabbled in astronomy while living in Trinco and discovered the Red Spot on Jupiter.

the height of the troubles are now returning to their home villages, under the auspices of the United Nations which houses the refugees in a local camp until it is safe for them to return to their homes. The town bustles with markets, general stores and numerous small tailor's shops, whose old treadle machines buzz with activity.

The Trincomalee Rest House, on the corner of Fort Frederick Road near the old Town Hall, has cheap accommodation and meals if you are looking for somewhere to stay, but there is not a great deal of interest in the town itself. **Fort Frederick**, originally built by the Portuguese, is now used as a barracks and is also home to a herd of wild spotted deer.

Lover's Leap

At the end of the road is **Swami Rock**, also known locally as Lover's Leap, on account of a Dutch official's daughter, Francina Van Reede, who threw herself off the rock after watching her unfaithful husband desert her by sea. Although her suicide attempt was unsuccessful, and she went on to marry for a second time eight years after her near-fatal fall, her father erected a pillar to mark the incident. At the end of the spit stands a Hindu temple which contains the temple lingam of an older temple thrown into the sea by the Portuguese in 1624, and later recovered by divers.

Inside the portals of the fort is a large residence known as **Wellington House**. In 1799 Arthur Wellesley stayed in Trincomalee to rest and recover from a bout of malaria after fighting Tippu Sultan in South India. He found his billet so comfortable that he managed to miss the boat to take him home. Since the ship sank in the Gulf of Aden with the loss of all hands, it was a fortunate mishap.

BELOW: buffaloes wallowing in mud.

Wellesley soon became the Duke of Wellington, and Wellesley Lodge was re-named Wellington House to reflect the new position of its famous resident.

The Mahaweli Ganga, Sri Lanka's longest river, begins at Adams Peak and finally reaches the sea about 12 km (7 miles) south of the town at the scenic **Koddiyar Bay**. If the ferry is running across the bay it is worth sailing to the Muslim town of **Mutur** to see a stone at the foot of an old tree bearing the inscription: "This is White Man's Tree, under which Robert Knox, Captain of the ship *Ann* was captured AD 1660. Knox was held captive by the Kandyan king for 19 years. This stone was placed here in 1893." The Robert Knox referred to here was the father of the young seaman who later related his tale of imprisonment by Rajasinha II in his *Historical Relation of Ceylon*. It is thought this book became the inspiration behind Daniel Defoe's *Robinson Crusoe*.

If you head southeast to **Toppur** you will come across the ancient Buddhist site of **Seruwawila**, built in the 3rd century BC by the Sinhalese King Kavantissa to enshrine the front collar bone of the Buddha.

Map on page 150–1

The perfect beach

The small fishing villages of **Nilaveli** and **Uppuveli**, north of Trincomalee, are still considered safe and the best places to stay at the time of writing. The wide stretches of soft white sand make a stunning location for bathing and basking. The Shahira Hotel at the 10th milepost has 27 simply furnished rooms just set back from the beach. A couple of kilometres further on is the Nilaveli Beach Hotel with 80 rooms, including a few deluxe and some luxury suites, most with ocean views. These are the only hotels to survive the ups and downs of the ethnic conflict and even they are only half full. The local fishermen are friendly, and from here you can hire a boat to take you to **Pigeon Island**, an islet where the rare blue rock pigeon breeds, and a paradise for snorkelling and skin diving.

If you enjoy wildlife, the Nilaveli Beach Hotel can (depending on security at the time) organise trips to **Bundala**, a sanctuary for flamingos, elephants and other wildlife. Much closer by is the vast shallow lagoon of **Kokkilai**, a bird sanctuary for such common species as wild pelicans, ducks and flamingos. Visitors will find that a rubber dingy is an ideal way to navigate the marshes.

The Hot Springs at **Kanniyai** are 8 km (5 miles) inland on the Anuradhapura road and are known for their therapeutic qualities. The coolest spring is 29°C (84°F) and the hottest not more than 46°C (115°F). The Tamils believe they were created by Vishnu and named after the mother of Ravanna, the demon king, to enable Vishnu to perform an ablutionary rite on his mother. Devout Hindus come here to perform religious rites after a loved one has died.

Batticaloa and the south east

Batticaloa, the next largest town on the coast, is famed for its singing fish. It is surrounded by a massive lagoon where a unique network of canals and waterways created from up-country rivers flow down towards the sea. There is an age-old controversy about the source of the sounds from this lagoon, which are

Wayside Hindu shrine.

BELOW: buffalo curd setting in shallow earthenware pots.

Map on pages 150–51

The East Coast receives a drenching from the northeast monsoons between October and January, but otherwise it is drier than the west.

RIGHT: East Coast traffic jam.
BELOW: the Lover's Leap at Swami Rock.

heard very clearly between April and September on moonlit nights. Some say the orchestra is made up of topsail catfish which congregate on the bed of the lagoon; others swear the sound comes from tides rushing through empty mollusc shells or fretted rocks. Place your ear on an oar thrust into the water to hear the full concerto.

For the time being "Batti", as it is known locally, is classified as a trouble spot owing to its mainly Tamil and Muslim population. It was hit by a cyclone in the late 1970s and this devastation was compounded by ethnic conflict. At the time of writing, Batticaloa is out of bounds to tourists.

Near Batticaloa, about 32 km (20 miles) north of the town, are two immaculate beaches where the waters are safe and crystal clear, thanks to a protective offshore reef that calms the waters. The white sandy crescent of **Kalkudah Bay** is splendid for children. There is a rest house at **Passekudah Bay** but it is currently closed due to the hostilities. Further down the coast, a short way south of Pottuvil, is **Arugam Bay** with its own picturesquely sited rest house by the sea. There are no offshore reefs here, so the waves can be dangerous for swimmers but great for experienced surfers. A Danish couple used to run a small hotel called the Stardust Club which was very popular with surfers (and may well be so again), but sadly it is also off limits to visitors at time of writing.

Although much of the East Coast is too dangerous to visit – and even those areas which are considered reasonably safe are not equipped for the demanding traveller – it does offer miles of beautiful unspoiled tropical beaches and vast areas of untamed jungle. If you can face the spiky sea urchins and the jelly fish, and can cope with the area's proximity to the stomping ground of the Tamil Tigers, you may very well be pleasantly surprised. ❑

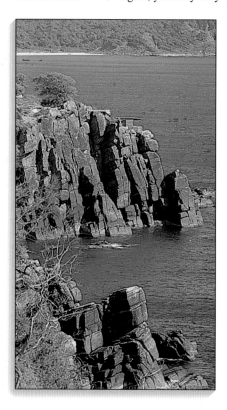

JAFFNA AND THE NORTH

The north of Sri Lanka has been ravaged by the civil war which has put a stop to any tourism, though this was minimal even before the conflict started. The Railway Ferry to India used to bring a few intrepid overlanders to **Mannar Island** but this dry and barren spot had few attractions, and the trains went straight through. The ferry has since ceased to make the short crossing to India.

Jaffna was fought over by the Portuguese and Dutch in 1658 in a prolonged siege. The population has recently suffered an even more prolonged siege, and much of the city, including a priceless library, has been destroyed. The independent Tamil kingdom was founded in the 15th century by Sempaha Perumal, whose royal palace stood at **Nallur**, 3 km (2 miles) from Jaffna Fort. Here the Kandaswamy Temple holds a spectacular festival in August when the chariot of Skanda is pulled along by thousands of devotees.

Evidence of an ancient Buddhist past is found at **Kantharodai**, where 100 miniature *dagobas* are clustered together. They are thought to be 2,000 years old, but their function is not known. Locals fervently hope that peace will soon come to the area, and with it a few more adventurous travellers.

INSIGHT GUIDES
Travel Tips

...AND THE LOCAL TIME AT YOUR DESTINATION IS 1

A MEMBER IN STAR ALLIANCE

S | M | O | O | T | H |

A.D.

Your specially tailored
Royal Orchid Holidays begin
the moment you board
when you fly with THAI,
official carrier to
Amazing Thailand.

Simply travelling safely

American Express Travellers Cheques

- are recognised as one of the safest and most convenient ways to protect your money when travelling abroad

- are more widely accepted than any other travellers cheque brand

- are available in eleven currencies

- are supported by a 24 hour worldwide refund service and

- a 24 hour Express Helpline service provides assistance and information when travelling abroad

- are accepted in millions of shops, hotels and restaurants throughout the world

Travellers Cheques

CONTENTS

Getting Acquainted

The Place

Situation Described as the "pearl of the Indian ocean", Sri Lanka lies between the northern latitudes 5°55' and 9°55' and the eastern longitudes 79°42' and 81°52', 650 kilometres (403 miles) north of the equator. The southernmost tip of India is located 30 kilometres (19 miles) to the northeast. To the south, there is nothing until Antarctica.

Capital The capital Colombo is the political, economic and cultural centre. Kandy is the unofficial capital of the Hill Country, as it was the last stronghold of the Sinhalese kingdoms.

Highest mountain Pidurutalagala, 2,524 m (8,200 ft).

Languages The official languages are Sinhala, Tamil and English. Many signposts bear all three.

Time Zone Sri Lanka Standard Time is 5 hours and 30 minutes ahead of Greenwich Mean Time. (Allowances should be made for summer time changes.)

International dialling code +94

Population

Sri Lanka has a population of roughly 18 million, with a population density of 270 people per sq km, one of the highest figures in Asia. With free education and healthcare, the literacy rate is 88.6 percent, again, one of the highest in Asia, and the infant mortality rate is one of the lowest. Life expectancy is 74 years for women and 69 for men. 56 percent of the population are under 25 years of age.

The majority of people live in the south-western regions. Much of the rural population works in agriculture and subsistence farming, or along the coast, fishing. There are vast differences in the distribution of capital and poverty is more of a problem in the inner-city areas, where living conditions in slums are giving rise to an increase in crime.

There are a number of ethnic groups in Sri Lanka. The Sinhalese, descendants of northern Indians who sailed to the island in the 6th century BC, amount to roughly 74 percent of the population. Sinhalese are mainly Buddhists, although some are Christian. The Tamils amount to roughly 18 percent, including both "Indian" and "Sri Lankan" Tamils. The latter are descendants of the ancient warriors who came from India to fight the Sinhalese for land over 1,000 years ago. The "Indian" Tamils came in the 19th century, employed by the British colonists to work on tea estates. Tamils are mainly Hindus.

Muslims account for seven percent of the population. These are mostly Moors (descendants of Arab and Indian Muslim traders during the Portuguese era) or Malays (descendants of Southeast Asian Muslims brought over during the Dutch era). A small percentage are more recent arrivals from India.

The Burghers are Christian descendants of the Dutch and Portuguese invaders but their numbers have decreased in recent years. The Veddhas, the indigenous inhabitants, were almost completely assimilated by the Sinhalese and their lifestyle has been largely destroyed. Sindhi and Parsee residents from India can also be found here.

Although over the centuries there has undoubtedly been much intermixing, Sri Lankans are very proud of their cultural heritage, whatever it may be.

Geography & Climate

This tear-shaped land mass spans 430 km (267 miles) north to south, 225 km (140 miles) east to west with an area of 65,608 sq km (25,322 sq miles).

Roughly 1,330 km (825 miles) of palm-fringed yellow-sand coastline provides an attractive landfall. The south-central Hill Country slopes down into the coastal plain. The arid north-central and northern plain extends up to the northern tip.

The island has an unusual blend of climatic features. It is possible to travel from tropical heat to cool, misty hills, then to the dry zone, all in one day. There are two main monsoon seasons, one in the northeast, the other in the southwest. While the northeastern monsoon blows, the southwestern side experiences peak weather and vice versa, so the weather is always perfect somewhere on the island.

The southwest monsoon, or *Yala*, brings rain from the Indian Ocean from May to September, commencing with a month of heavy rain, followed by short showers. At this time the coastal tides are dangerous and swimming is inadvisable – even the fishermen avoid it. *Maha*, the northeastern monsoon, blows in from the Bay of Bengal.

An inter-monsoon period in October and November can bring thunder-storms to any part of the country. However, most days are sunny and humid, so short bursts of heavy rain are a pleasure, bringing welcome coolness and freshness. These intense, short-lived showers fill up myriad small lakes and perfume the air with the smell of damp soil and bruised frangipani blossoms.

The low-lying southern coastal regions experience the warmest temperatures. Colombo averages 27°C (81°F). The sea remains at 27°C all year round. In the central highlands, temperatures become noticeably cooler and the nights can be decidedly chilly. At 305 m (1,000 ft) Kandy averages 20°C (68°F), and Nuwara Eliya, at 1890 m (6,200 ft), 16°C (61°F). These lush regions are home to tea plantations. The Mahaweli is the island's longest river.

Economy

Agriculture is the economy's basis, with rice as a major food crop, although some rice is imported.

The main export crop is the world renowned Ceylon tea. The newly implemented privatisation of the formerly nationalised plantations has seen a dramatic increase in cultivation. Tea crops are predicted to show an increase of up to 30 percent for 1998, and a 15 percent increase for 1999. The increase shown in 1997 was dramatic due to price rises, improved productivity and efficiency and a decline in costs, creating profits of up to 142 million rupees.

Other chief crops are rubber, coconuts and spices (mainly cinnamon), accounting for roughly a third of the island's exports. Gems, particularly Sri Lankan sapphires, are another major industry.

Currency

The Sri Lankan rupee is divided into 100 cents. There are notes and coins of many denominations and it is best to familiarise yourself with them: many of the notes are similar to look at. The most common error is mistaking the 500 rupee note for the 100 rupee one. When held up to the light the notes have the watermark of the Sinhalese lion.

Anywhere on the subcontinent, the term *lakh* denotes a sum of 100,000. The term is usually used in reference to money. Therefore, one lakh equals 100,000 rupees.

Government

The Democratic Socialist Republic of Sri Lanka is the current name of the former British Colony of Ceylon. The President, HE Mrs Chandrika Bandaranaike Kumaranatunga, is a representative of the People's Alliance Party, a coalition of several political parties which won a sweeping victory over the ruling United National Party. Her mother, Mrs Sirimavo Bandaranaike, was the world's first female Prime Minister.

Religion

There are four major religions in Sri Lanka – Buddhism, Hinduism, Christianity and Islam. Most people are Buddhist and the exquisite ancient temples are a focal point for many visitors. Breathtaking mosques and Hindu *kovils* can also be sighted around the island, as well as churches erected by the European colonists. If you wish to attend religious services, your local consulate may provide a list of establishments.

Public Holidays

Sri Lanka has a large number of holidays, so it is wise to arm yourself with a local calendar and plan your days accordingly. The Tourist Board publishes an annual Calendar of Events which provides a full listing of all notable dates and holidays. Travelling over a long weekend can be a nuisance, as services of buses and trains are likely to be delayed, overcrowded and frequently cancelled.

Alcohol cannot be purchased in shops on *Poya* days, and is not served in bars, except by prior arrangement with your hotel.

Culture & Customs

Courtesy is an inherent part of Sri Lankan culture – the warmth and hospitality of the people has always delighted visitors. Today, culture being an amalgamation of modern behavioural patterns and ancient beliefs, there are certain noteworthy points for visitors who wish to extend their courtesy.

When entering holy areas, it is customary to remove your shoes and walk barefoot within the designated area. (This may also be the case in people's homes.) Women should wear long skirts or loose trousers and a modest blouse, or a loose cotton dress. Men should wear long trousers. Even ancient temples are considered sacred, and should be treated as such.

Holidays

Public, bank, *Poya* (full moon) and mercantile holidays:
January
14 Tamil Thai Pongal
Duruthu Full Moon
February
4 National day
Maha Sivarathri
March
Medin Full Moon *Poya*
March/April
Good Friday
April
Sinhala and Tamil New
Year's Eve
Sinhala and Tamil New
Year's Day
Id-Ul-Fitr (Ramadan)
Bak Full Moon *Poya*
May
1 May Day
22 National Heroes' Day
Wesak Festival
May Day following Wesak
June
Id-Ul-Alha (Haj festival)
Poson Full Moon *Poya*
July
Esala Full Moon *Poya*
August
Nikini Full moon *Poya*
September
Milan-Un-Nabi (Holy
Prophet's birthday)
Binara Full Moon *Poya*
October
Wap Full Moon *Poya*
November
Deepavali
Full Moon *Poya*
December
Unduwap Full Moon *Poya*
25 Christmas
31 Special bank holiday

If you encounter a Buddhist monk or a Hindu *swami* and would like to greet him in the traditional way, hold your hands together as if in prayer and raise them to your forehead. Do not shake hands. If you wish to offer a gift to a monk, do so with both hands to show that it is given freely. (Gifts of money should be placed directly in the temple box.) When sitting with a Buddhist monk, try and sit at a lower level to him and avoid pointing your toes towards him, as this is seen as a lack of respect.

Culture also stems from livelihood and environment and so changes from place to place. As long as you show friendliness and courtesy, people will reciprocate. The questions Sri Lankans ask in conversation can be different to those asked by Westerners and may be considered as quite personal or rude by the foreigner. For instance, it is not unusual for people to ask you your age, marital status and the number of children and siblings you have in their first conversation. These are ordinary questions and simply reflect the emphasis Sri Lankans place on family life. People may also enquire about your religious beliefs, due to the emphasis on religion within their own culture.

Some Westerners instantly relax into the strolling pace of life in Sri Lanka, while others find it difficult to adjust to the ambling lack of time structure. Up-market hotels and establishments tend to have a more Western approach to time-keeping.

Body Language

The mannerisms of the people are another factor to take into account in communications. For example, the famous head "waggle" of the Indian subcontinent manages to confuse almost every foreign visitor. As in many parts of the world, shaking the head from side to side indicates a negative, while a nod indicates a positive response. However, the "waggle", a cross between a nod and a shake with the chin pointed outwards indicates a simple "yes" or "okay".

In Sri Lanka, eating with your hands is quite usual and considered appropriate. However, food should be handled with the right hand only, as the left is considered unclean. When handing objects to another person, either the right hand or both hands should be used.

Sri Lankans are also likely to stare at anyone new, which is not considered rude in the same way as it is in the West. Expect to be stared at by locals, but do not be offended by it – it simply shows that people are interested by you and your difference to them.

Electricity

Sri Lanka uses 230–240 volts, 50 cycles, alternating current. Most outlets are three-pronged and you are unlikely to find an American-type adaptor, so bring one with you.

If you are travelling with a laptop computer, bring a stabiliser as power often fluctuates, even in the cities, a laptop plug and adaptor.

It is also best to bring a hairdryer with you, and a powerful flashlight in case of electricity failures.

Weights & Measures

Sri Lanka officially converted from the English Standard system to the Metric system in late 1981.

The road system has markers with the distances shown on them, but to complicate matters, in the early 1980s most major roads were marked in kilometres, while secondary ones were marked in miles.

Business Hours

In Sri Lanka, most government offices are open by 8.30am at the latest and are closed by 4.30pm.

Most shops are open by 10am and close by 6pm during the week and on Saturday. During Christmas and New Year they remain open much longer. All shops and banks remain closed on public, bank and mercantile holidays, such as *Poya*. Also, most shops close on Sunday, or are open until 2pm.

Banks are open from 9am to 1.30pm, although some have later hours. Seylan Bank is open until 8pm and is open on Saturday from 9am to 11am. Many local and some foreign banks have automatic teller machines, so cash may be withdrawn using a teller card.

Planning the Trip

Visas

Nationals from over 50 countries do not require a visa to stay in Sri Lanka for a period of 30 days if arriving as tourists, and can extend their stay for another 30 days. These include the United Kingdom, France, Canada, Germany, the Netherlands and Japan. Nationals from Australia, New Zealand, Malaysia and the Philippines, among others, are entitled to 90 days as tourists, with the entitlement to extend for another 90 days. Check with your travel agent for the requirements. If you do require a visa, you can obtain one from a Sri Lankan Consular office, or, in the absence of one, through a British Consular office.

Visa extensions are given at the Department of Emigration and Immigration at Station Road, Bambalapitiya. The charge is based on what your own country charges a visiting Sri Lankan. Conditions for extensions are an onward ticket and proof of sufficient money for maintenance while in the country, at US$15 a day. Proof of money spent in the country may be required, so keep all traveller's cheque encashment receipts. Be warned – even the simplest matter takes an hour or two at this non-computerised visa office, where your application travels around the office to be processed by numerous operatives.

Customs Regulations

If you are bringing in over US$5,000, it should be declared at customs on arrival. Valuable equipment, gems and jewellery

More colour
for the world.

HDCplus. New perspectives in colour photography.

Probably the <u>most</u> <u>important</u> TRAVEL TIP you will ever receive

Before you travel abroad, make sure that you and your family are protected from diseases that can cause serious health problems.

For instance, you can pick up *hepatitis A* which infects 10 million people worldwide every year (it's not just a disease of poorer countries) simply through consuming contaminated food or water!

What's more, in many countries if you have an accident needing medical treatment, or even dental treatment, you could also be at risk of infection from *hepatitis B* which is 100 times more infectious than AIDS, and can lead to liver cancer.

The good news is, you can be protected by vaccination against these and other serious diseases, such as *typhoid, meningitis* and *yellow fever.*

Travel safely! Check with your doctor at least 8 weeks before you go, to discover whether or not you need protection.

Consult your doctor before you go... not when you return!

SB
SmithKline Beecham
VACCINES

Produced as a service to public health

should also be declared. Duty free allowances permit up to 2 litres of spirits, 2 bottles of wine, 200 cigarettes or 50 cigars and perfume in a quantity for personal use. Personal equipment such as radios, sports equipment, laptop computers, photographic equipment and so on is allowed. Import of illegal drugs, firearms or pornography of any form is an offence. Many bags are physically examined prior to departure and on arrival and all bags are x-rayed. If gems are purchased in Sri Lanka, keep the receipts.

Currency Restraints

Visitors are required to declare the amount of foreign currency they are bringing into the country upon arrival, on the official Exchange Control Form D, attached to the landing card. The card should be kept with you, as it is required to change foreign currency into rupees. In some instances, however, your passport is sufficient. Each time money is exchanged it is recorded on the form, or you should obtain a receipt. Do NOT lose your form or receipts, as rupees cannot be taken out of the country, and without your form you will be unable to exchange any unspent rupees.

What to Wear

In the intense heat of the low country regions, cottons and light natural fabrics such as linen are ideal. However, remember that in a conservative culture like this, skimpy skirts and brief shorts are not the norm or considered respectable, so if you do wear such items, be prepared for many stares and even a certain amount of hassle, especially outside tourist areas.

Take loose cotton skirts or trousers and tops, and a long dress or skirt and long-sleeved blouse for visiting temples. Men will feel comfortable in cotton trousers or shorts and a T-shirt or even the traditional sarong. Once you've

Embassies and Consulates in Sri Lanka

Australia
Sri Lankan High Commission
35, Empire Circuit
Forest, Canberra ACT 2603
Tel: 062 239 7041/2
Canada
Sri Lankan Commission
85, Range Road
Sandringham,
Ottawa KLM 816
Tel: 233 8440
Germany
Sri Lankan Embassy

Rolandstrasse 52,
5300 Bonn, 2
Tel: 0228 33205
United Kingdom
Sri Lankan High Commission
13, Hyde Park Gardens
London W2 2LU
Tel: 0171 262 1841
United States
Embassy of Sri Lanka
2148, Wyoming Avenue NW
Washington DC 20008
Tel: 202 483 4025/9

mastered the art of tying it, you may find it is cool and comfortable, and it also doubles as a changing tent on the beach! Take a sunhat and a good pair of sunglasses to protect against the ferocious afternoon glare and sandals, slippers or open shoes that are easy to slip on and off. If you intend to spend some time in the hills, take a couple of light sweaters or sweat-shirts. If you wish to visit areas such as Nuwara Eliya or Horton Plains, famous for their scenic trails, bring along a sturdy pair of walking shoes or trainers.

Travel light, as Western clothes are inexpensive and readily available – garments for many European chains (such as Gap, Marks and Spencer and C&A) are manufactured locally (*see Shopping section*).

If you are travelling with children, bring loose cottons for them and long-sleeved cotton tops to protect them from mosquito bites. Avoid jersey fabrics unless you intend to spend time in the hils. A sun hat, with straps that tie below the chin is also useful. Avoid bringing many white garments unless you intend to wash them by hand.

What to Bring

Sun protection should be number one on your holiday shopping list (good tanning lotion and sunscreen are hard to come by in Sri Lanka). If you plan to stay in inexpensive hotels, you may be glad to have a

travel-mosquito net. Bring along your favourite toiletries, as Western brands tend to be more expensive in Sri Lanka. Don't forget to bring a good travel wallet that you can wear under your clothing.

For Children
Nappies are also expensive but training pants can be a good alternative, as fewer layers of clothing make it quick and easy to clean your children. Buggies tend not to be so useful due to the condition of many of the roads and pavements, so a strong hands-free carrier would be useful. A couple of small tupperware containers are handy for packing meals and a spray atomiser of mineral water helps to cool children quickly and efficiently. A fabric mesh food cover also doubles as a portable, mini-mosquito net for babies.

Health

Officials do not require certificates of immunization unless you have passed through an infected area within 14 days prior to your arrival. It is recommended that travellers have standard vaccinations. Apart from these, cholera immunization is suggested. Anti-malaria tablets prescribed by your doctor should be started about a week before you plan to arrive and continued for at least two weeks after you depart, depending on the brand you have been prescribed. Additionally, mosquito repellents can be taken with you. Citronella oil, readily available in Sri Lanka, is an effective natural repellent.

Sun and Heat

Sri Lanka is a favourite destination for holidaymakers who want a sun-and-sea break. However, it won't be much of a holiday if you don't take adequate precautions against sunburn.

The heat is intense, especially in the afternoon when the sun is best avoided altogether. Use a maximum protection sunblock or tanning lotion that has a high protection factor. If you go out in the midday sun, take a large hat or a parasol (Sri Lankans often use umbrellas).

It is vital to drink plenty of fluids in the humid Sri Lankan climate, to avoid dehydration. Don't drink tap water at all, unless you know for a fact that it has been boiled. Many restaurants claim that their table water is boiled, but stick to bottled water or bottled or canned fruit juices and carbonated drinks to avoid any risk.

Mineral water is available at most restaurants and in all supermarkets. Stock up with small bottles to carry with you when you are out during the day. Avoid fresh fruit juices and cordials which tend to be made with tap water.

The best drink possible is King Coconut water – *thambili* – drunk straight from the shell. It is safe, a great thirst quencher, widely available and has remarkable rehydrating properties. Locals claim that if stranded on a desert island with nothing to eat except *thambili*, you would not only survive, but thrive!

If you start feeling the effects of excessive sun such as nausea, dizziness and headaches, find somewhere shady to rest, drink something cool, eat some salt and bathe your face in cool water.

Stomach Upsets

Diarrhoea can wreck a holiday, but can be avoided with a little care. Wash and peel fruit, and avoid raw vegetables unless they have been washed in boiled water. If you are

prone to "Delhi-Belly" carry some Lomatil or Pepto-Bismal with you.

Getting There

By Air

The main airport in Sri Lanka is Bandaranaike Memorial International Airport, more commonly known as the Katunayake International Airport. It is the only international airport on the island and is located 34 km (21 miles) north of Colombo, near Negombo.

The national carrier, **Air Lanka** (UL) provides a wide network of international flights spanning most major destinations.

Flights are available to and from: Europe (Amsterdam, Frankfurt, London, Paris, Rome, Vienna, Zurich); the Middle East (Abu Dhabi, Bahrain, Beirut, Dharan, Doha, Dubai, Muscat, Kuwait, Riyadh); India (Bombay, Madras, Trivandrum, Tiruchirappali); Pakistan (Karachi); East Asia (Bangkok, Hong Kong, Singapore, Kuala Lampur, Fukuoka, Tokyo) and the Maldives (Male).

Other international carriers are: Condor Airways (DF) – cargo and charters only; Gulf Air (GF); Indian Airlines (IC); Royal Jordanian (RJ); Kuwait Airways (KU); Bal Air (BB); Emirate Airways (EK); LTU (LT); Pakistan International Airline (PK); Singapore Airlines (SQ); Aeroflot (SU); Thai International (TG); Caledonian Airways (CKT); Bulgarian Airlines (LZ); Air Maldives (L6); Monarch Airlines (MON); Middle East Airlines (ME); Austrian Air (OS); Air Europe (PE); Qatar (Q7); Saudi (SV); and Oman Air (WY).

By Sea

Sea travel is no longer a common route to Sri Lanka, although some companies operate cruises. A tour operator in your home country may be able to offer it as a package. Liners such as P & O Lines and the Queen Elizabeth II stop here on round-the-world cruises, whereas others such as CTC offer regional cruises. Some freighters offer limited passenger space. Check with shipping lines for further information.

Airline Offices

Air Lanka
37 York Street, Colombo 1.
Tel: (ticketing) 581131;
(reservations) 421161;
(flight information) 446175.

Aeroflot
North Wing, Taj Samudra Hotel
Colombo 2.

Air India
108 YMBA building, Col 1.
Tel: 325832.

Cathay Pacific
186 Vauxhall Street, Col 2.
Tel: 421931.

Emirates
Hemas House,
Braybrook Place, Col 2.

Gulf Air
Mackinons Building,
11 York Street, Col 1.
Tel: 326633.

Japan Airlines
Galadari Hotel,
64 Lotus Road, Col 1.
Tel: 541291.

Korean Air
World Trade Centre, Col 1.
Tel: 449773.

Kuwait Airways
30–34 Cargills Building, Col 1.
Tel: 445531.

Pia
342 Galle Road, Col 3.
Tel: 573475.

Swissair
5th floor,
41 Janadhipathi Mawatha, Col 1.
Tel: 435403.

Thai International
Ceylon Intercontinental, Col 1
Tel: 438050.

Practical Tips

Credit Cards

Most major hotels, restaurants and shopping centres accept credit cards. However, some places accept one card and not another, so it is best to check and to have some cash as an alternative. Some places refuse to take American Express because of high commission charges. Note that some establishments may try and add a surcharge to your card. This is illegal, so you are justified in insisting that they remove the charge. Contact your card company.

Credit Card Organisations
American Express
104, Dharmapala Mawatha
Colombo 7
Tel: 439283
MasterCard
90, Chatham Street, Colombo 2
Tel: 436889
Visa
22nd floor
4, Bank of Ceylon Mawatha
Colombo 1
Tel: 447823

Exchanging Money and Banking

Local banks are slow in processing traveller's cheques. Unless you wish to spend half a morning waiting in a queue, go to the Hong Kong Bank or Grindlays. Money can also be withdrawn on credit cards but some refuse to cash traveller's cheques issued by Visa. Exchange rates fluctuate and any bank will give you a conversion estimate. All commercial banks are authorised to exchange money, as are many hotels, though hotels offer lower rates. Traveller's cheques attract a

better exchange rate than cash. Banks are open 9am–1pm, Monday and 9am–1.30pm Tuesday–Friday. They are closed Saturday, Sunday and all public holidays.

Foreign Banks
ANZ Grindlays Bank
Head Office
37, York Street, Colombo 1
Tel: 446150
Hong Kong Bank
Head Office
24, Sir Baron Jayatilaka Mawatha
Colombo 1
Tel: 446591
Deutsche Bank
Head Office
86, Galle Road, Colombo 3
Tel: 447062

Money Changers
Daya Authorised Money Changers
112, Sea Street, Colombo 11
Tel: 320345
Trust Lanka Money Changer
342, Sea Street, Colombo 11
Tel: 341250

Medical Services

Most hotels have a doctor on call, and most embassies can provide a referral list.
    Medical attention is available from many private hospitals, or from the state-owned Colombo General Hospital (Tel: 691111). It has the most advanced cardiology unit (Tel: 693039) on the island and provides medical attention free to Sri Lankans. Foreigners are required to pay for certain services. There are general hospitals in Kandy (Tel: 08 22261), Negombo (Tel: 031 2261) and Galle (Tel: 09 2261). Although many doctors have British qualifications, state hospitals have poor facilities and crowded wards.
    Private hospitals are well staffed, and are generally competently run and also comfortable. In the capital, you can choose from the following:
Asiri Hospital
181, Kirula Road, Colombo 5
Tel : 500608–12
One of the better hospitals, with 24-hour service and laboratory testing. Visited by many well-known medical practitioners.
Central Hospital
37, Horton Place, Colombo 7
Tel: 696411–2
Offers medical treatment at a very reasonable price.
General
Regent Street, Colombo 7
Tel: 691111
Excellent laboratory but not a comfortable place for a long stay.

Ayurvedic Centres

Homeopathic and herbal (Ayurvedic) medicine (see pages 138–9) is an alternative option available at hotels and health centres:
Barberyan Reef Hotel
Tel: 94-3476036.
Blue Oceanic
Tel: 94-3122377.
The Citadel, Kandy.
Tel: 08-25314.
Club Robinson
Tel: 94-3475167.
Deer Park Hotel
Tel: 94-2746470.
Giritale Hotel
Tel: 94-2746311.
Government Ayurvedic Hospital (Tel: 695855).
Hetigoda Group, Ratmalana.
Tel: 94-736910.
Hotel Club Lanka
Tel: 94-953296.
Kandalama
Tel: 94-6684808.
The Lodge, Habarana.
Tel: 94-254220.
Queens Hotel
Tel: 94-572806.
Royal Oceanic
Tel: 94-3122377.
Siddhalepa Wellness Centre, Mount Lavinia.
Tel: 94-738623.
The Tree of Life, Kandy.
Tel: 72-220334.
Villa Ocean View
Tel: 94-3432463.

Nawaloka
23, Sri Saugathodaya Mawatha
Colombo 2
Tel: 544444
Good laboratory and competent
staff, reasonably comfortable
rooms.

In an emergency, especially on a
Sunday, first telephone to find out
which specialists they have on call
and select your hospital accordingly.

Pharmacies

Most Western medicines are
available, but so are many Indian
substitutes – check where your
product is made. The Asiri hospital
has a pharmacy that is open quite
late, and the Osusala Pharmacy
(Tel: 694716) is open 24 hours.

Media

Newspapers are available daily and
mostly sell out by noon. There are
many special Sunday editions. Of
the English-language newspapers,
the *Daily News* and the *Observer*
are government-sponsored – one
appearing in the morning, the latter,
at noon. Private newspapers include
the *Island*, the *Times* and the
Leader. Most hotels and reputable
book shops carry international
magazines such as *Newsweek*,
Asiaweek, *Time*, *The Far Eastern
Economic Review*, *The Economist*
and some French and German
publications. The British
International Herald Tribune and
The Daily Telegraph arrive a day or
so late and are available in most
leading hotels.

Television has improved, with a
range of new channels that run to
later hours, and up-to-the-minute
international news services via Sky
News and CNN. There are seven TV
channels, showing English,
Sinhalese, Tamil and Hindi
programmes. Some channels have
a morning service, as well as the
usual evening service. Details of
programmes are available in the
newspapers.

Radio has also expanded over
recent years. The government-run
SLBC, an English service, now faces
stiff competition from other more

up-to-date and professionally-run
operations such as Capital Radio,
TNL and Yes FM. These offer DJ
music with chart hits, jazz and
classical music. Sinhala and Tamil
broadcasts are also widely
available.

Postal Services

These are not particularly reliable.
As there are periodic strikes and
delays, it is best to register urgent
post. The **General Post Office**, on
Janadhipathi Mawatha (Tel: 323140)
is open 24 hours a day. A tourist
counter, faster and less crowded is
usually open.

Postal rates are extremely cheap
in comparison to those overseas.
When sending airmail letters with
stamps, it is best to make sure that
they are "franked" in front of you, to
prevent them being steamed off
and re-used. All overseas packages
should be stamped with a green
customs label stating the contents
and value.

Post office working hours are
7am–5/6 pm on weekdays, and
9am–6pm on Saturday. Mail is
delivered every day except Sunday
and public holidays. The simplest
way to mail anything is through your
hotel, but there are reliable international courier services available.
TNT Express Worldwide
315, Vauxhall Street, Colombo 2
Tel: 447644
FedEx
300, Galle Road, Colombo 3
Tel: 577055
DHL
130, Glennie Street, Colombo 2
Tel: 338060
Sprint
(domestic courier service)
160/16, Kirimandala Mawatha
Narahenpita
Tel: 594001

Communications

Most major hotels have direct
international direct dialling facilities,
but their rates for both local and
international calls are high. Cheaper
alternatives include telephone
cards for use at international Lanka

payphones throughout the country
or using the series of small
communications bureaux (*see
below*) which include fax and
photocopying. These bureaux and
post offices also offer reasonable
rates for international calls. For
local calls, use a phone card instead
of your hotel phones, for which you
will be charged exorbitant sums.

Fax facilities and photocopying
are available from communications
bureaux as well as phone services.

E-mail and Internet is now
available in Colombo. There are
cyber cafés (such as the one on
Union Street) where for a charge,
you may use the Internet and send
e-mail. Another option is to hire your
own computer for the duration of
your stay. Companies that offer
hiring facilities and internet
services are:
• **Rent-A-Comp**
Tel: 589990
• **Computer Island (Pvt) Ltd**
Tel: 594369
• **IT Market**
Tel: 508988
• **pahana@slt.lk**
43c, Lauries Road, Colombo 4
Tel: 502416
Fax: 595548

The business centres of many
hotels also have secretarial
services, fax and e-mail at your
disposal.

Several companies rent mobile
telephones by the day/week/
month. Try **Mobitel** (Tel: 071-
55777; Fax 337005).

Communications Bureaux

**Cross Point Communication
Service**
301/A, Galle Road, Colombo 3
Tel: 575164
Deshan International (Pvt) Ltd
189, Bullers Road, Colombo 4
Tel: 585783
**Metalix Communication and
Services (Pvt) Ltd**
154 1/1, Havelock Road
Colombo 5
Tel: 503767

When you're
bitten by the travel bug,
make sure you're protected.

Check into a British Airways Travel Clinic.

British Airways Travel Clinics provide travellers with:

- A complete vaccination service and essential travel health-care items
- Up-dated travel health information and advice

Call **01276 685040** for details of your nearest Travel Clinic.

BRITISH AIRWAYS
TRAVEL CLINICS

New Insight Maps

Maps in Insight Guides are tailored to complement the text. But when you're on the road you sometimes need the big picture that only a large-scale map can provide. This new range of durable Insight Fleximaps has been designed to meet just that need.

Detailed, clear cartography
makes the comprehensive route and city maps easy to follow, highlights all the major tourist sites and provides valuable motoring information plus a full index.

Informative and easy to use
with additional text and photographs covering a destination's top 10 essential sites, plus useful addresses, facts about the destination and handy tips on getting around.

Laminated finish
allows you to mark your route on the map using a non-permanent marker pen, and wipe it off. It makes the maps more durable and easier to fold than traditional maps.

The first titles
cover many popular destinations. They include Algarve, Amsterdam, Bangkok, California, Cyprus, Dominican Republic, Florence, Hong Kong, Ireland, London, Mallorca, Paris, Prague, Rome, San Francisco, Sydney, Thailand, Tuscany, USA Southwest, Venice, and Vienna.

👁 INSIGHT GUIDES
The world's largest collection of visual travel guides

Area Dialling Codes

Aluthgama	034
Ambalangoda	09
Anuradhapura	025
Badulla	055
Bandarawela	057
Bentota	034
Beruwela	034
Colombo	01
Dambulla	066
Dehiwela	01
Ella	057
Galle	09
Giritale	027
Habarana	066
Hambantota	047
Haputale	057
Hikkaduwa	09
Jaffna	021
Kalutara	034
Kandy	08
Kataragama	047
Kurunegala	037
Matara	041
Mount Lavinia	01
Negombo	031
Nuwara Eliya	052
Polonaruwa	027
Ratnapura	045
Sigiriya	066
Tangalla	047
Tissamaharama	047
Trincomalee	026
Unawatuna	09
Weligama	041

Photography

Film and cameras are available on arrival at the airport duty-free shop and at a number of photographic shops in Colombo. Repairs can be carried out at Heladiva Camera Repairs, Cross Street, Pettah district, who also stock camera filters, polarisers and batteries.

A lens hood and/or polarising filter are useful for reducing flare from brilliant sunshine and reflection from bright colours. High temperature and humidity can play havoc with cameras so protect all equipment with silca gel crystals. A camera left in midday sun can result in fogged film. If professional film is used it must be refrigerated both before and after use.

Tipping

As a general rule tipping is not expected unless you feel a service has been special, although chauffeur guides (but not trishaw drivers) expect one. Hotel and restaurant bills include a 10 percent service charge as well as a 10 percent business turnover tax (BTT). The service charge is supposed to be distributed among hotel employees.

Touts

Touts frequent all main towns but are most prevalent around temples, train and bus stations, tourist sites and outside hotels. Their friendly over-helpfulness is designed to make you feel obliged to part with your money. They may come up with a convincing act, such as "the student" who is supporting a sick mother and three siblings. Many trishaw drivers meeting tourist trains at Kandy station are the worst touts, as they go to inordinate lengths to herd you into a hotel or guest house where they can claim a fee. The only way to deal with touts is with a very firm "No!"

Another brand of tout has an identity card saying he is collecting for charity. They usually have a plausible tale but are nothing more than con-men. If you are feeling charitable you can leave a donation in a temple or church.

Begging

Begging is a way of life in Asia, and while some cases are genuine there are others who seek to take advantage.

Tourists are easily categorised as having a surfeit of cash, so you can expect to attract a fair share of beggars. Do remember, however, that genuine beggars love to receive food of any sort since they can eat it on the spot – without having to share it with the racketeer who usually takes most of his earnings. Begging rackets exist mainly in Colombo, so you might consider carrying a bag of oranges to hand to beggars instead of cash, if you object to giving money.

Security & Crime

Unsafe Areas

Due to the conflict between the Government and the LTTE or 'Tamil Tigers', there are certain areas of the island that are not safe for foreign travellers. These are mainly in the north and visitors should note that everything north of Anuradhapura is off limits, including Wilpattu National Park. Some parts of Yala Sanctuary are also closed. Places on the east coast such as Trincomalee can also be problematic, so check with a reputable travel agent or the tourist board that it is safe to visit. Because of occasional bombings, commercial areas in Colombo such as Fort are best avoided. However this state of affairs seems not to deter visitors whose own cities have suffered terrorist activity. To play safe always check the current situation with the tourist board and heed local advice.

Being Safe in Colombo

Offences of mugging and street crime in Colombo are low but it pays to be careful. Avoid lonely places at night and be wary of accepting lifts from strangers. If you are staying in a hotel, your valuables should be placed in the safety deposit box. Remember that property left lying around may be very tempting to those who earn less in a year than many Westerners earn in a month. In case of an emergency a special unit called the "Tourist Police" is available to all visitors. The main office is on the ground floor of the New Secretariat Building, Colombo Fort (Tel: 26941 or 421111 ext. 219). There are branches located in Sigiriya, Bentota, Negombo and Hikkaduwa.

All city beaches should be avoided at night, especially those in Colombo, which take on a seedy and dangerous atmosphere after dark – muggings, robberies and worse have been known to take place on Mount Lavinia beach. Solo travellers should avoid the beach at this time altogether. Even if in a group, it is best not to carry money or passports.

Women Travellers

Sri Lankan society is conservative, and the way you dress contributes greatly to people's opinions of you, and also to the way they behave towards you. If you can avoid wearing provocative clothing in areas such as Fort and Pettah in Colombo, the chances are that you won't be harassed.

Female travellers in tourist spots, especially on beaches, are likely to attract unwanted attention. On the West Coast, around the vicinity of Unawatuna, beach bums solicit female European holiday-makers looking for a local gigolo, so you may be propositioned along these lines. Pests can be repelled effectively as long as you do not behave in a way that may be considered encouraging – just walk away, avoiding contact of any sort and say nothing. On the whole, eye contact is seen as a "come-on", so, even if simply walking along the road, avoid looking at men who are strangers.

Women should avoid going out alone at night. Never walk or take a trishaw and never accept a lift from a stranger, but hire a cab from a reputable company.

You may find yourself the victim of opportunistic groping on a crowded bus or train. Deal with this by drawing attention to the perpetrator and his actions. Be wary of the male who sits beside you when there are plenty of seats elsewhere. Your refusal or reluctance to move away will be interpreted as an invitation to take matters further.

Gay Travellers

Homosexual activity is officially illegal in Sri Lanka and there have been some convictions. Discreet gay travellers, however, are unlikely to encounter any harassment but public displays of affection are best avoided.

Travellers with Disabilities

Sri Lanka is not well equipped for those with physical disabilities. Only a few of the five-star hotels have access and facilities for people in wheelchairs – public transport has none, so a car and driver will be essential. Consult your travel agent for more specific information.

Useful Phone Numbers

- **Police** – 433333
- **Fire & Ambulance Service** – 422222
- **Accident Service** – 691111
- **Colombo General Hospital** – 691111

Call the Accident Service first in the event of an accident. Only some hospitals provide an accident service. Get a list from your local consular office in case of an emergency.

Children

Sri Lankans adore children of all ages and make a great deal of fuss over them – travelling with children is therefore a good way of meeting locals. Children are well catered for in restaurants, and hotels and guest houses often have triple or family rooms. Baby food and nappies are available in most supermarkets in major cities but tend to be very expensive. Good baby bottles are hard to find, so bring these with you. Cotton childrens' clothing of all sizes is easily available, inexpensive and cool to wear (see p293).

A good source of information for parents is Lonely Planet's *Travel with Children* by Maureen Wheeler, which contains a chapter specifically on Sri Lanka.

If you require more advice on arrival, a good contact is Keren Jayaratne at the Canadian High Commission (Tel: 01 695841/3), who runs an expatriate's childrens' play group in Colombo.

Toilets

Toilets in up-market hotels and restaurants in tourist spots are of the Western style. In less visited areas, expect to squat Eastern-style, with water provided in place of toilet paper (so carry some with you if you prefer to use it).

Public toilets should only be used in dire emergencies.

Religious Services

Places of worship available in Colombo are as follows:

BUDDHIST
Gangarama Temple
61, Jinaratna Road, Colombo 2
Isipathanarama Temple
Isipathana Road, Colombo 5
Vajiramaya Temple
Vajira Road, Colombo 5
For more information on Buddhist worship contact
All Ceylon Buddhist Congress
380, Baudhaloka Mawatha
Colombo 7
Tel: 691695
The Buddhist Information Centre
50, Ananda Coomaraswamy
Mawatha, Colombo 7
Tel: 23079

CHRISTIAN
Anglican
Cathedral of Christ the Living Saviour
Baudhaloka Mawatha, Colombo 7
Tel: 696363
St Luke's Church
Colombo 8 (Borella)
Tel: 691543
St Peter's Church
26, Church Street, Colombo 1
Tel: 422510
Baptist Church
331, Grandpass Road,
Colombo 14
Baptist Manse
120, Dharmapala Mawatha
Colombo 7
Tel: 695153
Bampalapitiya Dutch Reformed Church
Galle Road, Colombo 4
Tel: 580854

St Andrew's Church
Galle Road, Colombo 3
Tel: 23765

Methodist
Methodist Church
6, Station Road, Colombo 3
Tel: 23033

Mormon
Church of Jesus Christ of Latter Day Saints
102A, Horton Place, Colombo 7
Tel: 693794

Roman Catholic
All Saints' Church
Campbell Place
Colombo 8
Tel: 693051
St Mary's Church
Lauries Road
Colombo 4
Tel: 88745
St Theresa's Church
364, Thimbirigasaya Road
Colombo 5
Tel: 583425
Seventh Day Adventist
7, Alfred House Gardens
Colombo 3
Tel: 585851

HINDU
New Kathiresan Temple
Galle Road, Colombo 4
Bambalapitya
Sri Muthuvinayagam Swami Kovil
221, Sea Street, Colombo 11
Tel: 43515554
Sri Samankodu Kadirvekanda Swami Kovil
Main Street, Colombo 11

MUSLIM
Bambalapitiya Mosque
Buller's Road, Colombo 4
Jaim-ul-Alfar Mosque
2nd Cross Street, Colombo 11
Kollupitiya Mosque
Colombo 3

On Departure

Passengers must pay Rs 500 departure tax. Up to 3kg (6˘ lb) of tea can exported without restriction but each additional kilo will cost Rs 5 per kilo purchased with funds declared on entry (which is why you need to keep all your receipts) can also be exported. For gifts of gems, permits are issued by the Controller of Exchange, Central Bank, Colombo. The export of antiques over 100 years old is prohibited, as is the export of native fauna and flora, unless accompanied with adequate documentation.

Tourist Information Centres

Colombo
78, Steuart Place
Galle Road
Colombo 3
Tel: 437059/437060
(also in lobby at the Bandaranaike Airport)
Kandy
Headmans Lodge
3, Deva Veediya
Tel: 08 226661
Negombo
12/6, Ethukala
Lewis Place
(no phone)

Getting Around

From The Airport

Most travellers head first to Colombo and make an onward journey from there. An airport bus connects with designated hotels in the capital and your travel agent can make any necessary arrangements.

Taxis are inexpensive and comfortable and can be hired from car hire stands outside the airport or you can hire a chauffeur-guide. (*see p300*).

Trains leave the airport for the capital at 7.40am, 8.40am and 4.56pm but they are not clean or comfortable and the journey takes over an hour. For further information telephone 435838 or 421281.

Buses: The SLTB bus which is always crowded and slow, also makes the journey to Colombo but is not recommended if you have a lot of luggage.

Getting Around the Island

Security posts are stationed all over Colombo, particularly in Fort, and security checks are common. Sri Lankans are required to carry identity cards and foreigners must be in possession of passports at all times. If you are stopped, a police officer will simply check your passport and then hand it back to you.

On Foot
Colombo pavements are good in some places but many are bad and sometimes there are none at all. Getting around on foot can be an ordeal, particularly in the

midday heat, but is often the quickest form of transport during the rush hour.

An A–Z street map booklet of the city is available from the Survey Department in Colombo and is an invaluable aid to orientation.

Bus

A rush-hour bus journey in Colombo is the closest thing to hell on earth. Buses are dangerously overcrowded to the point that four or five people may be hanging out of the doorway, holding on perfectly calmly for dear life, while drivers barely stop long enough to allow anyone to get on or off the vehicle.

Bus journeys, whether short or long distance, are hot, slow and uncomfortable but they are cheap even if you are stifled, stepped upon and sometimes groped. Buses tend to better maintained than their Indian counterparts and in quiet periods, when the crowds aren't around, can be quite a pleasant experience. Some private bus companies operate vehicles equipped with something which passes for air-conditioning but check with a travel agent before booking.

Car Rental and Driving

A Westerner driving in Sri Lanka – and especially Colombo – needs to adopt a whole new set of driving rules. Forget about warning others of your intentions because Sri Lankan drivers simply expect every-one else to avoid them. Remember too that the size of your vehicle dictates the right of way; buses and trucks come first, followed by cars and three-wheelers and finally the humble cyclist. Expect the unexpected, and be prepared for both your driving skills and patience to be tested to the utmost limits.

Away from the traffic-infested capital, driving is much easier, but a good road map and phrase book are invaluable. Don't rely too much on verbal directions – Sri Lankans are so accommodating that many are only too happy to "help", even if they don't know the way. Hiring your own car and taking an obligatory

Getting Around Colombo

Trishaw

Trishaws (auto rickshaws in India) or three-wheelers are the best way of negotiating Colombo's busy streets if you don't mind the speed at which they travel.

Fix the fare beforehand which should be cheaper than hiring an air-conditioned taxi, but often isn't, as much depends on the whims of your driver. Change is rarely given so try to give the exact money or ensure that you have a supply of small denom-ination notes.

Taxi

Only a few taxi companies have metered air-conditioned vehicles. Yet despite the heat, you can feel comfortably safe using these, even late at night, and they can be just as cheap and sometimes cheaper than trishaws when there is little traffic.

high insurance premium is hardly worth the time or expense but you may be lucky with a package deal.

You'll need a temporary Sri Lankan licence, available from the Automobile Association of Ceylon (Tel: 421 528/9), 40 Sir Macan Markar Mawatha, Galle Face.

Car rental firms include:
Mal-Key Rent-A-Car
Tel: 584253
Casons Rent-A-Car
Tel: 074405070
Lespri Rent-A-Car
Tel: 320498
Airport Express
Tel: 687037
Tel: 698207 (24-hour line)

Chauffeur-driven cars

These are by far the most comfort-able way of getting around. There are several reputable agencies in Colombo, which offer both air-conditioned and non air-conditioned vehicles. Long-distance chauffeur-driven services are available from some hire car companies and only a

little more expensive than self-drive. Make sure you fully understand who is responsible for the driver's food and lodgings, or *batty*.

For reliable chauffeur/guides contact:
Mohamed Ghouse
Tel: 585051/077310091
Airport Express
(as above).

Train

Trains are marginally slower than buses and not very comfortable. The express trains tend to be a little better but are not air-conditioned. Seats for the inter-city trains must be booked in advance as they are very busy especially at weekends and on public holidays. By comparison with Indian trains, Sri Lankan trains are rackety, ancient and very dirty. Fares in 1st class are cheap, travelling 2nd class is even cheaper but bearable and 3rd class, if you can manage to find a seat, is purgatory. Train travel is not for the faint-hearted but is an excellent way of enjoying the scenery and getting close to the locals, even if they do hang out of doorways of moving trains and beggars and vendors fill up the aisles.

If you want stunning views of the lush landscapes on the Colombo-Kandy train, and peace and quiet, reserve a seat in the observation saloon. It is not air-conditioned but is offlimits to other passengers.

For more information contact: the **Railtours** office at Fort Station (Tel: 435838).

Motorcycle

Motor cycles afford a quick and enjoyable way of seeing the country. If you don't mind getting dusty, a range of motorcycles can be hired from:
Goldwing
346, Deans Road, Colombo 10
Tel: 698787

Air Taxi

Avoid the heat and dust and grime of traffic by hiring a two-seater Cessna plane or five-seater Bell Helicopter. Expensive but worth it

for the beautiful scenery alone.
Flights depart from Ratmalana
Airport but may be cancelled
without notice due to the security
situation. The following companies
offer air taxi flights:
• **John Keells Aviation**
Tel: 329881
A 24-seater helicopter offers
scheduled services to the south
and to other tourist attractions.
• **Ace Airways**
Tel: 447239
Rates are reasonable.
• **Apelli Aviation**
Tel: 328826

Maps

Tourist maps available from
bookshops are often out of date.
For a comprehensive map in four
sections try the Survey Department
in Colombo. Maps can be
purchased in the UK from Edward
Stanford, 12/14 Long Acre, Covent
Garden, London WC2E 9LP.

Guided Tours

The **Ceylon Tourist Board** organises
guided tours around Colombo.
Telephone 437056/437059 for
further details.
   Glen Hodgins has tailor-made
personal tours for a maximum of
four people. In a full- or half-day tour
in an air-conditioned saloon car, you
get a dose of history, culture and
some facinating details.
   Other guided tour operators are:
Colombo Then and Now Tours
Tel: 075 335059
E-mail: grhicomm@sri.lanka.net
J F Tours and Travel
Tel: 01587996
For steam train excursions on the
Viceroy Special.
Adventure Sports Lanka
For canoeing/trekking/ biking tours
on the coast, up-country and in the
cultural triangle. Also white-water
rafting on the Mahaweli Ganga.

Travel Agents

The following selection are
recommended by the Ceylon
Tourist Board:

Aitken Spence Travels Ltd
Lloyds Building
13, Sir Baron Jayatillake
Mawatha
Colombo 1
Tel: 436735/436755

Browns Tours Ltd
Taj Samudra Complex
25, Galle Face Center
Colombo 3
Tel: 446622

Ceylon Tours
67, Parsons Road
Colombo 2
Tel: 421722

Hemtours
24, Sir Earnest DeSilva Mawatha
Colombo 3

Jetwing Hotels & Travels
457, Union Place
Colombo 2
Tel: 698818

Lanka Sportszreisen
244/1, Hospital Road
Kalubovila
Dehiwela
Tel: 824955

Mackinnons Travels Ltd
4, Leyden Bastion Road
Colombo 1
Tel: 448065

Where to Stay

Where to Stay

Tourist accommodation ranges from
the lowliest one-star establishment
to the grandest five-star hotel.
There are also small guest houses,
which vary in degrees of comfort,
from the simple and rustic to the
truly luxurious: staying in one can
be an entertaining way to get to
know the country and its people.
   Government-run rest houses are
often converted colonial buildings,
sometimes set in beautiful and
peaceful locations with wonderful
views. They can be comfortable and
excellently run or quite the
opposite, depending on the general
management.
   Most tourist hotels quote in US
dollars and the price guide here
(*see page 302*) reflects this.
Government-run rest houses and
small guest houses price
themselves in rupees but to avoid
confusion they are priced in US
dollars in the following list.

Hotels and Guest Houses

COLOMBO
Hilton
Echelon Square
Tel: 544644
Top class city hotel with the finest
restaurants in the country. Excellent
entertainment facilities, including
a horse riding centre, an aerobics
gym, swimming pool, tennis,
discotheque, pub and karaoke
lounge. **$$$$**
Taj Samudra Hotel
25, Galle Face
Tel: 446622
Lacks the lustre of its more
glamorous sisters in this chain but
has a good cake shop in the lobby

and all amenities. Large, beautifully laid out gardens. Some excellent restaurants with authentic Indian cuisine. Tennis and squash courts, swimming pool and sports and fitness centre with sauna and steam rooms available to guests. **$$$$**

Trans Asia Hotel
115, Sir Chittampalam A Gardiner Mawatha
Tel: 544200
Five-star hotel with non-smoking areas and specially designed rooms for disabled guests. Extremely comfortable, with beautiful gardens and a large pool. Tennis, squash and volleyball courts, jogging track, gym, herbal baths and massage. **$$$$**

The Galle Face Hotel
Tel: 541072
A gracious old relic of Colombo's colonial past, this hotel is in a time of its own. Although it provides the standard amenities such as air-conditioned rooms, TV and mini bar, the service is as relaxed and erratic as in days of yore – some messages and phone calls may not reach you. Otherwise, a delightful location, with a large sea-water swimming pool overlooking the sea itself. **$$$**

Hotel Sapphire
371, Galle Road
Tel: 583306/8
Comfortable air-conditioned rooms, with all basic facilities and a convenient location on Galle Road. Credit cards are accepted. **$$**

Hotel Galaxy
388, Union Place
Tel: 696372
Air-conditioned rooms, swimming pool. The restaurant serves good steaks. **$$**

Hotel Nippon
123, Kumaran Ratnam Road
Air-conditioned rooms, childcare facilities. Rooms can be booked on room only or bed and breakfast basis. **$$**

Mount Lavinia

The Falado
20, Beach Road
Tel: 941-716203
A small and intimate German-run guest house set in a cool old Portuguese villa very near the beach. Some rooms have air-conditioning. **$**

Blue Seas Guest House
De Saram Road (off Beach Road)
Tel: 01-716298
Well-run and friendly guest house with 20 rooms. Pass the Falado and follow signs. Fascinating and entertaining hosts. **$**

Mount Lavinia Hotel
102, Hotel Road
Tel: 715221/7
Old-fashioned, charming and comfortable with a rather good seafood restaurant. **$$$**

Price Guide

Prices are all for two including breakfast.
$$$$ more than US$150
$$$ US$50–100
$$ US$25–50
$ less than US$25

WEST COAST
Ahungalla

Triton Hotel
Tel: 09-54041/4
Unadulterated five-star comfort. Several excellent restaurants and one of the loveliest pools in the region. Advisable to book ahead. **$$$$**

Ambalangoda

Sumudu Guest House
418, Main Street, Ambalangoda
Tel: 09-58832
Turn left just after the Mask Museum and head northwards out of town. On your right is a basic but friendly guest house with just 6 rooms in an old, airy family home, run by a licensed gem dealer. **$**

Bentota

Saman Villas
Aturuwella
Tel: 439792
Absolute luxury, lovely rooms with TV, mini bar and CD player. Ideal for spoiling yourself. **$$$$**

Bentota Beach Hotel
Tel: 034-75176/9
Comfortable hotel, right on the beach. Large swimming pool.

Weekly entertainment programmes on a seasonal basis. **$$$**

The Villa
Mohotti Walauwa
138/18 & 138/22, Galle Road
Tel: 034-75311
An original 1880's villa now renovated, with additions by the eminent Sri Lankan architect Geoffrey Bawa. It has 15 large suites, with antique furnishings and fittings, and is just a short walk from the beach. **$$$**

Hotel Serendib
Tel: 034-75253
Directly on the beach. With 90 air-conditioned rooms with sea views, large gardens and swimming pool. **$$$**

Confifi Beach Hotel
Moragalla,
Tel: 034-76217
Not by the greatest beach, but there is a swimming pool and a kid's pool, and tennis and table tennis are available. **$$$**

Beruwela

Eden Hotel
Kaluwamodara
Tel: 034-76181
A large modern hotel with TV and piped music. Large swimming pool, and excellent water sports. **$$$$**

Neptune Hotel
Moragalla
Tel: 034-76031/3
All inclusive sports/recreation, with a swimming pool, a large stretch of beach and elephant rides. **$$$$**

Riviera Beach Resort
Moragalla
Tel: 034-76245
Set on the beach, with a pool and a spacious garden. Other amenities, however, are basic. Rooms are not air-conditioned. **$$**

Hikkaduwa

Coral Gardens Hotel
Tel: 09-77023
On a lovely stretch of beach, where boat-rides to view corals are available. A large swimming pool and air-conditioned rooms. **$$$**

Coral Rock Hotel
Tel: 09-77021
On the beach, some air-conditioned rooms. Very basic. **$$**

Indiruwa
Long Beach Cottage
(200m north of Induruwa railway
station)
Tel: 034-75773
Eat the best food ever in a friendly
family atmosphere in this small
guest house on one of the quietest
beaches. Run by a German/Sri
Lankan couple. Guests have been
coming back for decades. **$**

Kalutara
Tangerine Beach Hotel
De Abrew's Road
Waskaduwa
Tel: 034-22295
On a not very impressive beach but
relaxing ambience, with comfortable
rooms and large pool. **$$$**
Royal Palms
Tel: 034-28113/7
Lush and comfortable, with 7 suites
and 117 deluxe rooms. **$$$$**

Katunayake
Airport Garden Hotel
Negombo Road
Seeduwa
Tel: 252950/4
Air-conditioned rooms and conve-
nient for the airport. Swimming
pool. By the lagoon. **$$$**

Negombo
Browns Beach Hotel
Lewis Place
Tel: 031-22031/2
One of the oldest hotels on this strip
of beach which has been upstaged
by perkier rivals. Air-conditioned
rooms and a swimming pool. **$$$**
Blue Oceanic Beach Hotel
Ethukala
Tel: 031-22377
105 air-conditioned rooms with sea
views, swimming pool, tennis and
squash courts. **$$$**

SOUTH COAST
Galle
The Sun House
18, Upper Dickson Road
Galle
Tel: 074-380275/09-22624
E-mail: sunhouse@sri.lanka.net
American ex-model Mary has
converted this old Dutch

merchant's villa into a sumptuous
country house hotel, with pool. A
worthwhile stop at Galle. **$$$**
The New Oriental Hotel
10, Church Street
Fort Galle
Tel: 09-34591
Colonial atmosphere in this tired
but spacious hotel (35 rooms, 12
suites, all non-air-conditioned)
inside the fort itself. Its claim to
fame is that it's the oldest hotel in
the country. **$$**
Lighthouse Hotel
Dadella
Tel: 09-23744
Comfortable rooms, and a
remarkable stairway designed by
artist Laki Senanayake, depicting
the Portuguese invasion of Ceylon,
makes it well worth a visit. On-site
swimming pool, with water sports
and a good beach nearby. **$$$$**
Closenburg
Tel: 09-32241
Built on the site of an old Dutch
fortress. A palatial white villa
offering seafood and Italian dishes
as well as rice and curry
"Southern" style. **$$$**

Unawatuna
Unawatuna Beach Resort
Parangiyawatte
Galle
Tel: 09-32247
Rooms both with and without air-
conditioning. Basic, but peacful
year-round bathing in idyllic bay. **$$**

Wadduwa
Villa Ocean View
Molligodawatte
Tel: 034-32463
Ideal for a day trip from Colombo,
this comfortable beach hotel has a
swimming pool and tennis courts.
Unspectacular beach. **$$$**

Yala
Yala Safari Beach Hotel
Tel: 047-20472
Offers both air- and non-air-
conditioned rooms. **$$**

Uda Walawe
The Bungalow
Tel: 580156
Basic accomodation. **$$**

KANDY
Le Kandyan Resorts
Heerassagala, Peradeniya
Tel: 070-800268
One of the most beautiful views in
the area, overlooking Kandy.
Tastefully furnished, with air-
conditioned rooms, swimming pool
and Ayurvedic health centre. **$$$**
The Chalet Hotel
70, Frederick E. De Silva Mawatha
Tel: 08-234571
The eclectic décor has to be seen
to be believed but is distinctly
interesting. Rooms are comfortable
but non air-conditioned and, windows
must be kept shut at all times to
keep out marauding monkeys. **$$$**
Queens Hotel
Dalada Veediya
Tel: 08-222813
Old hotel in the city. With 5 air-
conditioned rooms. **$$**

Bed and Breakfast in Kandy

Prices for accommodation rocket
during the Kandy *Perahera*
festival in August when every
guest house and hotel in town is
fully booked. The rest of the year,
prices can be as low as RS
300–400 per person. Bed and
breakfast accommodation,
however, is dotted around Kandy.
Contact the numbers below for
more information:
Grassmere Holiday Home
Tel: 94868329
Lake Cottage
Tel: 94822832
Lake Mount Inn
Tel: 948233204
The Scenic Summit
Tel: 948232636
The Palanquin
Tel: 948233169
Blue Haven
Tel: 948232453
Bonavista
Tel: 94874255
Castle Hill
Tel: 948232739
Old Empire
Tel: 948222208
Elephant Bath
Tel: 948225167

UP COUNTRY

Ella

Lizzie Villa Guest House
Tel: 057-23243
Clearly signposted off the main Ella road. A path meanders up-hill to a peaceful haven where delicious home-made curries are served on the verandah overlooking a lush herb garden. **$**

Kandapola

The Tea Factory
Nuwara Eliya
Tel: 052-3600
A former tea factory, this hotel commands a unique position in the lush surroundings of the Hill Country. Stunning views, heated rooms, excellent food and popular with tour groups. **$$$**

Nuwara Eliya

Grand Hotel
Tel: 052-2881
This colonial buiding may be tired but has tasteful décor. All rooms have fireplaces. Adjoining golf course. **$$$**
Windsor Hotel
Tel: 052-2554
Absolute comfort with 44 double rooms and 5 luxury suites. Charming hotel with excellent service, close to the Botanical Gardens. **$$**

CULTURAL TRIANGLE

Anuradhapura

Hotel Palm Gardens Village
Puttalam Road
Pandulagama
Tel: 947228974
The hotel has 50 air-conditioned rooms, including 10 suites, and the largest swimming pool in the Cultural Triangle. **$$$**
Tissawewa Resthouse
Old Town
Tel: 942522565
Comfortable, basic rooms with an extra charge for air-conditioning. Easy access to archaeological sites and museum. Some credit cards are accepted. **$$**

Dambulla

Culture Club Resort
Kandalama,
Tel: 94663500

Comfortable accommodation with air-conditioned chalets. Outdoor activities galore, including a swimming pool. Set in a beautiful location – a lake full of white lotus and a mature parkland. Easy access to historical sites. A bird watcher's paradise. Two intimate resorts which provide the ultimate in service. **$$$**
Kandalama Hotel
Tel: 0663475/7
Absolute comfort, lovely setting with the lake on one side and forest on the other. Outdoor activities include horse-riding and beautiful swimming pools. Easy access to cultural sites, and a peaceful and private atmosphere. **$$$**

Price Guide

Prices are all for two including breakfast.
$$$$ more than US$150
$$$ US$50–100
$$ US$25–50
$ less than US$25

Giritale

The Deer Park Hotel
Polonnaruwa
Tel: 027-46470
Two hours from Wasgamuwa National Park, eight minutes from Polonnaruwa, overlooking Giritale tank. Comfortable rooms, swimming pool, sports and recreational facilities. **$$$**

Habarana

The Lodge
Tel: 025-4821
Enjoy colonial grandeur at the Lodge, as well as fishing, tennis and outdoor activities; there is in-house entertainment, too. The hotel shares 40 acres of unforgettable landscape with its sister hotel, The Village, described below. **$$$**
The Village
Bungalow-style accommodation is available here, with the emphasis placed on indigenous culture. **$$**

Sigiriya

Sigiriya Village Hotel
Tel: 94254716
Perfect views of the Rock Fortress

and an exotic garden reflect the intimacy of this well-appointed hotel. Relatively comfortable chalet-type rooms, some air-conditioned. There is a pool. **$$$**

EAST COAST

Trincomalee

Nilaveli Beach Hotel
Nilaveli
Tel: 343720
In a beautifully tranquil location by an isolated, unspoiled and tout-free beach – one of the best in the country. There is a swimming pool and both air- and non air-conditioned rooms. **$$**

Cottages and Bungalows

For cottages on coconut estates and up-country tea estates, contact Roland Holidays bungalows.
Tel: 072 277015/24756/844815.

Wildlife Sanctuaries

Bungalows within the sanctuaries are in great demand. For bookings contact the Department of Wildlife Conservation. Tel: 433012/433787.

Youth Hostels

The following are all in Colombo:
Boy Scouts Hostel (men only)
65/9, Sir Chittampalam A Gardiner Mawatha, Colombo 2
Tel: 433131
Girl Guides Hostel (women only)
10, Marcus Fernando Mawatha
Colombo 7
Tel: 697720
Horton Youth Hostel
35/1, Horton Place, Colombo 7
Youth Council Hostel
50, Haig Road
Colombo 4

Specialist Holidays

Jungle Safaris

Transasia Safari Kamp Services
Dehiwela
Tel: 941738714
Prime Destinations
Colombo
Tel: 94 1575300

Weddings

The following agents will arrange tailor-made itineraries at hotels owned by the John Keels group:

Kuoni
Kuoni House
Dorking, Surrey
Tel: 01306 740500

Inspirations
Victoria House
Victoria Road, Horley
Surrey RH6 7AD
Tel: 01293 820207

Whittall Bousted
148, Vauxhall Street, Colombo 2
Tel: 329682
Fax: 432780

The internationally growing interest in eco-tourism has not been ignored in Sri Lanka. Being a developing country, Sri Lanka has not lost its ancient methods of living, and the **Ulpotha Sanctuary** has been set up in the spirit and practice of old local traditions. This self-sustaining village community is a living example of how human beings can live in harmony with nature. Visitors stay in comfortable mud huts and meals are traditionally prepared with locally grown organic food. A traditional medicine man will treat any complaints with remedies prepared from herbs and leaves. In this naturally re-generative environment, you can practise Yoga, enjoy a massage and watch village life. Ulpotha's forest also includes walking trails frequented by wild animals, including elephants. Stays can be arranged in the UK through Jilly Batchellor at Free Spirit Travel (Tel: 01273-564230).

Where to Eat

What to Eat

Sri Lankan cuisine has its own distinctive and delicious blend of flavours based on local ingredients. Many Sri Lankans will eat rice and curry three times a day and curries can be made with meat, fish or vegetables, flavoured with a heady blend of condiments such as chillies, cinnamon, lemon grass, curry leaves, coriander, cumin, saffron, tamarind and coconut. Have a go at eating rice and curry with your hands – watch the locals to pick up some tips. Don't forget to try the sweetmeats and snacks. Most famous are stringhoppers and egghoppers.

If you fall in love with Sri Lankan cuisine, you can obtain a copy of the *Ceylon Daily News Cookery Book*, which provides a broad range of recipes in a small, travel-friendly format.

Do not leave the island without tasting the amazing tropical fruits on offer. There are many varieties of dwarf bananas – some locals are banana connoisseurs and will happily tell you which ones are the best. Red-sugar bananas must be tried, if you can find them. Papaya, or pawpaw, should be tried for breakfast, squeezed with lime. Also try custard apples from the up-country region. Rambutan, a cousin of the lychee, is a local favourite, as are mangosteens and mangos.

The durian is delicious, if you can get beyond its infamously ferocious smell. Also try the juice of woodapples, which is wonderfully creamy if prepared in the traditional way. Jack fruit is another widely available local speciality, and curries made from breadfruit have a remarkable texture.

Drinking Notes

All imported beverages (wines, spirits and beers) carry a whopping 100 percent tax so this can double or triple an otherwise inexpensive meal. Try local beers brewed in the highlands or cocktails make from *Arrack* rather than imported spirits.

Where to Eat in Colombo

Eating out in Colombo is surprisingly cheap and even five-star restaurants are good value. Vegetarian food is easy to find in all Chinese, Indian, Italian, Sri Lankan and Muslim restaurants. A pleasant surprise when eating at Chinese places is that even smart restaurants are quite happy to pack a "doggy-bag" in a white cardboard box in much the same way as is done in America. This is just as well as the portions in Sri Lankan Chinese restaurants are large, to say the least.

Prices are based on a two-course meal for two and are categorised as follows:
RRRR 1,500 Rupees plus
RRR 1-1,500 Rupees
RR 500-1,000 Rupees
R less than 500 Rupees

CONTINENTAL
Chesa Swiss
3, Deal Place, Colombo 3
Tel: 573433
Serves an expensive but tasty classic cheese fondue. **RRR**
Le Palace
79, Gregory's Road, Colombo 7
Tel: 695920
Italian and French *nouvelle cuisine* in a colonial mansion with a pretty garden ideal for outdoor wedding and birthday celebrations amongst the wealthy locals. Less crowded for lunch and tea when Parisian chef Jean Piérre Piallier turns out *pâtisserie* which is art on a plate. **RR**
Verandah Restaurant
Galle Face Hotel, Colombo 3
Tel: 28211.
Even if you don't want to eat, come for a drink in the famous bar (*see page 165*). **R**

Cricketer's Pub
34, Queens Road
Colombo 3
Tel: 501384
Tasty burgers and fries, omelettes
and BLT's for those tired of spices. **R**

FAST FOOD
Kentucky Fried Chicken
Majestic City
10, Station Road, Colombo 4
Tel: 581747
Open even on *Poya* Days for
burgers and fast food. **R**
Pizza Hut
312A, Union Place
Colombo 2
Tel: 334763
Some Lankan flavoured spicy pizzas
as well as salad and soup bar. **R**
The Golden Rooster
407, Galle Road
Colombo 3
Tel: 576507
This Sri Lankan chain is fast catching
on due to its Halal menu and close
attention to cleanliness. Particularly
good take-away roast chicken. **R**
Food Court
Majestic City
Colombo 4
An inexpensive way to try several
different types of cuisine for under
Rs 100 a go. **R**
Burgerland
215, R. A. De Mel Mawatha
Colombo 3. **R**
Food Court
225, Galle Road
Mount Lavinia
Reasonable burgers and fries. **R**
Garfields
11C, Race Course Avenue
More expensive than most fast food
places for really good burgers and
hot dogs. **R**
Deli Mart
21, De Vos Avenue
Colombo 4
Home of Izza Pizza and also a good
sandwich and snack bar, with
lampreis (traditional rice packet,
wrapped in a banana leaf). **R**
Morley's
365, Galle Road
Colombo 3
Tel: 565015
Rather good burgers and fries. **R**

Price Guide

The prices are based on a two-
course meal for two.
RRRR 1,500 Rupees plus
RRR 1–1,500 Rupees
RR 500–1,000 Rupees
R less than 500 Rupees

INDIAN AND MOGHUL
Navaratne
Taj Samudra
25, Galle Road
Colombo 3
Tel: 446622
A good lunch-time buffet at this
plush Moghul restaurant. **RRR**
Alhambra at Holiday Inn
Mohammed Marcan Markan
Mawatha
Colombo 3
Tel: 422001
Consistently good food, courteous
service, in an elegant setting. **RR**
Shanthi Vihar
3, Havelock Road
Colombo 5
Tel: 580224
Popular Indian takeaway for excellent
vegetarian food at reasonable price.
Air-conditioned dining area. **R**
Greenlands Hotel
3/A, Shrubbery Gardens
Colombo 4
Tel: 81986
Best *masala dosais* in town. The
dining section is very basic and
unless you feel particularly brave and
ethnic, just take the food home! **R**

ITALIAN
Il Ponte Ristorante
Hilton Hotel
Echelon Square
Colombo 1
Dining *al fresco* by the pool is
romantic by night. But don't expect
serious Italian food here. Good
pizzas. **RRR**
Il Cappriccio
29, De Fonseka Road
Colombo 5
Tel: 594663
A charming old house of quiet
elegance with a limited but
thoughtful menu for excellent Italian
food – especially the truffles. **RRRR**

JAPANESE
Ginza Hohsen
Colombo Hilton
Echelon Square
Colombo 1
Undoubtedly the best Japanese
food in town. Extensive menu
offering smoked eel and other
delicacies flown in from Japan twice
a week. *Teppan Yaki* tables, and
excellent service. The lunch time
menu prices are more moderate
than those for dinner. Sushi bar and
private *Tatami* rooms. **RRRR**
Sakura
14, Rheinland Place
Colombo 3
Tel: 573877
Popular little restaurant, with
traditional Japanese tables, or
standard dining. Delicious *sushimi*.
Service is attentive and very prompt.
RR
Moshi Moshi
594/2, Galle Road
Colombo 3
Tel: 500312
A rooftop bar and *karaoke* are
sufficient attractions to offset
the mediocre Japanese food. **RR**
Hakata
110, Havelock Road
Colombo 5
Tel: 501397
Conveniently located, offering a
choice of traditional Japanese
seating or standard tables. The
muted décor makes it a cool
lunchtime haven at noon. **RR**

KOREAN
Han Gook Gwan
25, Havelock Road
Colombo 5
Tel: 587961
The "steamboat" speciality here is
always good. **R**

PAKISTANI
Kebabish Restaurant
526, Galle Road
Colombo 3.
Tel: 574479
Moderately good Pakistani food
and a top floor room for parties or
conferences. Occasional *Buriyani*
festivals. **RRR**

SEAFOOD

Beach Wadiya
2, Station Avenue
Wellawatta
Tel: 585868
Advisable to book. Tables available both inside and on the beach. A fish tank reveals an ever changing display of tropical fish and eels while a feast from the sea is laid before you. Enormous portions of lobster, crayfish, prawns and crab will defy even the most gargantuan diner. **RRR**

The Seafood Cove
Mount Lavinia Hotel
Mount Lavinia
Tel: 715221.

Orient Hong Kong Seafood
1A, Race Couse Avenue
Colombo 7
Tel: 699007

Seaspray
Galle Face Hotel
Colombo 3
Tel: 28211
Set in Colombo's oldest and most beautiful colonial hotel. Good food, with a pleasant ambience but erratic service. **RR**

Gourmet Palace
399/A R.A. de Mel Mawatha
Colombo 3
Tel: 596700
This bustling Chinese restaurant does a very brisk trade at lunchtime when queues form for its good value take away menu of the day. Inside, *dim sum* served daily between 11am and 3pm.

SRI LANKAN FOOD

The Curry Leaf Garden Restaurant
Colombo Hilton
Tel: 544644
The fame of its delicious *kotthu rottis* is widespread. *Al fresco* dining under the stars with authentic Sri Lankan barbecue and freshly caught seafood.

Palmayrah Restaurant
Hotel Renuka
328 Galle Road
Colombo 3
Tel: 26901
Renowned for delicacies such as *milk hoppers* and *prawn poriyal*, traditional foods of Northern Sri

Lanka. A definite "must-visit" for discerning gourmets wishing to sample Jaffna cuisine. **RR**

Green Cabin Cafe
453, Galle Road
Colombo 3
Tel: 88811
This bustling lunchtime café is also good value in the evenings. **R**

Banana Leaf
86, Galle Road
Colombo 4
Tel: 584403
Eat off a banana leaf plate. Good crab. Also take away. **R**

Curry Bowl
24, Deal Place
Colombo 3
Tel: 570157
All manner of spicy Lankan food. **R**

Ibn Batuta
Trans Asia Hotel
Tel: 544200 **R**

Where to Eat Outside Colombo

Outside Colombo the best places for meals on the go are the rest houses which are moderately priced, have good local cooking and can muster up simple Western food if given notice. Resort hotels tend to provide bland pseudo-European food that they believe tourists want. Be adventurous if you are after great culinary experiences.

Aluvihara Kitchens

Don't miss the Aluvihara Kitchens, on the main road through Matale between Kandy and Dambulla (*see page 238*). The restaurant offers lodgings as well as food, but there is only a very small number of rooms. The restaurant serves Sri Lankan home cooking at its best, and in generous portions. Aluvihara Kitchens also sells homemade sweets, pickles and chutneys of high quality that make excellent gifts. This is a thriving cottage industry managed by Ena de Silva, who also runs woodcarving and fabric-printing workshops nearby: another source of gifts.

Nightlife

Any kind of nightlife in Sri Lanka is located in Colombo, although the city is not known for its nightlife. Eating out alone is considered a night out to most Sri Lankans, although these days there is rather more to do on a Saturday night than there was a few years ago.

Nightlife in Colombo

Karaoke Bars
Showboat
104, Reid Avenue, Colombo 4
Not noted for the quality of the food, Showboat is still popular because of its state-of-the-art Karaoke Lounge (with English, Thai, Korean, Chinese and Japanese songs) and its MTV lounge providing daily movies and sports coverage. **RRRR**

Hilton Karaoke
A wide range of music, a well-stocked bar, and an easy-going atmosphere make this one of the most popular karaoke bars around. **RRRR**

Pubs
Echelon Pub
Colombo Hilton, Lotus Road
Colombo 1
Tel: 544644
An English pub in a five-star hotel. Seats are grouped cosily round large TVs. A pool table is on offer, as are televised sporting events on a large screen. Up-market ambience.

Cricketer's Pub
34, Queens Road, Colombo 3
Tel: 501384
Intimate atmosphere, as authentic as a pub can be in Sri Lanka. TVs show non-stop cricket and tables are made out of large beer barrels.

Frankfurt Lavinia Beer Garden
34/8A, De Saram Road
Mount Lavinia
A short distance from the sea.

Known for the generous quantity of the food they serve.

Casinos

Casinos offer complimentary drinks and snacks and even taxi transport to and fro if you become a member.
Bally's Club
14, Dharmapala Mawatha, Colombo 3
Tel: 573497
Open 24 hours, offers Baccarat, Roulette, Black Jack and Banco.
Ritz Carlton
433, Galle Road, Colombo 3
Tel: 589731
Black Jack, Baccarat and Roulette. Complimentary Chinese dinner buffet, drinks and live entertainment.
Star Dust Club
9, 5th Lane, Galle Road, Colombo 3
Tel: 573493
24 hour. Conveniently located within easy reach of most leading hotels. Call GNTC cabs on 688688 for free transport to the club. Roulette, Black Jack and Baccarat, with complimentary bar and food service.

Nightclubs

Blue Elephant
Colombo Hilton
Lotus Road, Colombo 1
Tel: 544644
Theme nights and DJ music. Membership offered to club regulars.
Cascades
Hotel Lanka Oberoi
77, Steuart Place, Colombo 3
Tel: 320001
The current popular hangout for the younger party set. Newly refurbished, with a pool room.
The Library
Trans Asia Hotel
115, Sir Chittampalam A Gardiner Mawatha, Colombo 2
Tel: 544200
An up-market alternative, with more conservative music. Popular with young professional community.
Legends
Majestic City
5th Floor, Colombo 4
Occasionally has live bands, both local and foreign. A great night, if a good band is playing.
The Venue
The only club in Colombo that plays house music. Has a huge bar.

Culture

The visual beauty of Sri Lanka and the mythological splendour of the ancient beliefs are two factors that have inspired artists over the ages. In museums, the styles and concerns of the ancient artists can be seen and compared with those of the many contemporary artists whose works can be viewed in numerous Colombo galleries. Established modern favourites to look out for are Laki Senanayake, LTP Majusri, George Keyt, George de Neise and David Paynter.

Art Galleries

Art Gallery
101, Ananda Coomaraswami Mawatha, Colombo 7
Tel: 693965
Open 8am–5pm daily except *Poyas*.
Mountcastle Gallerey
2, Arunachalam Avenue
Off 36, Horton Place, Colombo 7
Kalagaraya Art Gallery
54, Ward Place, Colombo 7
Tel: 694162
At the Alliance Francais.
Open 9am–1pm, 5–7pm Monday–Friday.
Lional Wendt Memorial Art Centre
18, Guildford Crescent, Colombo 7
Tel: 695794
Manjasuri Home
215, 2/E block
Anderson Golf Links Flat
Park Road, Colombo 5
Tel: 582417
By appointment only.
Sapumal Foundation
32/4, Barnes Place, Colombo 7
Tel: 695731
Sometimes erratic opening hours so best to telephone first.
Serendib Gallery
36 1/1 Rosemead Place, Colombo 7
Tel: 697467
Antique maps and prints of Ceylon.

Barefoot Galleries
704 Galle Road, Colombo 3
Tel 589305
Contemporary art and photographs.

Cinemas

English-language films are shown at the cultural centres listed below and the following cinemas:
Liberty
38, Dharmapala Mawatha, Colombo 3
Tel: 25265
New Olympia
Jaya Mawatha, Colombo 10
Tel: 693141
Savoy
12, Galle Road, Colombo 6
Tel: 588621

Libraries

Public libraries are usually a waste of time, as the concept of libraries, research and book-lending has not evolved enough for Sri Lankans to understand that they are there as a public service. You will generally be regarded as a nuisance and given very little or no help. There are also no borrowing facilities for tourists.
American Centre
39, Sir Earnest de Silva Mawatha
Colombo 7
Tel: 691461
British Council
49, Alfred House Gardens, Colombo 3
Tel: 581171/2
Colombo Public Library
Sir Marcus Fernando Mawatha
Colombo 7
Tel: 695156
University of Colombo Library
Colombo 7
Tel: 586432

Cultural Centres

Alliance Français
11, Barnes Place, Colombo 7
Tel: 694162
The British Council
49, Alfred House Gardens, Colombo 3
Tel: 581171
German Cultural Centre
39, Gregory's Road, Colombo 7
Tel: 694562

Shopping

What to Buy

Sri Lanka is an excellent place to shop if you have foreign currency, as the conversion rate ensures that clothes, spices and household items are at a considerably lower price than in the West – many holiday-makers go home with a whole new wardrobe! There is a booming market for designer "fakes", so be aware when purchasing CK jeans, Armani shirts and Tommy Hilfiger clothing that they are only good copies and not of the same quality as originals.

Other good buys are tea, spices, handlooms, masks and carvings and gems such as moonstones. Read the tips on gem buying in the Crafts chapter before purchasing any jewellery or gems.

Outside Colombo, go for items that are traditionally made locally. For example, beautiful hand-made lace can be bought in Galle. (Some elderly women sell their own skillful pieces of work outside the New Oriental Hotel and on the ramparts.) If in Wewelbeniya, on the Kandy road, look out for hand-woven baskets. Mask carvings can be bought anywhere on the island, you are likely to find lovely pieces at a fair price at Ambalangoda, the centre of Sri Lankan mask carving.

Gems

To export gems received as gifts, permits from the **Controller of Exchange**, Central Bank Colombo and the **Controller of Imports and Exports**, National Mutual Building, Chatham Street, Colombo 1, are required.

Antiques

The export of antiques over 50 years old is banned. So is the export of wild animals, birds and reptiles unless with the proper documentation and licences.

Shopping in Colombo

Clothes

Barefoot
704, Galle Road, Colombo 3
Tel: 589305
Exclusive range in vivid cottons and linens created by Sri Lankan artist and designer Barbara Sansoni and her skilled team. This is a great shop for buying gifts. Café and gallery on the premises.
The London Shop
252, Galle Road, Colombo 4
Tel: 502552
For St Michael from Marks and Spencer.
Elle
Ground Floor Majestic City and 1st Floor Liberty Plaza
Ready-made garments, such as T-shirts, casuals.
Levis
39A, Queensway Building
Duplication Road, Colombo 3
Tel: 581024
The only authentic Levis outlet.
Odel Unlimited
5, Alexandra Place, Colombo 7
Best selection of casual and "designer" clothing.
Cotton Collection
Flower Road, Colombo 7
Cotton clothing for everyone.
Kidz
169, Kynsey Road, Colombo 8
Tel: 688558
For children's wear.

Household and Handicrafts

Barefoot
704, Galle Road, Colombo 3
Tel: 589305
Odel Home Shop
38, Dickmans Road, Colombo 5
Tel: 589618
Paradise Road
36, Flower Road, Colombo 7
Tel: 07123287
Promenade
213, Dharmapala Mawatha
Colombo 7
Tel: 686943
Lanka Ceramics
696, Galle Road, Colombo 3
Tel: 589349
Lakpahana
21, Rajakeeya Mawatha, Colombo 7

Gifts

Aluthgama Wood Carvings
25/3, Riverside Avenue
Aluthgama (on the west coast)
Barefoot
704, Galle Road, Colombo 3
Tel: 589305
The Oasis Company
18, Station Road, Colombo 4
Tel: 597097
Odel Unlimited
5, Alexandra Place, Colombo 7
Thimble
32, Duplication Road, Colombo 4
Tel: 597196

Gems and Jewellery

Colombo Jewellery Stores
1, Alfred House Gardens
Galle Road, Colombo 3
Hemachandra Brothers
229, Galle Road, Colombo 3
Tel: 325147
Zam Gems
81, Galle Road, Colombo 4
Tel: 589090
Ridhi Design Studio
Zays Pvt. Ltd
15, Skeleton Road, Colombo 5
Tel: 595955

Sunglasses

Fashion Optic (Eric Rajapakse)
2–9, Majestic City,
Colombo 4
Tel: 592710

Tea and Spices

Mlesna
Colombo Hilton
Also at Liberty Plaza and Majestic City.
The Shoppe
Shop No. 5
Crescat Boulevard, Colombo 3
Tel: 698015

Books

Barefoot Bookshop
704, Galle Road, Colombo 3
Tel: 589305
Bookland
430–432, Galle Road, Colombo 3
Tel: 074714444

Vijitha Yapa Bookshop
Unity Plaza
376, Galle Road, Colombo 3
Tel: 577624

Shopping Malls
Majestic City
Galle Road
Bambalapitiya
Liberty Plaza
Duplication Road
Kollupitiya
Crescat Boulevard
Galle Road
Colombo 3

Duty Free Shopping

After completing your check in and immigration formalities, you are free to embark on a shopping spree! The Colombo duty-free shops are located only at the Bandaranaike International Airport and sell a good range of clothes, watches, jewellery, liquor, tobacco and so on. On departure, foreign passport holders can "strike gold" at the gold shop in the transit lounge and purchase unlimited quantities. Anyone landing in the country and leaving the airport, for even an hour (your passport is stamped by immigration) is eligible for this facility.

The duty free shop at the airport is open to travellers on the way in and out. Prices are said to be the lowest in Asia. In addition to the usual items you can buy audio and video appliances, camera and photographic equipment and gold.

Sport

Sri Lankans are sports-conscious people, the favourite games being cricket and rugby.

Many sports clubs and associations accept foreign visitors as temporary members. Also, most of the major hotels have swimming pools and tennis courts.

Cricket

The cricket season begins in September and ends in April with the Lackspray Trophy.

Clubs which accept temporary foreign members are as follows:
Nondescripts Cricket Club
29 Maitland Place, Colombo 7
Tel: 95293
Bloomfield Cricket and Athletic Club
Reid Avenue, Colombo 7
Tel: 914119.
Dikoya and Maskeliya Cricket Club
Tel: 0512216
Uva Club
Bailey Road, Badulla
Tel: Badulla 216

Fishing

Freshwater Fishing
Department of Wildlife Conservation
82 Rajamalwatta Road
Battaramulla
Tel: 433012/433787
The Ceylon Anglers Club
Chatiya Road, Colombo 1
Tel: 421752
Accepts temporary members and can provide much information on fishing throughout the country.

Deep-sea fishing
Deep-sea fishing is growing in popularity in Sri Lanka. **Sunstream Boat Services**, at the National Holiday Resort in Bentota, and the

Sea Anglers Club, on China Bay, can help organise trips for visitors. Trincomalee, on the east coast, also has deep-sea fishing facilities.

Golf

Golfing facilities are available at the beautifully maintained golf clubs in Colombo and Nuwara Eliya.
The Royal Colombo Golf Club
Model Farm Road
Colombo 8
Tel: 695431
Has a 9-hole course.
Nuwara Eliya Golf Club
Tel: 052-3833
Considered one of the best in Asia, is 1,890 m (6,200 ft) above sea level and offers a challenging hilly terrain with an 18-hole course.

Mountain Biking

For organised bike rides through rubber estates and downhill rides through tea estates contact
Adventure Lanka Sports
12a, Simon Hewavitharane Road
Colombo 3
Tel: 074-713334
Fax: 01-577951

Tennis

Sri Lanka Tennis Association
45, Marcus Fernando Mawatha
Colombo 7
Tel: 695293
Oberoi Tennis Courts
Lanka Oberoi, Colombo 3
Tel: 420001
The Womens International Club
16, Guildford Crescent, Colombo 7
Tel: 695072
The Colombo Hilton
Echelon Square, Colombo 1
Tel: 544644
Orient Club
Racecourse Avenue, Colombo 7
Tel: 605068

Watersports

Canoeing
Adventure Sports Lanka
Tel: 074-713333
A wide-ranging organisation, offering some original locations in jungles,

Dutch spice canals and the Sinharaja rainforest with experienced guides from US$20 or $30 for a full day.

Rowing
Colombo Rowing Club
Five minutes' walk from the Ramada Renaissance Hotel
Tel: 433758

Scuba Diving
An increasing number of operators offer scuba diving trips in Sri Lanka and differ only in the level of insurance cover they provide.

Many places along the Galle Road in Hikkaduwa will hire out masks, snorkels and fins for around Rs 50 for each hour or Rs 250 per day.

Some of the best companies are:
Lanka Sports Riezen
Confifi Marina, Beruwala.
Scuba Safaris
Coral Gardens Hotel, Hikkaduwa.
Prices start from Rs 1,000 per dive (including equipment). PADI international courses available.
Underwater Safaris Ltd
Padi Dive Centre
25 C, Barnes Place, Colombo 7
Tel: 694012
Poseidon Diving Station
Galle Road, Hikkaduwa
Tel: 09-23294
Aqua Tours Ltd
108, Rosmead Place, Colombo 7
Tel: 69170

Surfing and Windsurfing
Surf boards to suit different skill levels as well as wetsuits, fins and body boards can be hired from many shops, hotels and guest houses in Hikkaduwa from Rs 50 per hour and upwards. Midigama and Polhenha also offer some hire facilities.

An hour's windsurf will cost around US$5 per hour or US$100 for a ten-hour course. All tour operators should offer full briefings and go through overboard drills before you set off.
Blue Oceanic Water Sports Limited
Blue Oceanic Hotel, Negombo
Tel: 031-2377
Sun Stream Boat Services
National Holiday Resort, Bentota
Club Nautique Boat House
Bentota Beach Hotel, Bentota

Tel: 034-75176. ext. 370
Lanka Sportsreizen
244/1 Hospital Road, Kalubowila, Dehiwela
Tel: 824500

Swimming
Most hotels have a pool available free to hotel guests, and at a fee of about Rs 200 to visitors. Clubs offer membership and use of club facilities including tennis courts, squash courts and the bar.
Otter Aquatic Club
380/1, Bauddhaloka Mw.
Colombo 7
Tel: 695070
Sinhalese Sports Club
35, Maitland Place
Colombo 7
Tel: 695362
Kinross Swimming and Lifesaving Club
10, Station Avenue, Colombo 6
Tel: 586461
Sea bathing, lifesaving, skin diving.
Colombo Swimming Club
Storm Lodge
Galle Road, Colpetty
Temporary membership available.

White-Water Rafting
Adventure Lanka Sports PVT Ltd
12a, Simon Hewavitharane Road
Colombo 3
Tel: 074-713334
For up to grade 4 rapids on the Kelani river.

Yachting and Coastal Cruising
Ceylon Motor Yacht Club
Indebedda Road
Bolgoda Lake, Moratuwa
Sailing, windsurfing ,swimming.
Kelani Yacht Co
1A Dharmaraja mw.
Colombo 3
Tel: 587507
Coastal cruising.
Island Yatch Tours
102/11, Templers Road
Mount Lavinia
Tel: 737483
Offer cruises on a 60-foot yacht between Tangalle and Negombo.

Language

Most Sri Lankans will not allow you to practise your Sinhala words, so eager are they to practise their generally fluent English. Even in rural areas there will be someone who will translate before you can reach for your phrasebook. But once you get into a flow the language is not difficult, and you may find you have a rudimentary understanding by the time you leave.

Greetings and Phrases

Yes	Ou
No	Naa
Hello/good day	Ayubowan
Thank you	Istuti
Thank you very much	Bohoma istuti
How are you?	Kohomode?
Fine	Varadak neh
Please	Karunakerela
What is your name?	Nama mokadhdha?
My name is....	Mage nama....
OK/very good	Hari hondai
Delicious	Hari rasai
I don't understand	Mata terinneh neh
Very expensive	Hari ganan
No sugar please	Seeni netuwa
Please stop here	Metana nawaththanna
What?	Mokadhdha?
Where?	Kohedha?
Where is the hotel?	Hootale kohedha?
Where is the station?	Stesemeta eka ko?
What is this?	Mekeh mokadeh?
May I telephone?	Mata call ekak gand poluwandeh?
How much (is this)	(Meeka) kiyadha?

Days of the Week

Monday	*Sanduda*
Tuesday	*Angahauwada*
Wednesday	*Badada*
Thursday	*Brahaspathinda*
Friday	*Sikurada*
Saturday	*Senesurada*
Sunday	*Irida*

Place Names

Many Sinhalese place names are long but quite logical as they are nearly always a compound, so remember a few rules and you will pronounce them like a native.

island	*duwa*
village	*gama*
river	*ganga*
street	*mawatha*
city	*nuwara*
stream	*oya*
town	*pura*
port	*tota, tara*
temple	*vihara*
lake	*weva*

Useful Vocabulary

bank	*bank eka*
breakfast	*udee tee*
clean	*pirisidu*
coffee	*kipi*
dinner	*paa kaama*
dirty	*kilutu*
food	*kaama*
hotel	*hotela*
lunch	*dawal kaama*
small	*punchi*
pharmacy	*bet sappuwa*
restaurant	*apana sala*
room	*kaamare*
soap	*saban*
tea	*tey*
this/that	*mee/oya*
water	*watara*
one	*eka*
two	*deka*
three	*tuna*
four	*hatara*
five	*paha*
six	*haya*
seven	*hata*
eight	*ata*
nine	*namaya*
ten	*daaha*

Further Reading

History and Politics

An Historical Relation of Ceylon, Robert Knox. Knox was captured near Trincomalee in the 17th century and held under "house arrest" for the next 19 years by the king. His description of the Kandyan kingdom became a best-seller and is still one of the best on pre-European Lanka.
Prehistory of Sri Lanka I & II, SU Deraniyagala. A little heavy-going but one of the most authoritative works on Sri Lankan history.
Sri Lanka Island of Terror, EM Thornton and R Niththyananthan (1984). The Tamil version of events about the countries ethnic conflict, more readable than it sounds, traces events from the 1940s to mid-1980s.
Only Man is Vile: The Tragedy of Sri Lanka, William McGowan (1993). Mixes history, travelogue and reportage and lays the blame squarely between the Sinhala élite and the British colonialists.

Fiction

Running in the Family, Michael Ondaatje. Some flashes of brilliance and humour as he re-visits Sri Lanka to explore the land of his upper-class relations.
Savage Sanctuary, R.L. Spittel. The writer spent a good deal of time living with the Veddhas, Lanka's own aborigines, and getting to know them. This is his novel about their lifestyle.
Colombo, Carl Muller. You may never want to venture into the island's capital after reading this, a mix of history, reportage and faction, and it is perhaps the reason why the writer chooses to live in Kandy. The Jam Fruit Tree and Yaka-de-Yaka, two of this trilogy about a Burgher family in Ceylon, are vintage Muller as well as being a lot less stomach-churning.
The Village in the Jungle, Leonard Woolf. The author who went on to become part of the Bloomsbury set spent a term of office in the Ceylon civil service. Novel is set in a backward farming village around 1900.

Tourist Publications

A Guide to the Waterfalls of Sri Lanka, Eberhard Kautzsch (1983). A fabulous memento of the island and a beautiful and unusual guide book.
Trekkers Guide to Sri Lanka, Trekking Unlimited of Colombo. Where to walk while passing paddy fields, temples, tea estates, the vast inland seas built by the ancient kings, as well as seashore and city treks in Kandy, Galle and Colombo.
The Thorana Guide to Sri Lanka, Lever Brothers Cultural Conservation Trust (1979). Full of interesting material on temples and old buildings that you won't find anywhere else.
The Linc is a free magazine produced for the Lankan International Community and is a good current listing of events. Available at large hotels or else contact linc@sri.lanka.net to find out where you can get a copy.
Travel Lanka and **Explore Sri Lanka**, available from the tourist board and hotels, are free magazines which list current events.

Wildlife

A Field Guide to the Birds of Sri Lanka, Sarath Kotagama and Prithiviraj. Illustrated in colour and giving the common names of wildlife in Sinhala and English.
Sinharaja: a Rainforest in Sri Lanka, Neela de Zoysa and Rhyana Rahem. Details flora and fauna of Sinharaja and the region.

Miscellaneous

Viharas and Verandas, Barbara Sansoni (1980). This renowned colourist and designer has always been an inspiration to architects and in this beautifully illustrated book, you will understand why.
A Personal Odyssey, Nihal Fernando. The grand photographer of Sri Lanka has collected his most stunning pictures into this one collection. An excellent memoir of your stay.

ART & PHOTO CREDITS

All photography by R. Ian Lloyd except:
Martin Adler/Panos Pictures 62, 63
Roland Ammon 80, 81, 94/95, 99R, 100, 102, 200, 201, 209R, 283
J.G. Anderson 28, 83, 98, 177, 195, 205, 230, 232, 242, 261, 284
Ravindralal Anthonis 122/123, 124, 126, 127, 130, 131
Associated Newspapers of Ceylon, courtesy of Asiaweek magazine 60/61
Edmund Bealby-Wright 50, 215R, 271, 273, 276
Keith Bernstein/Impact 164
Marcus Brooke 19, 76, 101, 110, 118, 185
John Brunton 66/67, 169, 194T, 260
Linda Carlock 135, 233, 240, 243, 244, 267
Howard J. Davies 59, 91
A. Evans/Panos Pictures 48
Alain Evrard 112, 187
Nihal Fernando 24
Michael Freeman 212
Manfred Gottschalk 49, 159, 211, 236, 265, 280/281
Hans Höfer 14, 193
Rodney Jonklaas 220/221, 270, 286, 287
Jill Jones/ffotograff 215T, 266
Philip Little 8/9, 86/87, 115, 197, 285
Ben Nakayama 58
Eric Oey 75, 120, 125, 219
Christian Petron/Planet Earth Pictures 121
Photobank 16, 144/145
Jonathan Pile/Impact 162
Lesley Player 2, 74, 92, 103,

158T,161, 178, 181, 182, 183T, 184T, 199, 199T, 207, 207T, 214, 215L, 218T
Louise Renkema 70R
Eric Roberts 129, 177T, 229
Dominic Sansoni 36, 71, 88, 93, 166, 183T, 245, 252, 258, 162T, 168T, 233T, 265T, 267T, 275T, 285T
Dominic Sansoni/Impact 184
Dominic Sansoni/Panos Pictures 4/5, 138, 139, 154/155, 181T, 183, 186T, 227R, 227T, 231T
Thomas Schoellhammer 179, 254, 259
Henry Sofeico/from the Bevis Bawa Collection 64/65
Studio Times 256
Tom Tidball 77, 90, 97, 104, 105, 106, 111, 132/133, 136L&R, 137L&R, 156, 157, 163, 167, 171, 186, 190/191, 223, 231
Alexis Wallerstein/ Impact 89, 165
Bill Wassman 17, 25, 27, 31, 73, 107, 128, 134, 196, 209L, 227L, 228, 239, 239T, 248T, 251T, 257T, 263T, 255, 257, 269
Jan Whiting 52, 213
From the P.R. Anthonis Collection 20/21, 40/41, 51
From Capt. O.C. O'Brien, Views in Ceylan, 1864 29, 32, 44
From Philip Baldeus, A True and Exact Description ... of Ceylan 1703 39
From the Leo Harks Collection 158
From Robert Knox, An Historical Relation of Ceylan, 1681 42, 43, 70L
From Senanayake Family Collection 23, 57
From the K.V.J. de Silva Collection 34/35, 37, 160

Picture Spreads

Pages 84/85 *clockwise from bottom left-hand corner.* Dominic Sansoni; Roland Ammon; Dominic Sansoni; Piers Cavendish/Impact; Lesley Player; Dominic Sansoni/ Imapact; Dominic Sansoni/Impact; Lesley Player; Lesley Player; N. Cooper/Panos Pictures.

Pages 140/141 *clockwise from bottom left-hand corner.* Michael Freeman; Michael Freeman; Eric Roberts; Dominic Sansoni; Eric Roberts; Manfred Gottschalk; Lesley Player; Lesley Player.

Pages 188/189 *clockwise from bottom left-hand corner.* Katerina and Eric Roberts; Lesley Player; Eric Roberts; Lesley Player; Dominic Sansoni; Dominic Sansoni; Lesley Player.

Pages 278/279 *clockwise from bottom left-hand corner.* Dominic Sansoni; Linda Carlock; John Brunton; Lesley Player; Linda Carlock; Dominic Sansoni; Dominic Sansoni; Ian Lloyd.

Map Production Berndtson & Berndtson Productions
© 1998 Apa Publications GmbH & Co. Verlag KG, Singapore.

Cartographic Editor **Zoë Goodwin**
Production **Stuart A. Everitt**
Design Consultants
Klaus Geisler, Graham Mitchener
Picture Research **Hilary Genin**

Index

Numbers in italics refer to photographs

A
B
C
D
E
F
G
H
J
a
b
c
d
e
f
g
h
i
j
k